Accounting Workbook *for* Peachtree® 5.0

Prepared by
Warren Allen

Problem Material Prepared by
James A. Heintz
University of Kansas

and

Robert W. Parry
Indiana University

South-Western College Publishing
an International Thomson Publishing company I(T)P®

Cincinnati • Albany • Boston • Detroit • Johannesburg • London • Madrid • Melbourne • Mexico City
New York • Pacific Grove • San Francisco • Scottsdale • Singapore • Tokyo • Toronto

Publishing Team Director:	Richard Lindgren, CPA
Acquisitions Editor:	Alex von Rosenberg
Developmental Editor:	Sara Wilson, CPA
Production Editor:	Marcella Dechter
Production House:	Navta Associates, Inc.
Manufacturing Coordinator:	Gordon Woodside
Marketing Manager:	Matthew Filimonov

ISBN 0-324-00722-1

5 6 7 8 9 GP 5 4 3 2 1 0
Printed in the United States of America

I(T)P®
International Thomson Publishing
South-Western College Publishing is an ITP Company.
The ITP trademark is used under license.

CONTENTS

SECTION 1 INSTALLING AND OPERATING THE PEACHTREE ACCOUNTING SOFTWARE

SECTION 2 INSTRUCTIONS FOR SOLVING SELECTED PROBLEMS USING PEACHTREE ACCOUNTING SOFTWARE

SECTION 3 SETTING UP A NEW COMPANY

SECTION 4 DEMONSTRATION PROBLEM SOLUTIONS

SECTION 1

Installing and Operating the Peachtree Accounting Software

INSTALLING THE PEACHTREE ACCOUNTING SOFTWARE

You must install Peachtree Accounting from within Windows™. If you plan to run Peachtree Accounting on a network, you must install Peachtree Accounting on each workstation. The procedure for installing the Peachtree Accounting software is detailed below:

▶ **Turn on the computer and start Windows.**

▶ **Place the Peachtree Accounting CD into the CD-ROM drive.**

▶ **From the Windows Program Manager, select Run from the File menu. In Windows 95, select Start, then Run.**

▶ **Type D:SETUP substituting the appropriate drive letter for D (for example, E:SETUP).**

A window displays up to four choices depending on whether you are a new or previous user.

Standard This option installs everything you need to begin running Peachtree Accounting. You cannot change the location of where the program will be installed if you select this option.

Upgrade This option upgrades you from a previous version of Peachtree Accounting, maintaining your current program and data path settings. This option only appears if you have previously installed an earlier version of Peachtree Accounting.

Custom You can set a different path for the program or data files using this option or choose which components of Peachtree Accounting you want to install.

Network This option allows you to install program and data files in a network environment.

▶ **Select either Standard (new users) or Upgrade (previous users) for quick installation.**

▶ **Select Install to continue. If you are installing from diskette, follow the prompts and insert additional diskettes as needed.**

▶ **Select Ok to close the system modification window, if displayed.**

Once the program and data files have been installed, a window is displayed, and you may decide whether to install a program group and icons for Peachtree Accounting.

▶ **Select Install to create program icons in the group displayed in the drop-down list. If you do not want to install program icons, select Skip.**

A window may display the question of whether you want to install Microsoft Video for Windows. Video for Windows is necessary to run the multimedia version of New Company Setup available on CD-ROM. Select Yes to have the Video for Windows setup program run when installation of Peachtree Accounting has finished. If you do not want to install Video for Windows, select No.

▶ **A window indicating the successful completion of the Peachtree Accounting portion of the installation is displayed. If any of your system files were modified during installation, you will see different options.**

If you *received* a message that one or more of your system files were modified, the following options appear:

Read Select this to view the Peachtree Accounting Read Me file.

Reboot Select this to restart your computer. You must restart to run Peachtree Accounting.

Windows Select this option to return to Windows.

If you *did not* receive a message that any of your system files were modified, the following options appear.

Read Select this to view the Peachtree Accounting Read Me file.

Install Select this to load PeachLink (for Windows 95 users only). You can load PeachLink later or load it now.

Begin Select this option to launch Peachtree Accounting.

Windows Select this option to return to Windows.

INSTALLING THE DATA FILES

The opening balance files for selected problems are included on the Peachtree Accounting CD. The setup program and files are contained on the Peachtree CD in a directory named ACCNTNG. Each problem requires a unique data file containing the opening balance data for that problem. To solve a particular problem, you will open the data file that contains the opening balances. As you solve the problem, the computer will be updating information in this file; therefore, each user must have his or her own unique copy of the respective file. If available disk storage is limited or you do not always have access to the computer that contains your data files, there are several options described within the instructions that will accommodate these circumstances. The step-by-step instructions for installing the Peachtree Data Files are detailed below:

- **Place the Peachtree Accounting CD into the CD-ROM drive.**
- **From the Windows Program Manager, select Run from the File menu. In Windows 95, select Start, then Run. Type the command to run the setup program from the directory named ACCNTNG on the CD-ROM drive (e.g., D:\ACCNTNG\SETUP, assuming the CD-ROM is drive D).**
- **The Setup Type window shown in Figure 1.1 allows you to select which of the available problems you wish to install. The options are described on page 3.**

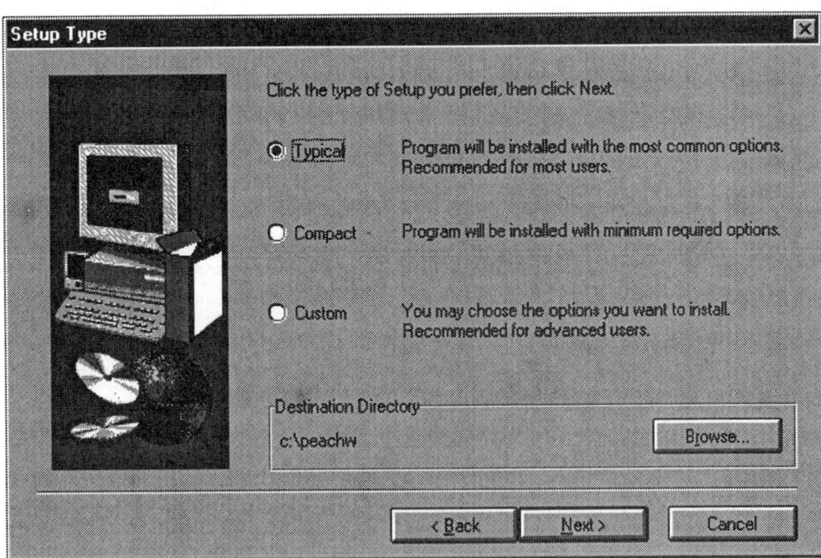

FIGURE 1.1 Setup Type Window

Typical. If you choose the Typical option, all of the problems will be installed. This option requires approximately 50 megabytes of hard disk storage for its use. ***All*** of the files will be installed to the default directory, PEACHW. Choose the Custom option to install to a different directory.

Compact. If the Compact option is chosen, only the Demonstration problems will be installed. This option requires approximately 11 megabytes of disk storage. Again, if this option is chosen, each student will be installing a complete set of the data files for the Demonstration problems in his or her own directory.

Custom. With this option, you can choose which files are to be installed. You can install the files for several chapters, just one chapter, or just one problem. This option is especially useful if either available storage space is limited or it isn't always possible to access the same directory from one session to the next because the directory you need is on a different computer from one session to the next. The Select Components window is illustrated in Figure 1.2. Notice that the list on the left shows the Accounting Chapters available. Notice that each has a check mark next to it. The check mark indicates that the problems for that chapter will be installed. If you do *not* want the files for that chapter installed, click on the check mark to toggle it off. The list on the right shows the problems available for the currently highlighted chapter. Again, if the file name is checked, it will be installed. In the example shown in Figure 1.2, only the four files will be installed.

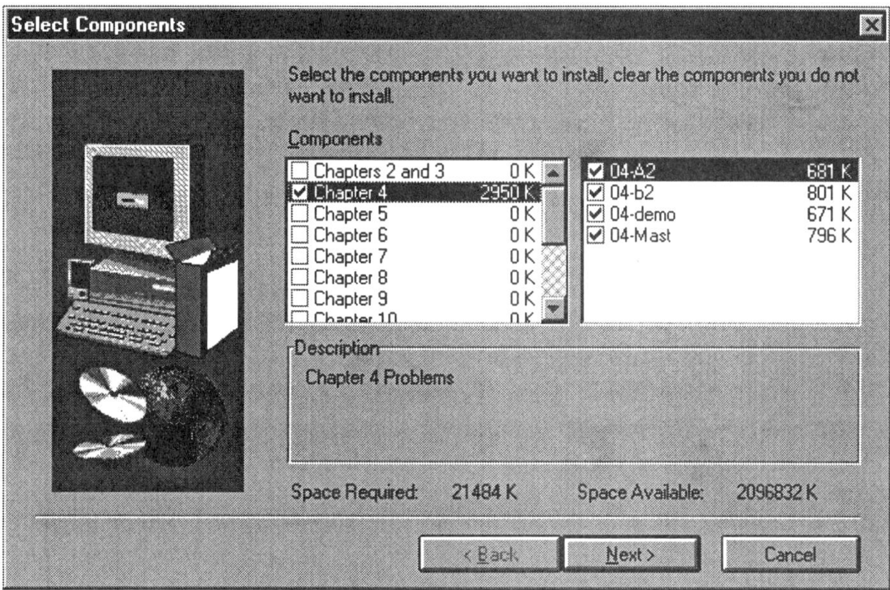

FIGURE 1.2 Select Components Window

- **The default directory into which the data files will be installed is PEACHW. To install into a different directory, click on the Browse button. When the Choose Directory window illustrated in Figure 1.3 (shown on the next page) appears, enter or select the drive and directory where you would like your file(s) to reside.**

If you are installing the Peachtree data files on your own personal computer or one where there are no other Peachtree users, then you should install to the default, PEACHW directory. If you are installing on a computer or network file server shared by other users who are also using Peachtree 5.0, you should click on the Browse button and enter or choose a unique directory name. The directory name you enter must be 8 characters or less and cannot have embedded blanks. For easy identification, you might use your name or an abbreviation thereof.

- **Click on the Next button to proceed with the installation.**
- **When the Setup Complete dialog appears, click the Finish button.**

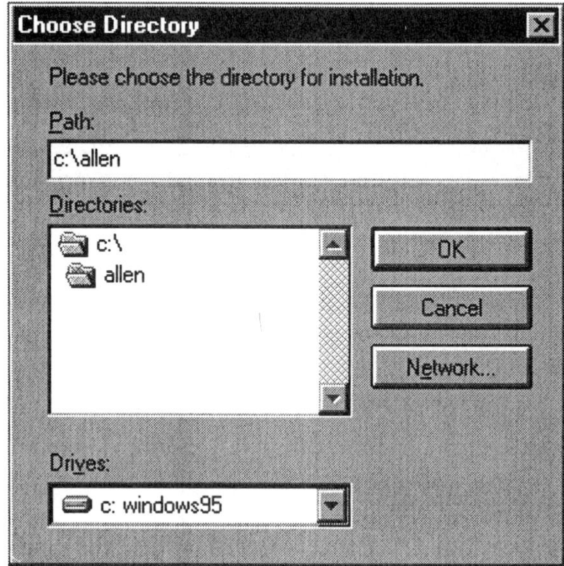

FIGURE 1.3 Choose Directory Window

PEACHTREE ACCOUNTING OPERATING INSTRUCTIONS

Peachtree accounting follows Windows standards for program navigation. Therefore, if you have used other Windows programs, you will have few problems navigating the Peachtree menus and entering data into the Peachtree data entry windows. If you are unfamiliar with the Windows environment, it is recommended that you view the Windows online tutorial lesson in the Peachtree Accounting Help menu.

Enter or Tab Keys

In most Windows programs, you use the Tab key to move from field to field. However, most people find the Enter key more natural. Peachtree Accounting gives you the choice; both Enter and Tab move the cursor to the next field. Shift+Tab or Shift+Enter will move you backward to the previous field.

Case Sensitivity

Some software programs are case sensitive and others are not. If a program is not case sensitive, then "apple," "Apple," and "APPLE" would all be interpreted the same by the software. However, Peachtree Accounting *is* case sensitive, so each of the above examples would be interpreted differently. This will have implications for you as you work with the software. For example, one of the companies you will be working with has a sales tax code named "Indiana." While you most likely would select the code from a drop-down list, if you chose to key it instead, you would have to key it exactly as shown. If you key "indiana" rather than "Indiana," Peachtree would not calculate sales tax correctly.

The Startup Screen

When you first start Peachtree Accounting, the Startup Screen shown in Figure 1.4 will appear. From the Startup Screen, you can open a company, set up a new company, convert the records from another accounting system, explore the sample company, or access the Peachtree online tutorial.

The Startup Screen is just a convenient way to get you started. All the options available on the Startup Screen are also available via the Peachtree menus. There is a checkbox option near the bottom of the screen

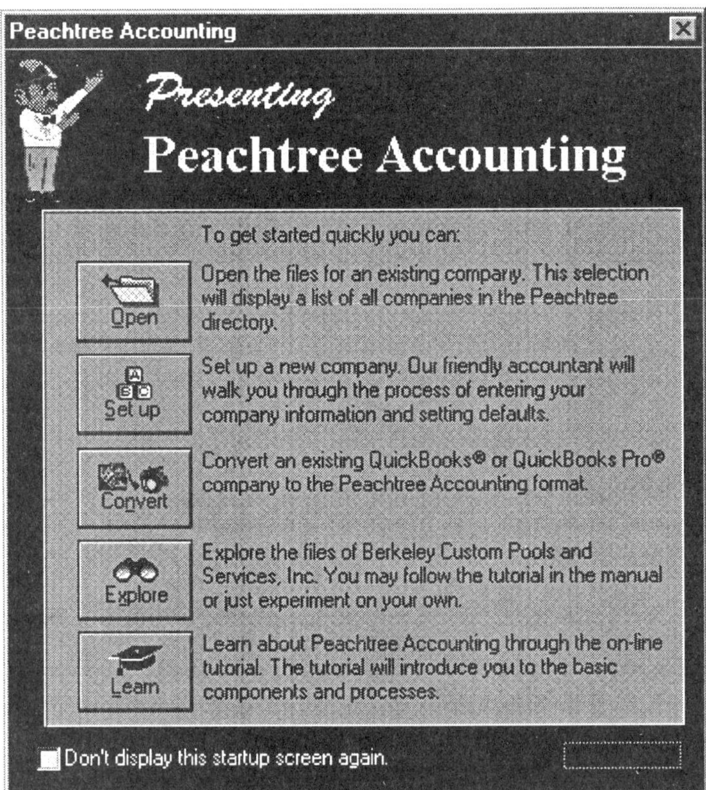

FIGURE 1.4 Peachtree Startup Screen

that allows you to turn off the Startup Screen so that it will not reappear the next time Peachtree Accounting is started. You can always change this later from the Options menu.

PEACHTREE ACCOUNTING MAIN MENU OPTIONS

The Peachtree Accounting Main Menu allows you to access the various features of the software. There are nine pull-down menus available. The Peachtree menus with the File menu pulled down are shown in Figure 1.5.

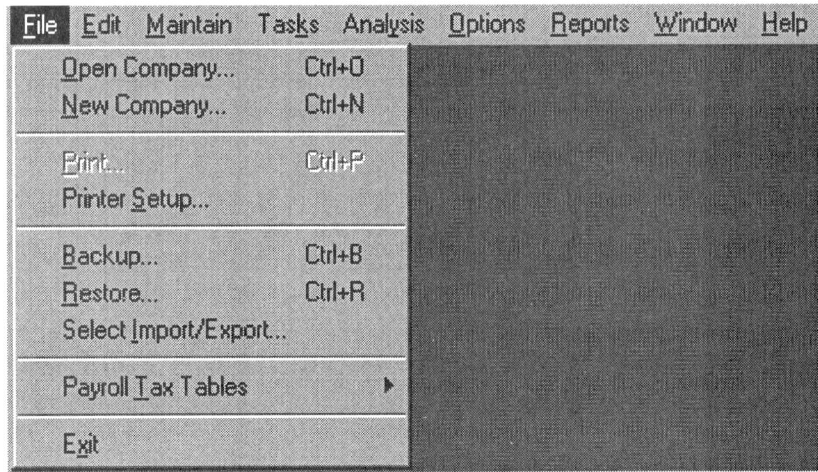

FIGURE 1.5 Peachtree Accounting Menus

▶ **Click on the desired menu to pull it down.**

▶ **Click on the menu option you would like to choose.**

Each of the main menu options is described below:

File. This menu option allows you to open an existing company, create a new company, print, do printer setup, back up a company, restore a previously backed up company, import and export data, set up taxes for payroll, and exit.

Edit. This menu provides the standard Windows cut, copy, and paste options.

Maintain. This menu allows you to access the various data entry windows to maintain the accounting data base by entering or editing the chart of accounts, customers, vendors, and employees.

Tasks. This menu allows you to enter the various accounting transactions such as general journal entries, sales invoices, purchase invoices, payments, and payroll transactions.

Analysis. This provides access to graphical overviews of cash flow, collections from customers, and payments due.

Options. These menu options allow you to change the system date, toggle the Smart Guide, Status Bar, Navigation Aid, and Startup Screen.

Reports. This menu allows you to access the various accounting reports by accounting system (accounts receivable, accounts payable, payroll, and general ledger).

Window. This menu allows you to arrange the displayed windows on your desktop, arrange the icons on your desktop, and close all open Peachtree windows.

Help. This menu allows you to open the Peachtree Help system.

The various menu options can also be accessed from the keyboard. To open one of the Main Menu options, press the Alt key and the underlined character. For example, press Alt+F to open the File menu. You can use the up and down arrow keys to move through the menu options, then press Enter to select the option. As an alternative, once the menu is displayed you can key the underlined letter to select the menu option.

THE NAVIGATION AID

In addition to the menu options, you can also utilize the Navigation Aid feature to access these same options. The Navigation Aid allows you to click on icons instead of choosing menu options. The Navigation Aid simplifies the selection of options because it is organized by accounting system (general ledger, accounts payable, accounts receivable, or payroll), so you only need be concerned with options within the system in which you are working. The Navigation Aid is shown in Figure 1.6. If you don't see the Navigation Aid at the bottom of your screen, it has been turned off. To turn it back on, select the View Navigation Aid from the Options menu.

FIGURE 1.6 Navigation Aid

As an example, the general ledger navigational aid is illustrated in Figure 1.7. Notice that the various options are illustrated as icons. To access the desired option, simply click on the appropriate icon.

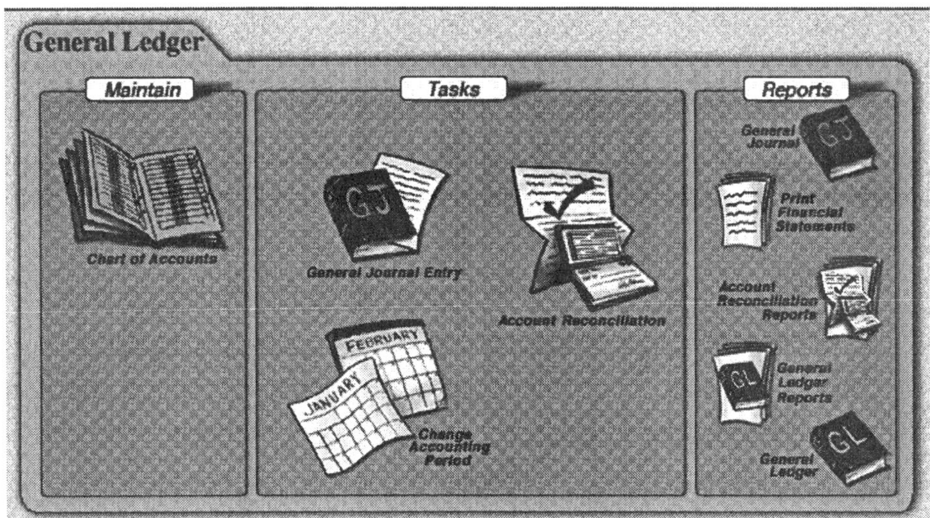

FIGURE 1.7 General Ledger Navigational Aid

OPENING A PEACHTREE COMPANY DATA FILE

The Open Company option allows you to access previously created company files. Each of the selected problems has been set up as a company. Follow the steps below to open a company file.

- ▶ **From the File menu, select Open Company. The Open Company window shown in Figure 1.8 will appear.**
- ▶ **Select the data file you wish to open from the Company Name field and click Ok.**
- ▶ **If the company name you wish to work with does not appear, go to the Directories field and double-click the directory containing your data files. The list of data files will appear in the Company Name field. Select the data file you wish to open and click Ok.**

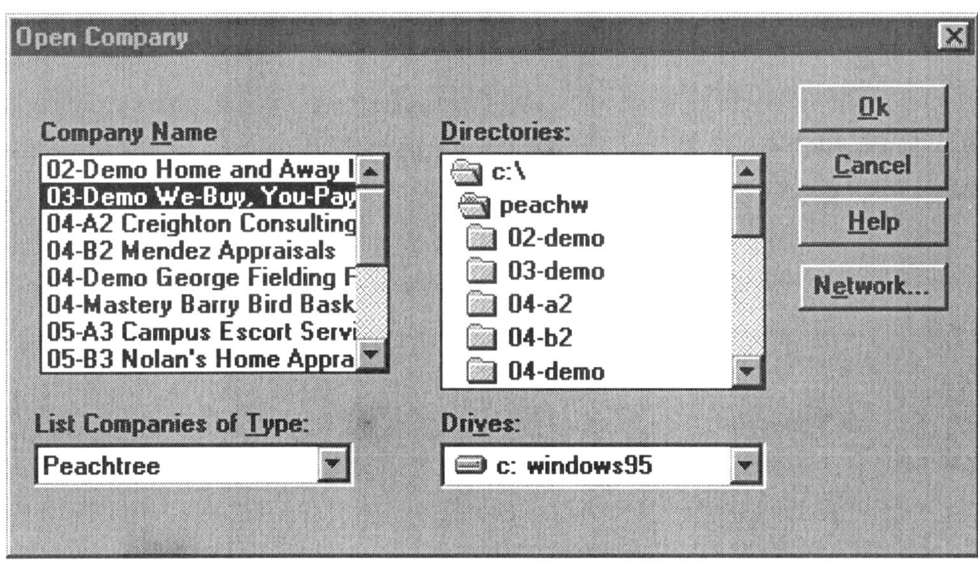

FIGURE 1.8 Open Company Window

PEACHTREE ACCOUNTING WINDOWS

When you select a menu option, a data entry window will often appear. The Maintain Chart of Accounts window, a typical data entry window, is illustrated in Figure 1.9.

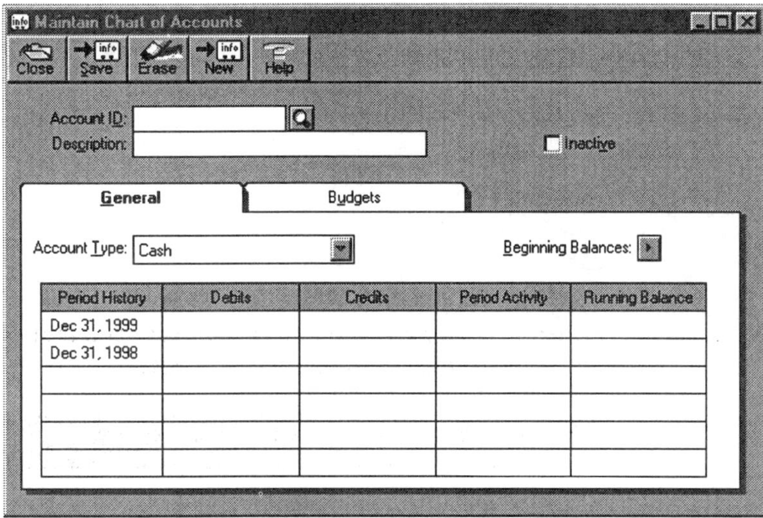

FIGURE 1.9 Peachtree Data Entry Window

Icon Bar. The strip of buttons near the top of the window is called the Icon Bar. The Close button will exit the window without saving any work entered since the last Save. The Save button saves the Chart of Accounts entry just entered. The Erase button causes the entry you are working with to be deleted. The New button will clear the window and allow you to enter a new entry. The Help button calls up the context-sensitive help system and provides useful information about the current activity.

Folder Tabs. Notice the General and Budget Folder Tabs. Many windows in Peachtree Accounting have Folder Tabs that allow easy navigation between sections of the window. You can visualize them as file-folder tabs that you can flip through by simply clicking on the appropriate Folder Tab.

Lookup Boxes. Lookup Boxes are indicated by a button with a magnifying glass. Click on the magnifying glass button to display a list from which you may select an option. An example of the Chart of Accounts Lookup Box is shown in Figure 1.10. You can also display the Lookup Box by typing a ? or by clicking the right mouse button from within the associated text box.

101	Cash	Cash
103	Accounts Receivable	Accounts Receivable
105	Office Equipment	Other Assets
107	Computer Equipment	Other Assets
201	Accounts Payable	Accounts Payable
203	Notes Payable	Long Term Liabilities
301	Celia Pints, Capital	Equity-Retained Earnings
303	Celia Pints, Drawing	Equity-gets closed
401	Shopping Fees	Income
501	Rent Expense	Expenses
503	Telephone Expense	Expenses
505	Commissions Expense	Expenses

Ok Cancel Find Next Help

FIGURE 1.10 Chart of Accounts Lookup Box

Drop-Down List. A down-arrow button to the right of the field indicates that a drop-down list is available. Only the options in the list are allowable for the associated data field. The Account Type drop-down list is shown in Figure 1.11.

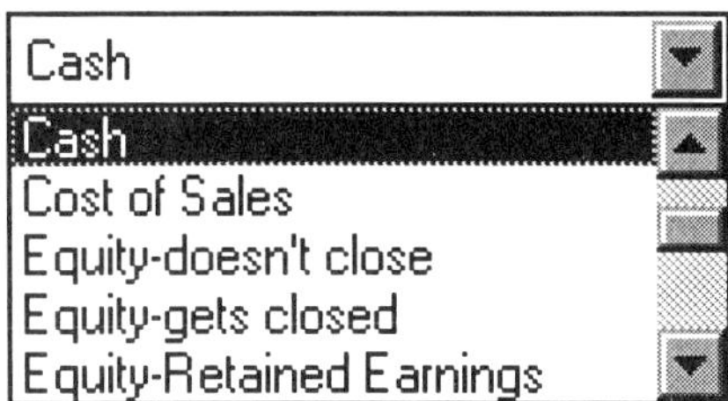

FIGURE 1.11 Account Type Drop-Down List

Status Bar. The status bar at the bottom of the screen provides a brief explanation of the current field. It also shows the current system date and the current accounting period. An illustration appears in Figure 1.12.

Select from the list the account type for this account. | 4/7/98 | Period 1 - 1/1/99 to 12/31/99

FIGURE 1.12 Status Bar

Smart Guide. The Smart Guide is a window that pops up and provides an explanation of the current field. The Smart Guide can be turned on or off with the Smart Guide menu option from the Options menu. The Maintain Chart of Accounts window is shown with Smart Guide active in Figure 1.13.

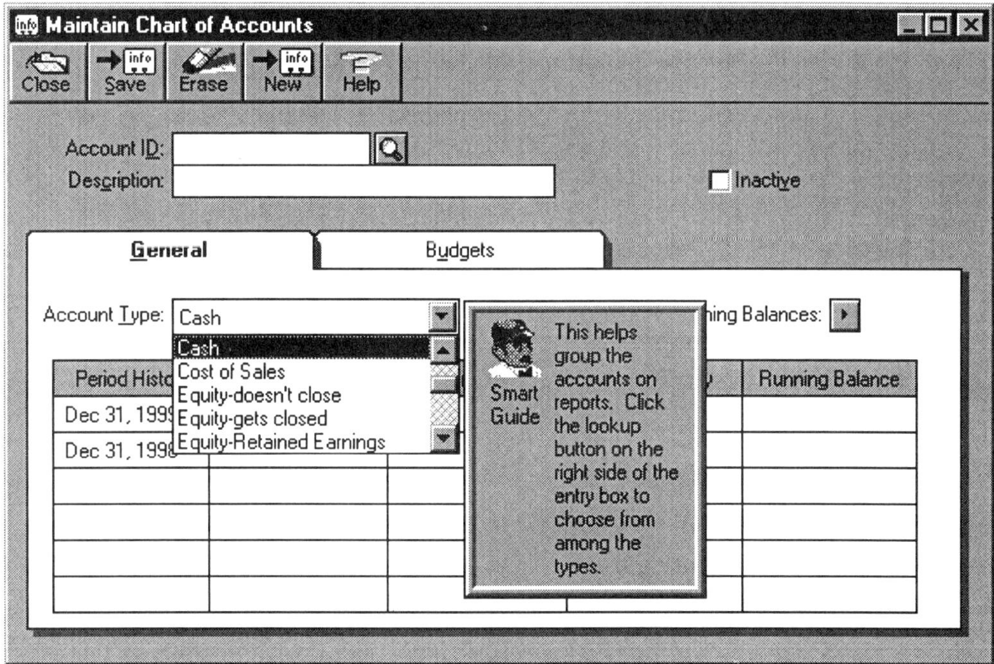

FIGURE 1.13 Maintain Chart of Accounts Window with Smart Guide Active

Pop-Up Calendar. All data entry windows that have a date field have available the pop-up calendar shown in Figure 1.14. To bring up the calendar, simply click on the calendar icon next to the date field. There are arrow buttons next to the year and month which can be clicked on to increase or decrease the year or month. Once you have set the calendar to the correct month and year, click on the day of the month. The calendar will close, and the selected date will appear in the date field. A shortcut method of entering the date is available if the month and year of the date are correct and you only wish to change the day of the month: you can simply enter the two-digit day of the month into the date field.

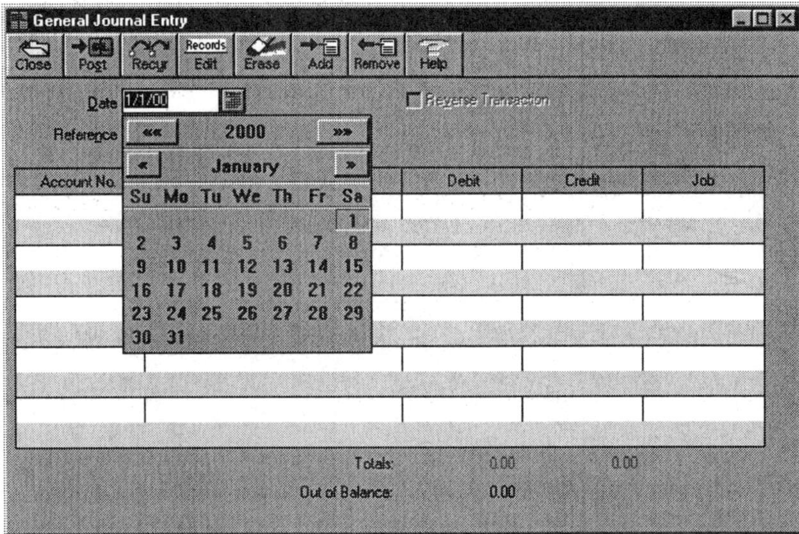

FIGURE 1.14 Pop-Up Calendar

CHART OF ACCOUNTS AND ENTERING BEGINNING BALANCES WINDOWS

The Maintain Chart of Accounts window shown in Figure 1.15 is used to add new accounts, to modify existing accounts, and to delete an existing account.

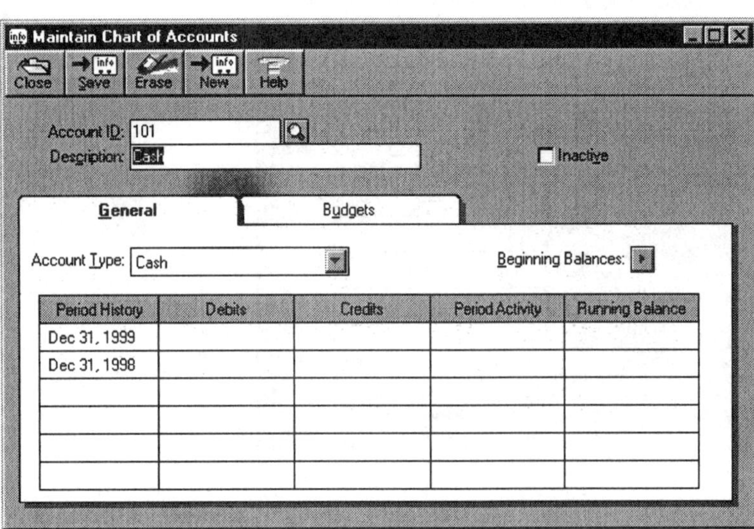

FIGURE 1.15 Maintain Chart of Accounts Window

To add a new account to the chart of accounts, complete the following:

- ▶ **Enter the Account Number in the Account ID field.**
- ▶ **Enter the Account Title in the Description field.**
- ▶ **Select the Account Type from the drop-down list.**
- ▶ **Click on the Save button to record the account.**

To make a change to an existing account, complete these steps:

- ▶ **Click on the magnifying glass button next to the account number, then select the account you wish to modify.**
- ▶ **Enter the changes to the account.**
- ▶ **Click on the Save button to record the changes.**

Complete the following steps to delete an account:

- ▶ **Click on the magnifying glass button next to the account number, and choose the account you wish to delete.**
- ▶ **Click on the Erase button.**

To record beginning account balances, complete the following:

- ▶ **Click on the arrow button labeled "Beginning Balances:" near the center of the window to the right of the Account Type field.**
- ▶ **When the Select Period dialog box appears, choose the accounting period for which you wish to enter opening balance data and click on Ok.**
- ▶ **When the Chart of Accounts Beginning Balances window shown in Figure 1.16 appears, enter the account balances. Make sure that you enter the decimal point. After entering each account balance, press Tab to move to the next account.**
- ▶ **After all balances are entered, click on the Ok button.**

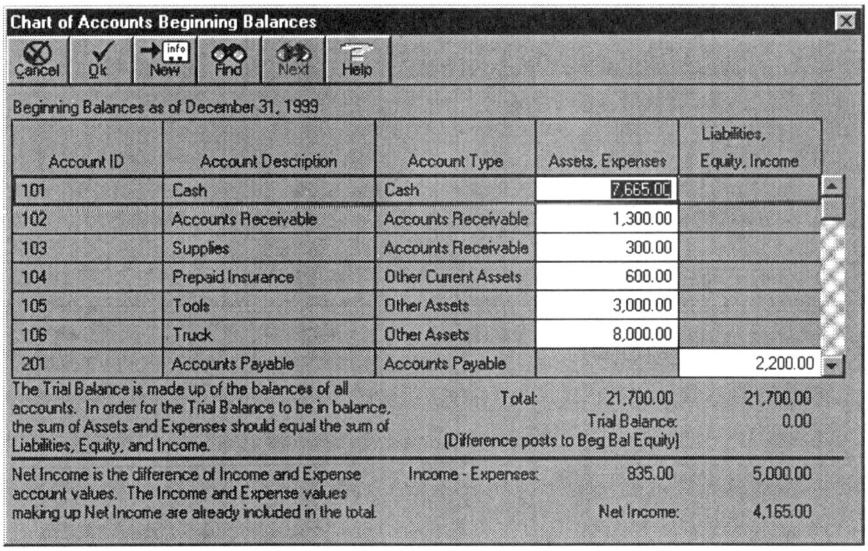

Chart of Accounts Beginning Balances

Cancel | Ok | New | Find | Next | Help

Beginning Balances as of December 31, 1999

Account ID	Account Description	Account Type	Assets, Expenses	Liabilities, Equity, Income
101	Cash	Cash	7,665.00	
102	Accounts Receivable	Accounts Receivable	1,300.00	
103	Supplies	Accounts Receivable	300.00	
104	Prepaid Insurance	Other Current Assets	600.00	
105	Tools	Other Assets	3,000.00	
106	Truck	Other Assets	8,000.00	
201	Accounts Payable	Accounts Payable		2,200.00

The Trial Balance is made up of the balances of all accounts. In order for the Trial Balance to be in balance, the sum of Assets and Expenses should equal the sum of Liabilities, Equity, and Income.

Total: 21,700.00 21,700.00
Trial Balance: 0.00
(Difference posts to Beg Bal Equity)

Net Income is the difference of Income and Expense account values. The Income and Expense values making up Net Income are already included in the total.

Income - Expenses: 835.00 5,000.00
Net Income: 4,165.00

FIGURE 1.16 Chart of Accounts Beginning Balances

You will notice that as you enter the account balances two totals are updated near the bottom of the window. The first is the total of Assets and Expenses; the second is the total of liabilities, equity, and income. After all balances have been entered, the two totals must be equal. If they are not, you must find and fix any errors or the software will not allow you to proceed.

GENERAL JOURNAL ENTRY WINDOW

The General Journal Entry window is illustrated in Figure 1.17. Follow the steps below to enter general journal transactions.

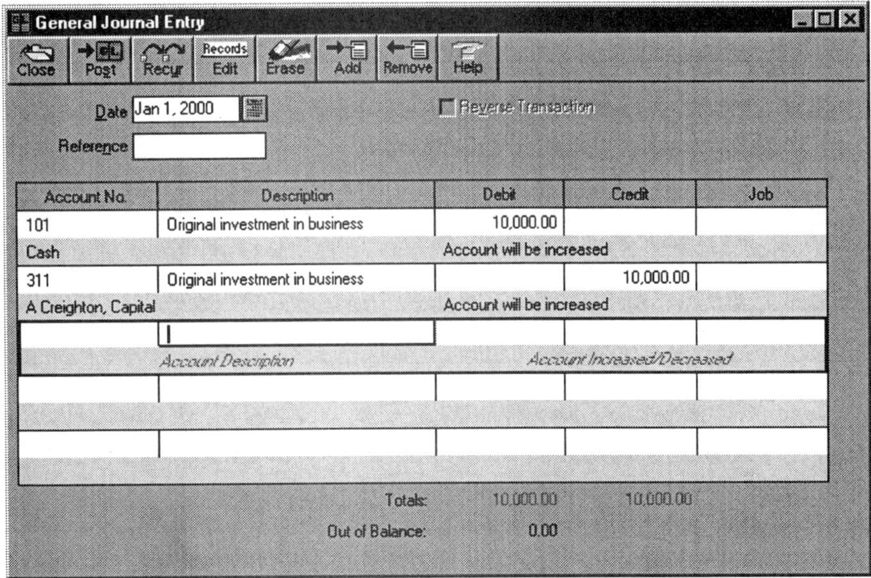

FIGURE 1.17 General Journal Entry Window

- **From the Tasks menu, select the General Journal Entry option.**
- **Enter the date of the transaction. Click on the Calendar icon next to the Date field to select the date from the pop-up calendar. If the month and year are correct, you can use the shortcut method of just keying the two-digit day of the month.**
- **Enter the reference, if one is provided, up to twenty characters in length. If none is provided, leave the reference blank. Examples would be check number, invoice number, or other meaningful transaction reference that will provide an audit trail to the original transaction source document.**
- **Enter the account number or select it from the drop-down list.**

You can add a new account to the chart of accounts by keying a +, by double-clicking in the Account Number text box, or by clicking on the magnifying glass icon, then selecting Records New.

- **Enter a description of the transaction.**
- **Enter the debit or credit amount (key the decimal point).**
- **After all the parts of the entry have been entered, click on the Post button to save and post the transaction.**
- **If you wish to insert a leg to the transaction between two existing legs, simply position the cursor to the point where you would like to insert the entry and click on the Add Icon Bar button. The software will open up a space to insert the entry.**
- **If you wish to remove a leg of a transaction, position the cursor to the line you wish to remove and click on the Remove Icon Bar button.**

To make changes, corrections, or deletions to existing journal entries, click on the Edit Icon Bar button. The Select Journal Entry window shown in Figure 1.18 will appear.

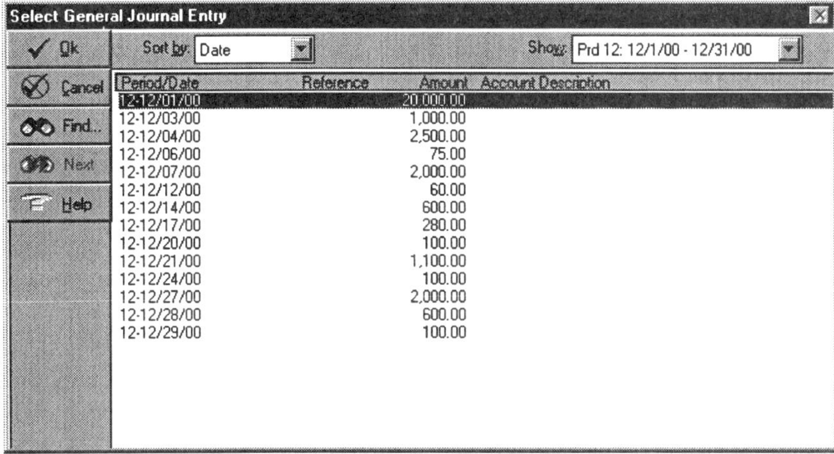

FIGURE 1.18 Select General Journal Entry Window

- ▶ **Highlight the journal entry you wish to change or delete and click on the Ok button.**
- ▶ **To locate a journal entry, you can use the Find button. A text box will appear. Enter the search argument you wish to search for such as an amount, description, or reference. The journal entry will be located and highlighted. Click Next to find the next occurrence of that search argument.**
- ▶ **Click on Cancel to return to the General Journal Entry window without selecting a journal entry.**

Notice that the upper right corner of the window contains a drop-down list labeled "Show" that displays the current accounting period. If you wish to access transactions from a different (not previously closed) accounting period, select that period from the drop-down list. The general ledger transactions for that period will be displayed so that you can make changes and corrections to them.

ACCOUNT RECONCILIATION WINDOW

The Account Reconciliation window illustrated in Figure 1.19 allows you to reconcile your bank account.

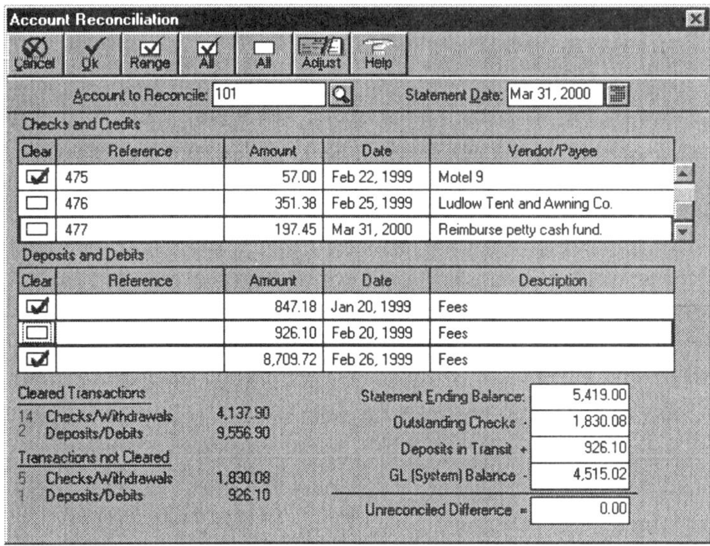

FIGURE 1.19 Account Reconciliation Window

The procedure for reconciling a bank account is detailed below:

- ▶ **From the Tasks menu, select Account Reconciliation.**
- ▶ **Select the account you want to reconcile.**
- ▶ **Enter the closing date from the bank's statement as the Statement Date.**
- ▶ **Enter the Statement Ending Balance from the bank statement in the lower right section of the window.**
- ▶ **Mark the Checks and Credits that have cleared (those not marked represent the outstanding checks). Checks and Credits can be marked as cleared by clicking in the Clear box to place a check mark there indicating the item has cleared.**
- ▶ **Mark the Deposits and Debits that have cleared by clicking in the Clear box associated with that item.**
- ▶ **If there are additional withdrawals or additional deposits, click on the Adjust Icon Bar button.**

The Additional Transactions window appears in Figure 1.20. Follow the steps below to enter any additional withdrawals or deposits.

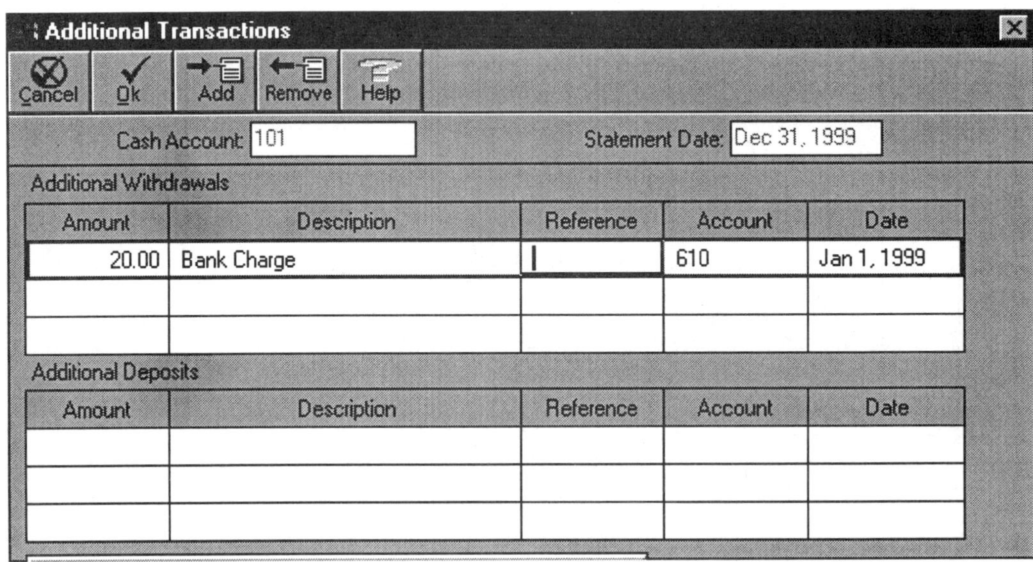

FIGURE 1.20 Additional Transactions Window

- ▶ **Enter the adjustments.**
- ▶ **Click on Ok when finished.**
- ▶ **These transactions will now appear in the Account Reconciliation window.**
- ▶ **Mark the new adjustments as cleared.**
- ▶ **When you are finished reconciling, click on Ok.**

DISPLAYING AND PRINTING REPORTS

Reports can be directed either to the screen display or to an attached printer. While many standard reports are available, reports can be customized to meet specific needs. Often, the data files will contain reports customized to meet the needs of a particular accounting problem. Follow the steps provided to display and/or print reports.

- **Select the menu option you want from the Reports menu shown in Figure 1.21.**
- **Select the area of Peachtree you want from the Report Area. The reports available for that area will display in the Report List section.**
- **Select the report you want from the Report List.**
- **Click the Screen Icon Bar button to display the highlighted report. A window will appear that will allow you to customize the report just selected. Because any needed customization has already been done for the files, simply click on the Ok button. For transaction reports or list reports, you may want to use the Filter option to limit the entries listed on the report. Refer to the Section titled "Using the Report Filter" for details on using that feature.**
- **To print the report, click on the Print Icon Bar button.**
- **Click on the Close Icon Bar button to exit from the currently displayed report.**

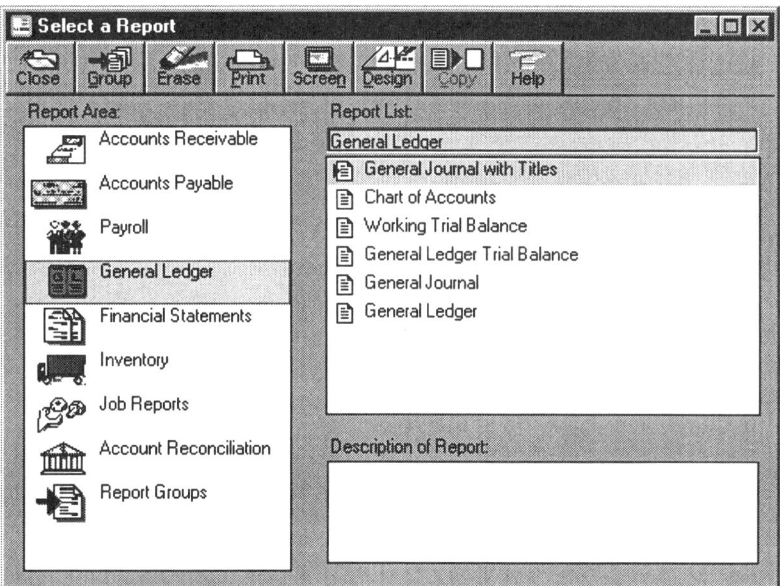

FIGURE 1.21 Select a Report Window

USING THE REPORT FILTER

The Report Filter option allows you to select which transactions or list items are to appear on the report. Follow the steps below to use this feature:

- **Select the Screen icon after you have selected the report. The Filter folder shown in Figure 1.22 will appear.**

Note: If you double-click on the report, the Filter window will be skipped.

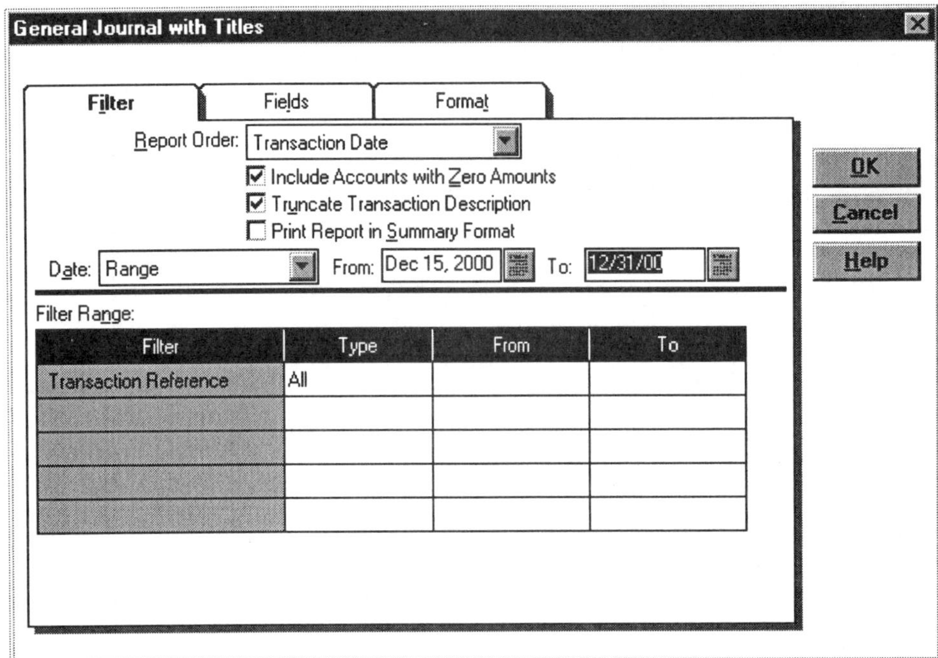

FIGURE 1.22 General Journal Filter Tab

- ▶ **To accept the defaults and display the report, just click on Ok.**
- ▶ **To filter the report entries, make any entries you want in the fields to establish the kind of information you want to include in the report and then click on Ok to display the report.**

Figure 1.22, for example, allows you to filter the general journal entries. You can restrict the general journal entries to a date range or restrict by transaction reference. In the example, only transactions in the December 15th to December 31st range will be displayed. An example of filtering by Transaction Reference field would be to list only transactions with references in the range of 1,000 to 1,100.

VIEWING REPORT DETAIL

When displayed on the screen, some areas on reports are outlined in a box and the cursor changes to a magnifying glass as illustrated in Figure 1.23. This signifies that the drill-down feature is available for this data. This means you can access the transaction that resulted in this report entry and make changes and corrections to it. This is a very convenient way to make corrections to transactions. This means, for example, if you are viewing a general journal report and discover an error in a journal entry, you can access and correct that journal entry by simply double-clicking on the transaction within the report.

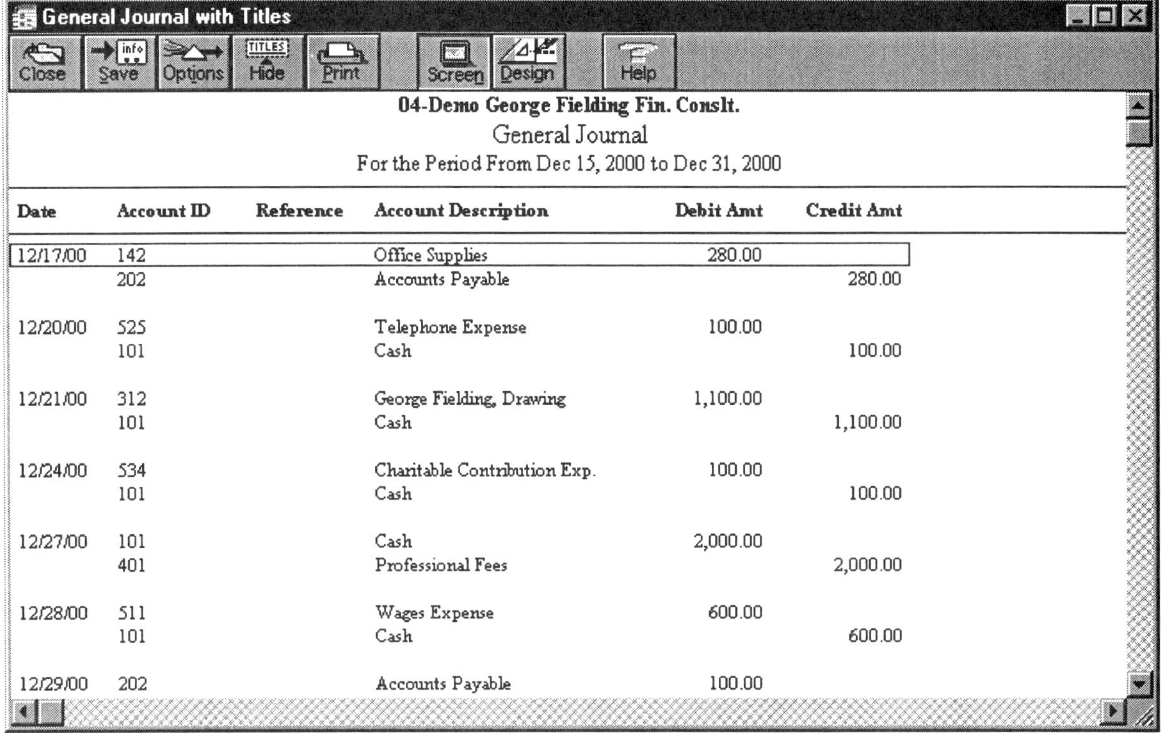

General Journal with Titles

04-Demo George Fielding Fin. Conslt.
General Journal
For the Period From Dec 15, 2000 to Dec 31, 2000

Date	Account ID	Reference	Account Description	Debit Amt	Credit Amt
12/17/00	142		Office Supplies	280.00	
	202		Accounts Payable		280.00
12/20/00	525		Telephone Expense	100.00	
	101		Cash		100.00
12/21/00	312		George Fielding, Drawing	1,100.00	
	101		Cash		1,100.00
12/24/00	534		Charitable Contribution Exp.	100.00	
	101		Cash		100.00
12/27/00	101		Cash	2,000.00	
	401		Professional Fees		2,000.00
12/28/00	511		Wages Expense	600.00	
	101		Cash		600.00
12/29/00	202		Accounts Payable	100.00	

FIGURE 1.23 General Journal Report (Drill-Down Feature)

▶ **Move the mouse pointer over a transaction outlined by the blue box. The cursor changes to a magnifying glass. Double-click the detail area you want to correct. The corresponding data entry window with the transaction display will appear as shown in Figure 1.24.**

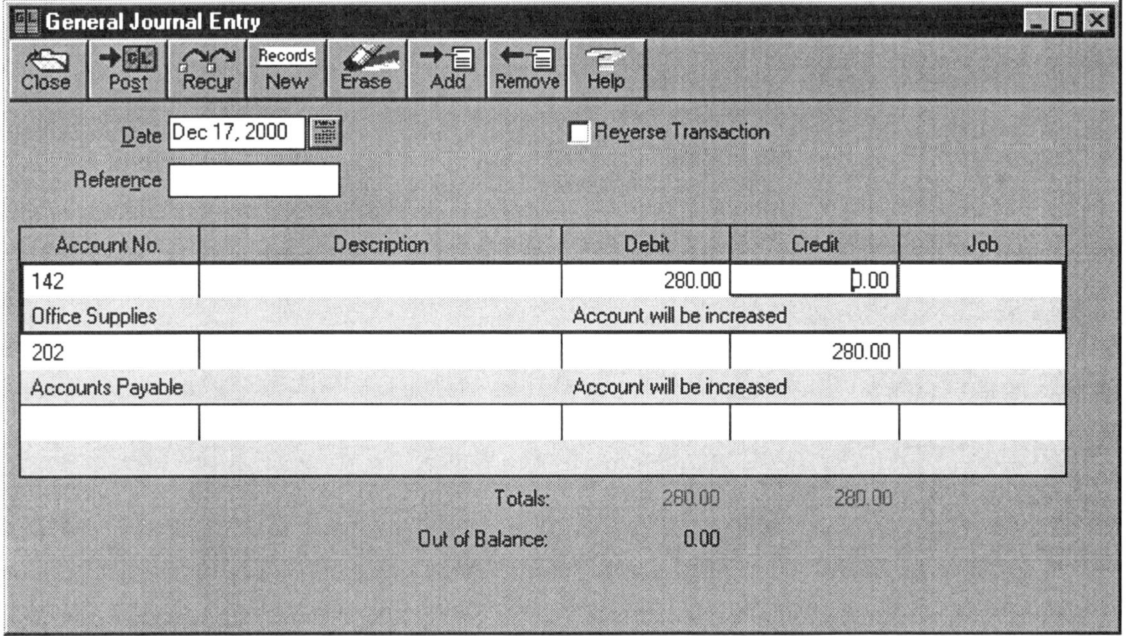

FIGURE 1.24 General Journal Entry (Making a Correction from Journal Report)

- ▶ **Make any change you wish to make to the transaction.**
- ▶ **Click on the Post icon to save your changes.**
- ▶ **Click on the Close button.**

CHANGING ACCOUNTING PERIODS

In Peachtree Accounting, accounting periods are established when the company is created. Each fiscal year is separated into anywhere from 1 to 13 accounting periods. You can have up to 26 periods or two fiscal years available at one time. This means you can have last year's history available for editing or adjusting throughout the current year. Before beginning processing for the next accounting period, you must change accounting periods. The process of changing accounting periods is identified in the following steps:

- ▶ **From the Tasks menu, select System then Change Accounting Periods from the submenu. The Change Accounting Period window shown in Figure 1.25 will appear.**
- ▶ **Select the accounting period to which you want to change, and select Ok.**
- ▶ **A message box appears, reminding you to back up and to print applicable reports. If you have already printed reports, choose No.**

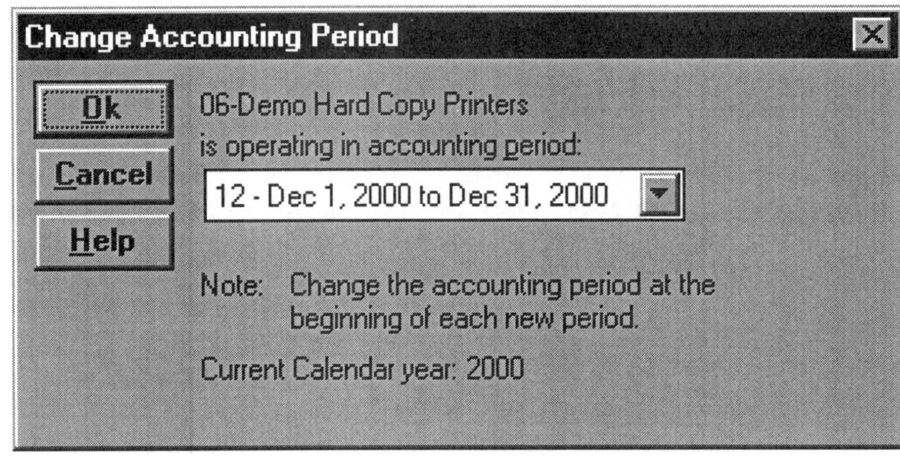

FIGURE 1.25 Change Accounting Periods Window

PAYROLL ENTRY

The Payroll Entry window allows you to select the employees to be paid this period and to enter hours and other pertinent information related to the current pay period. The computer will calculate and display earnings and withholdings data which you can modify if need be. Follow the steps listed below.

- ▶ **From the Tasks menu, select the Payroll Entry option. The Payroll Entry windows shown in Figure 1.26 will appear.**

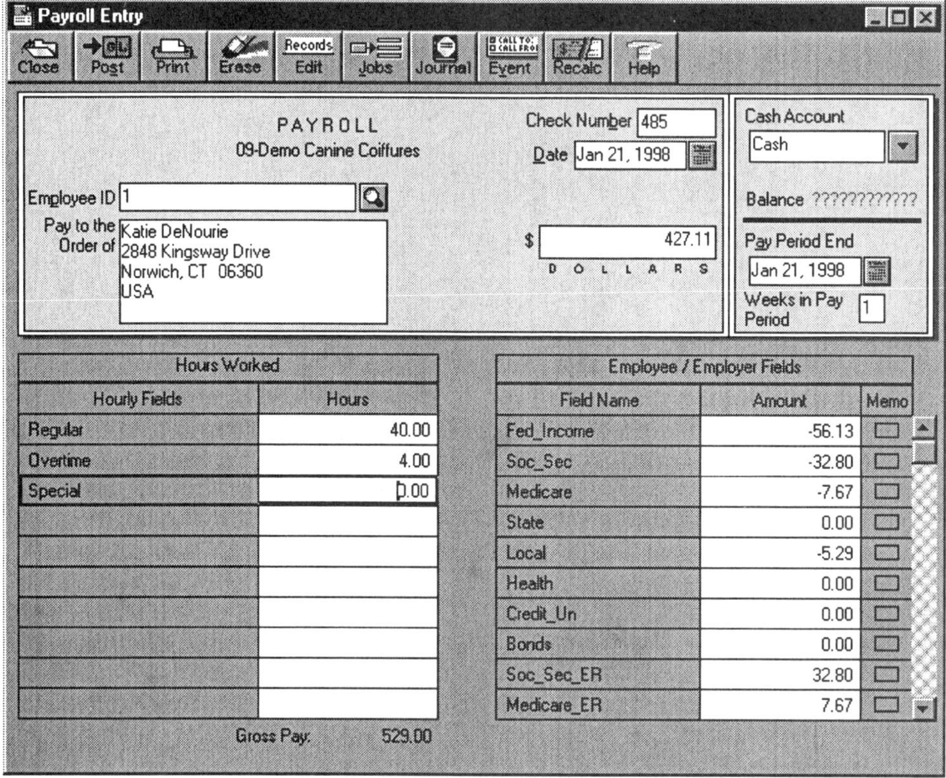

FIGURE 1.26 Payroll Entry Window

- **Enter or select the Employee ID code.**
- **Enter the Check Number.**
- **Enter the Date of the check for this pay period.**
- **Enter the Pay Period Ended date if different from the Date of the check.**
- **Verify the Hourly or Salary amounts assigned. Make changes if necessary.**
- **You may click on the Journal Icon Bar button to view the journal entry that will be generated as a result of this entry. You can review the accounts affected and change the accounts if incorrect. The Accounting Behind the Screens journal window is illustrated in Figure 1.27.**
- **Click on the Post Icon Bar button to save the transaction.**

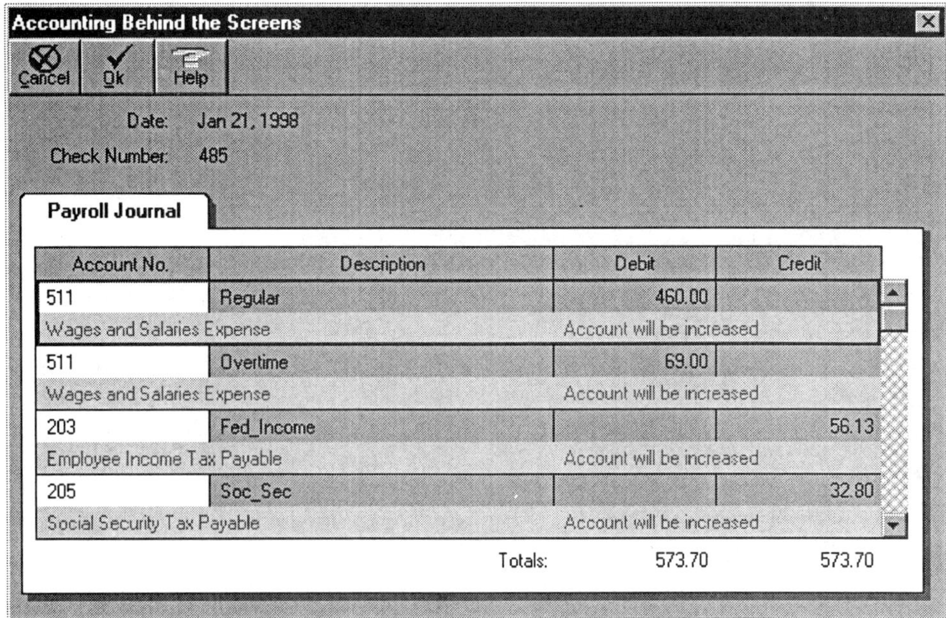

FIGURE 1.27 Accounting Behind the Screens Journal Window (Payroll Entry)

SALES/INVOICING WINDOW

Sales on account and credit memo transactions are entered into the Sales/Invoicing Window. The Sales/Invoicing Window is illustrated in Figure 1.28.

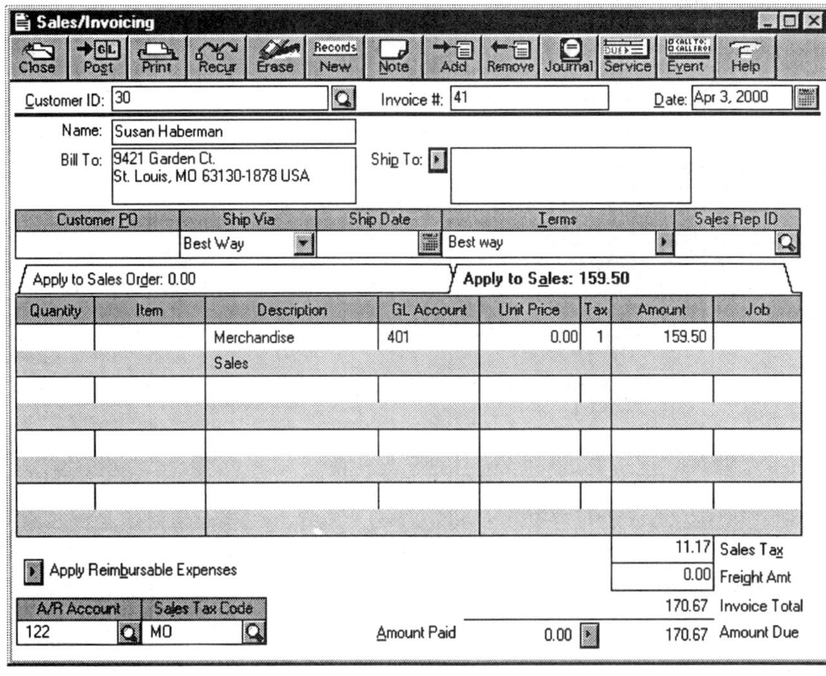

FIGURE 1.28 Sales/Invoicing Window (Sale on Account)

Sale on Account

- **From the Tasks menu, select Sales/Invoicing.**
- **Enter or select the Customer ID. When the customer is selected, Peachtree supplies customer default information including sales account, payment terms, and sales tax code.**
- **Enter the Invoice Number.**
- **Enter the Date of the transaction.**
- **Peachtree uses the default terms for that customer. When a receipt that qualifies for an early payment discount is applied to the invoice, Peachtree will calculate the discount. Therefore, it is most important that the terms shown are correct.**

You can select the Terms button to change the default discount dates or amounts for the invoice. Since the discount amount is recalculated each time the invoice amount changes, change the default discount information after you have finished entering all line items or it will be overwritten and recalculated with the customer default information.

- **Enter the description.**
- **Enter the account number of the revenue account to be credited in the GL Account field.**
- **Accept the default Tax Code, or select a different one. Tax Code 1 indicates that the item is taxable. Tax Code 2 indicates that it is exempt from sales tax.**
- **Enter the amount sold for this item.**
- **Verify the Sales Tax Code displayed in the lower left corner of the window. If it is incorrect, select the applicable Sales Tax Code.**
- **You can view the journal entry resulting from this transaction by clicking on the Journal Icon Bar button. An example is shown in Figure 1.29.**
- **Post the invoice by clicking on the Post Icon Bar button.**

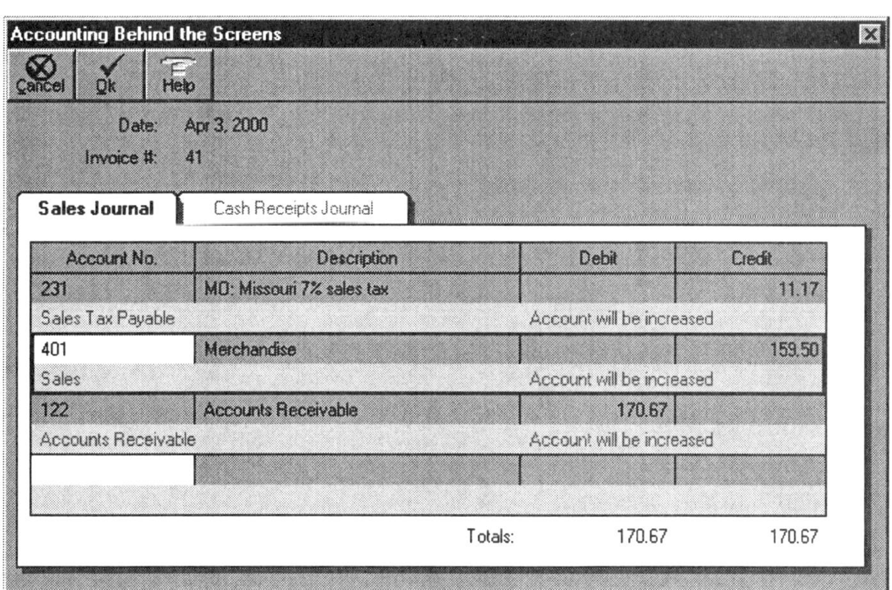

FIGURE 1.29 Accounting Behind the Screens (Sales Journal Entries)

Credit Memo

Credit Memos are entered in essentially the same way as normal invoices. The primary difference is that the amount is entered as a negative number. An example of a Credit Memo transaction is shown in the Sales/Invoicing window illustrated in Figure 1.30. The steps necessary for entering a sales return or allowance transaction follow the illustration.

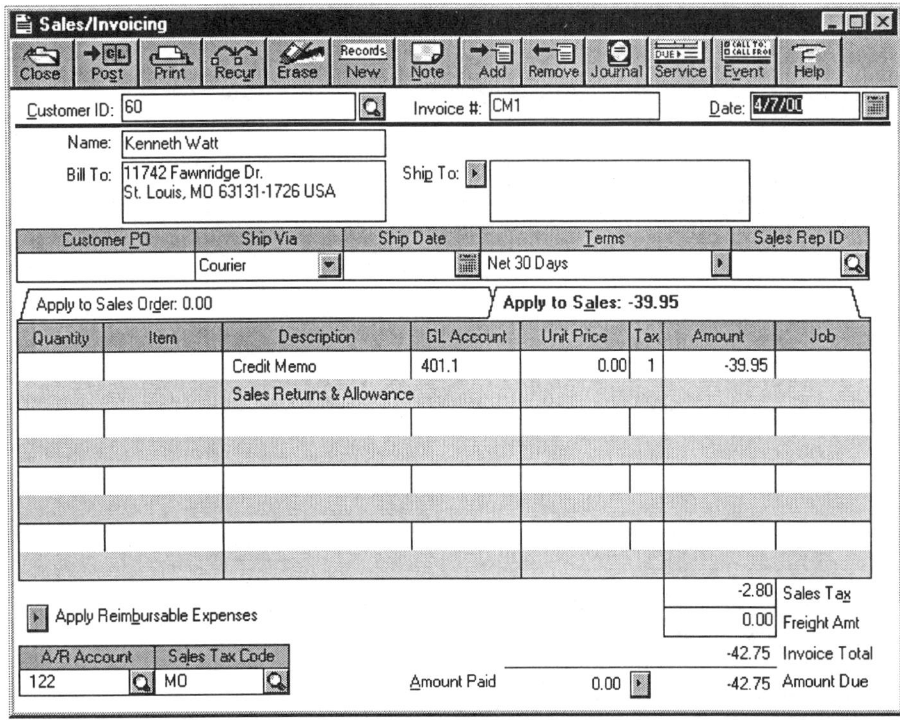

FIGURE 1.30 Sales/Invoicing Window (Credit Memo)

- **From the Tasks menu, select Sales/Invoicing.**
- **Enter or select the Customer ID.**
- **Enter a credit memo identifier in the Invoice Number field. If a credit memo number is provided, enter it. If not, key CM plus the original invoice number (CM801, for example). If the original invoice number is not provided, key CM plus part of the customer name so the item is easily identifiable.**
- **Enter the Date of the credit memo. It is important that you enter the correct date, since Peachtree uses this date to determine whether partial discounts will be applied.**
- **Enter "Credit Memo" in the Description field.**
- **Enter the account number of the Sales Returns and Allowances account in the GL Account field.**
- **Accept or change the Tax Code (1=taxable, 2=exempt).**
- **Enter the amount of the credit memo as a negative number as illustrated in Figure 1.30.**
- **Verify that the correct Sales Tax Code is displayed in the lower left corner of the window. The Sales Tax Code is usually the name or abbreviation of the respective state. In the example in Figure 1.30, the code MO represents Missouri.**
- **You can view the journal entry resulting from this transaction by clicking on the Journal Icon Bar button. An example is shown in Figure 1.31.**
- **Post the Credit Memo by clicking on the Post Icon Bar button.**

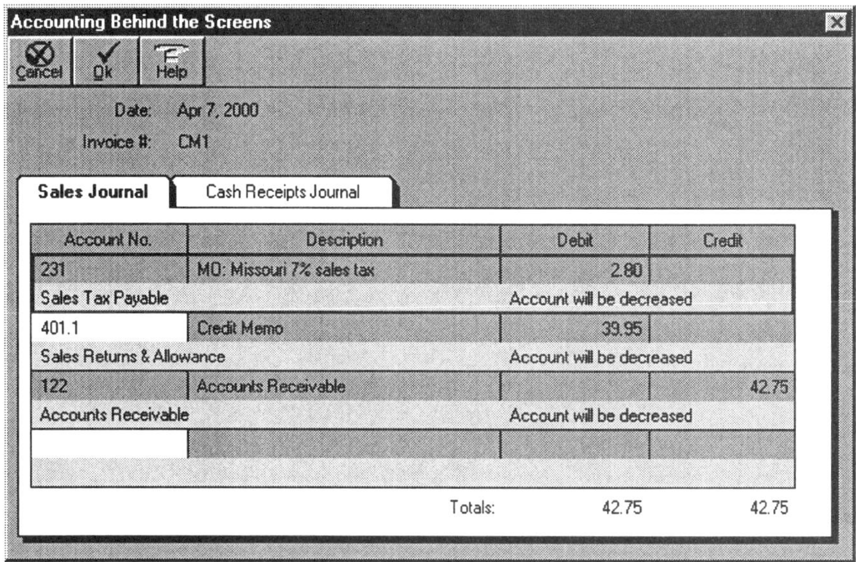

FIGURE 1.31 Accounting Behind the Screens (Credit Memo Journal Entry)

PURCHASE TRANSACTIONS

The Purchases/Receive Inventory task allows you to enter purchases on account and credit memo transactions. The Purchases/Receive Inventory window is illustrated in Figure 1.32.

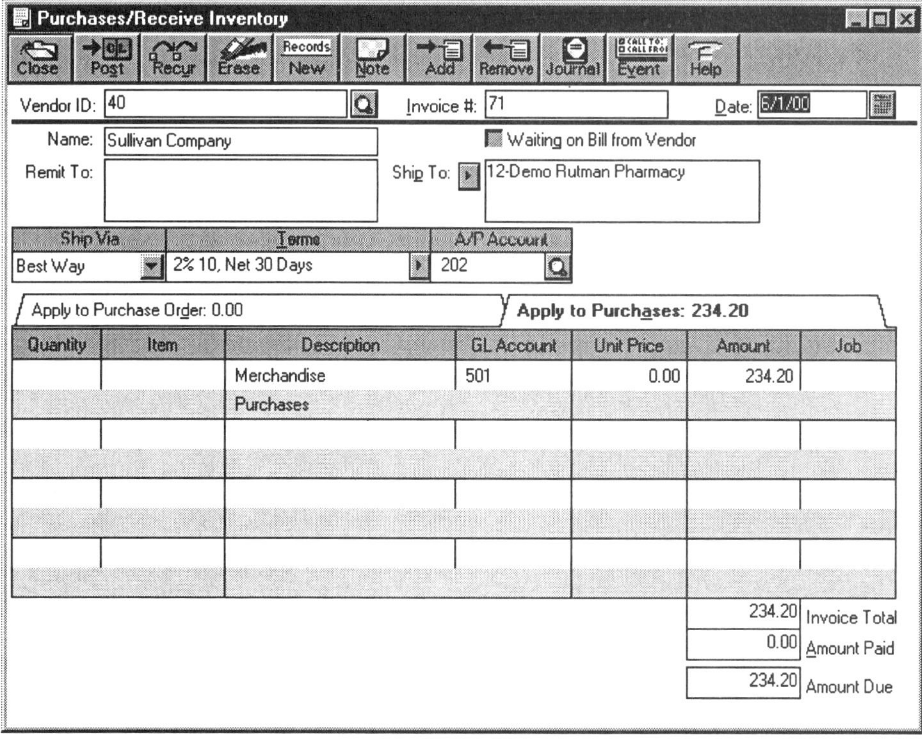

FIGURE 1.32 Purchases/Receive Inventory Window

Purchase on Account

- ▶ From the Task menu, select the Purchases/Receive Inventory option.
- ▶ Enter or select the Vendor ID code in the Vendor ID field.
- ▶ Enter the vendor's invoice number in the Invoice Number field.
- ▶ Enter the Date of the transaction.
- ▶ If the shipping instructions and terms of the invoice displayed are not correct, click on the right arrow button to make changes.
- ▶ If you are not using the Inventory system, leave the Quantity and Item fields blank.
- ▶ Enter a description of the transaction in the Description field.
- ▶ Enter or select the account number of the account to be debited. The default is the Purchases account.
- ▶ If you are not using the Inventory system, leave the Unit Price field blank.
- ▶ Enter the amount of the debit in the Amount field.
- ▶ Leave the Job number field blank.
- ▶ Continue entering transaction lines until the Invoice Total box equals the total balance of the vendor invoice.
- ▶ Click on Post to record the transaction.

Credit Memo (Purchases Returns and Allowances)

Purchases returns or allowances are entered in essentially the same way as normal invoices. The primary difference is that the amount is entered as a negative number. An example of a purchases allowance transaction is shown in the Purchases/Receive Inventory window illustrated in Figure 1.33. The steps necessary for entering a sales return or allowance transaction follow the illustration.

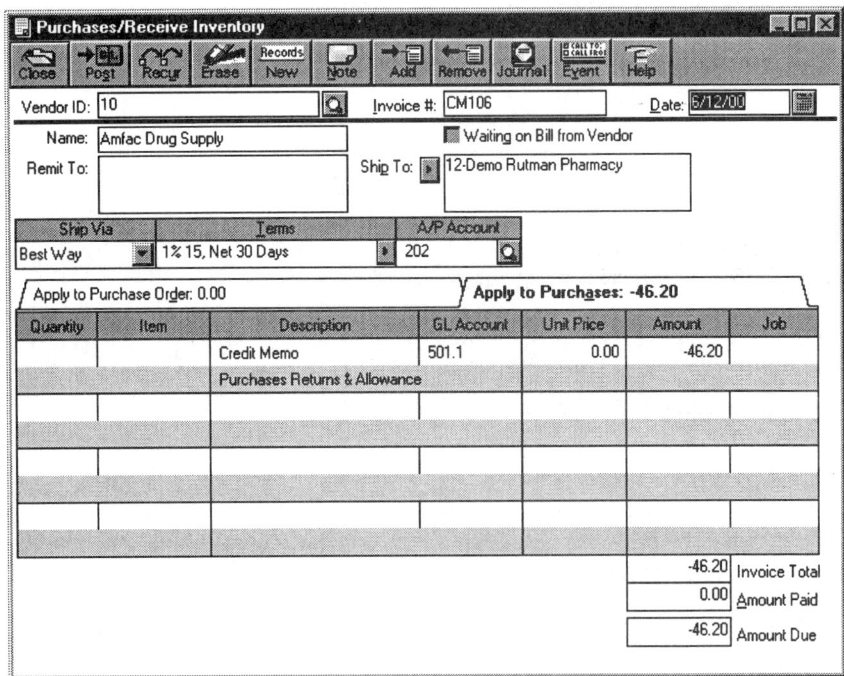

FIGURE 1.33 Purchases/Receive Inventory Window (Credit Memo)

- From the Task menu select the Purchases/Receive Inventory option.
- Enter or select the Vendor ID code in the Vendor ID field.
- Enter the CM followed by the original vendor's invoice number in the Invoice Number field (e.g., CM106).
- Enter the Date of the transaction.
- If the shipping instructions and terms of the invoice displayed are not correct, click on the right arrow button to make changes.
- If you are not using the Inventory system, leave the Quantity and Item fields blank.
- Enter a description of the transaction in the Description field.
- Enter or select the account number for Purchases Returns and Allowances.
- If you are not using the Inventory system, leave the Unit Price field blank.
- Enter the amount of the return or allowance in the Amount field as a negative number.
- Leave the Job number field blank.
- Click on Post to record the transaction.

PAYMENT TRANSACTIONS

The Payments window is illustrated in Figure 1.34. As you enter checks, a "stub" is displayed to the right of the check where you can select the cash account you want to use for the checks you are writing. The Payments window displays a check form at the top of the window in which you enter the Vendor information, Check Number, and Date. The bottom half of the window is divided into two tabs, Apply to Invoices and Apply to Expenses.

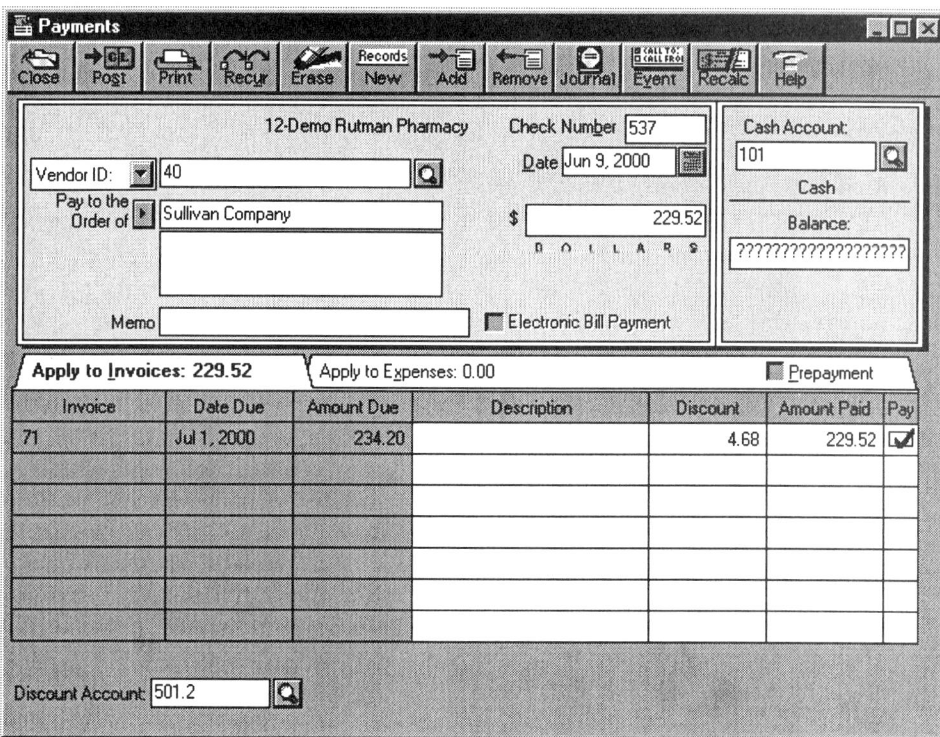

FIGURE 1.34 Payments Window

When you enter a Vendor ID, any open purchases invoices previously entered for that vendor display in the Apply to Invoices tab section as illustrated in Figure 1.34. You can then select the invoice(s) in the list. Next, either select the Pay box or enter the amount to apply against the invoice(s). If this is a cash purchase (direct payment as opposed to a previously-entered vendor invoice), the Apply to Expenses tab will be active.

Payment on Account

- ▶ **From the Tasks menu, select Payments.**
- ▶ **Enter or select the Vendor ID code of the vendor you want to pay.**

When you select a vendor with open invoices, the Apply to Invoices tab appears by default as illustrated in Figure 1.35. Notice that all the open invoices and credit memos for that particular vendor are listed.

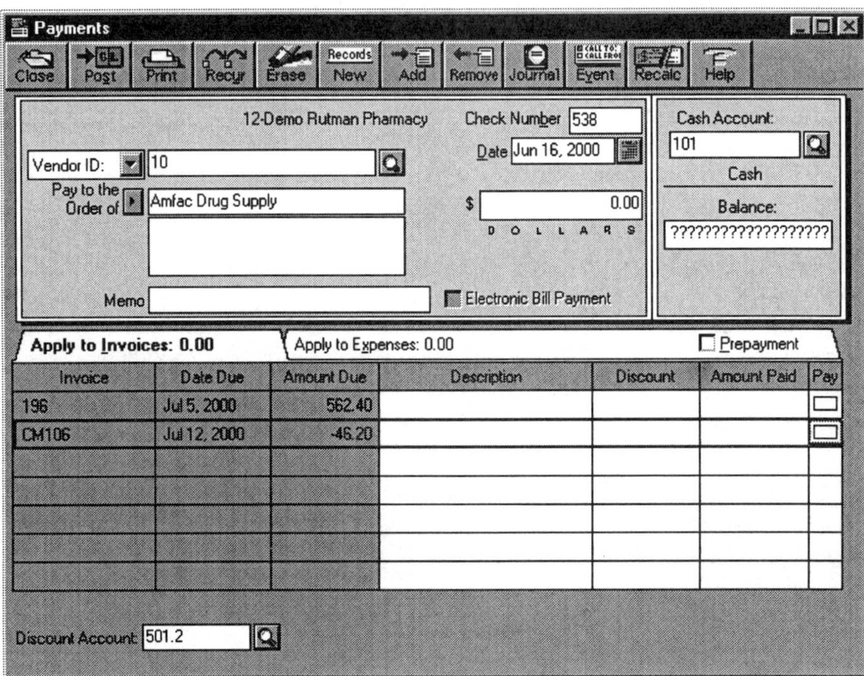

FIGURE 1.35 Payments Window (Apply to Invoices Tab)

- ▶ **If you are entering a handwritten check, enter the check number in the Check Number box. If you want Peachtree Accounting to print the check, leave this field blank.**
- ▶ **Enter or select the Date of the check.**
- ▶ **Change the Cash Account if necessary.**
- ▶ **To pay the invoice in full, you can select the Pay box next to the invoice and the amount will be entered automatically and a red check will appear in the Pay box.**
- ▶ **Enter a description of the transaction in the Description field.**
- ▶ **If you want to change the discount amount, do so after you check the Pay box.**

The check window displays the amount to be paid on this check and updates the amount as you select the invoices.

- ▶ **When you have completed paying invoices for a single check (the Check Amount box keeps a running total), select the Save or Post icon.**
- ▶ **Select the Journal Icon Bar button to display the Accounting Behind the Screens journal entries resulting from this transaction as illustrated in Figure 1.36.**

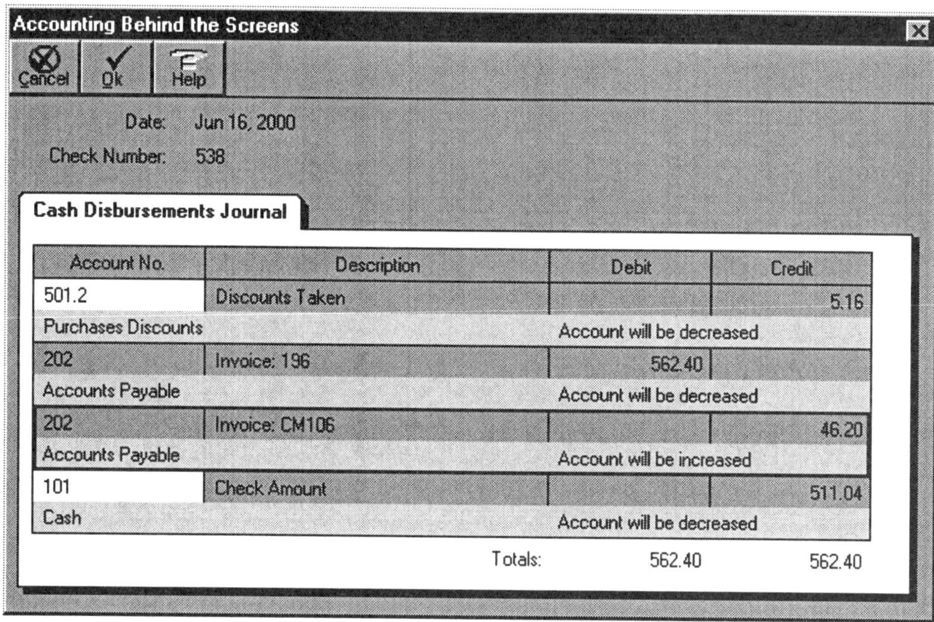

FIGURE 1.36 Accounting Behind the Screens (Payment on Account)

Cash Purchases (Direct Payment)

Instead of entering a Vendor ID, you can simply key the Payee into the Pay to the Order of field. In this case, the Apply to Expenses tab will be activated. This allows you to enter direct payments, such as rent payments, for which a vendor has not been set up. A direct payment is illustrated in Figure 1.37.

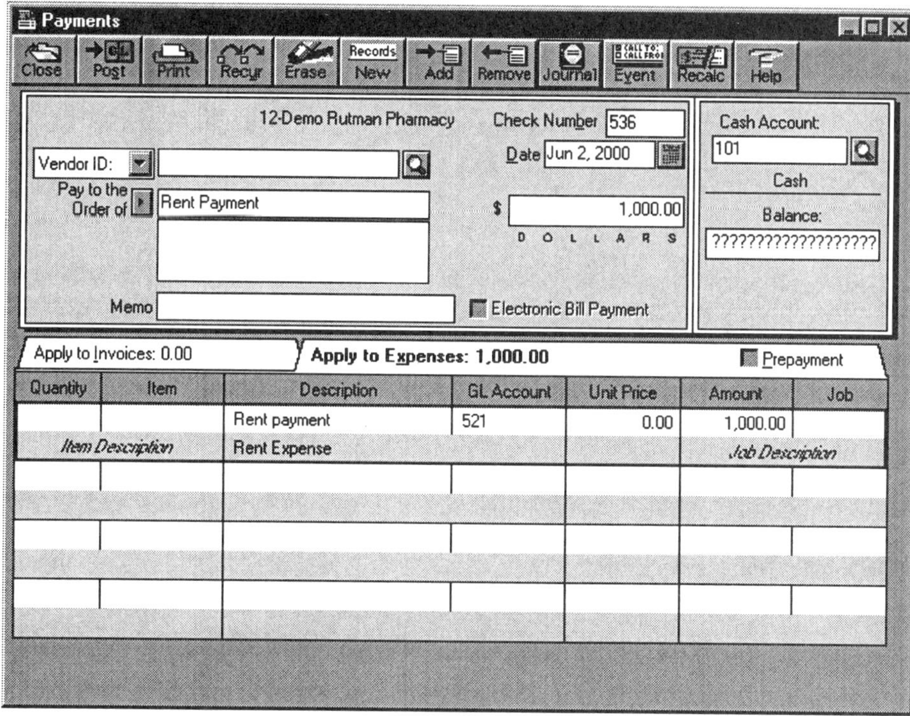

FIGURE 1.37 Payments Window (Direct Payment)

- **Enter the Payee in the Pay to the Order of field.**
- **Enter the Check Number.**
- **Enter the Date of the transaction.**
- **Enter a description in the Description field.**
- **Enter the account number of the account to be debited in the GL Account field.**
- **Enter the amount to be paid in the Amount field.**
- **Click on the Post button to record the transaction.**

REAL-TIME VS. BATCH

The decision to process transactions in real-time or by batch is made at the time a company file is set up. All of the companies in these materials are set up to process transactions in real-time. When the batch posting mode is used, as transactions are entered they are stored in a temporary holding area where you can review them before posting the batch to the general ledger. In real-time posting, the transactions are posted immediately as they are recorded. The mode to be used is established on the Maintain Company Information window available from the Maintain menu.

BACKING UP AND RESTORING DATA FILES

Peachtree has the built-in capability to backup (make a copy of) a set of company data files. The backup option will make a mirror-image copy of an existing set of data files on another drive and/or directory.

Backup

To backup or make a copy of the company data files that are currently open, complete the steps listed below:

- **From the File menu, select the Backup option. The Backup Company Data Files window shown in Figure 1.38 will appear.**

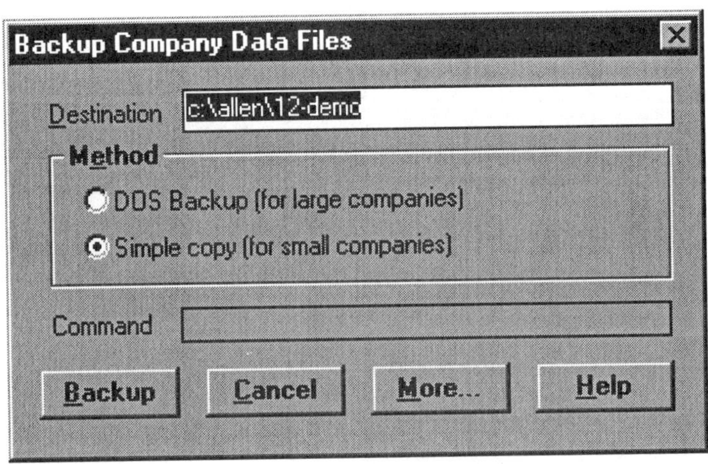

FIGURE 1.38 Backup Company Data Files Window

- Enter the path to the directory to which you wish to create the copy of the company data files. In the example, the current company files will be copied to the subdirectory 12-DEMO within the directory named ALLEN. In this example, the directory named ALLEN would have to exist; however, the subdirectory 12-DEMO would be created if necessary.
- Make sure that the "Simple copy (for small companies)" option button is selected.
- Click on the Backup button.

Restore

To restore the company data files for a company previously backed up with the backup procedure described above, complete the following steps:

- From the File menu select the Restore option. The Restore Company Data Files window shown in Figure 1.39 will appear.

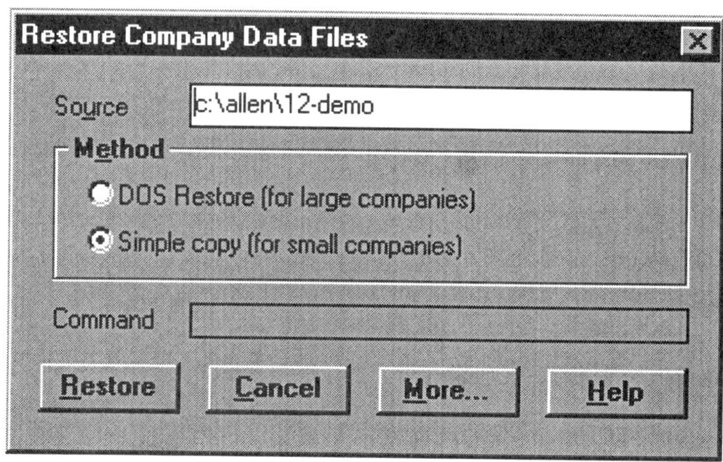

FIGURE 1.39 Restore Company Data Files Window

- Enter the path to the directory that contains the previously backed up company data files that you wish to restore.
- Make sure that the "Simple copy (for small companies)" option button is selected.
- Click on the Backup button.

SECTION 2

Instructions for Solving Selected Problems Using Peachtree Accounting Software

This section contains the instructions for solving problems using the Peachtree Accounting software. The beginning balance data for selected problems are included on the accompanying install disk(s) labeled "Peachtree 5.0 for Accounting." The Install program stores a master copy of the Peachtree data files for the problems on your computer's hard drive. Without these data files, you would be required to enter the chart of accounts, vendor, customers, employees, and beginning balances for each problem before proceeding to solve it using Peachtree software.

When the beginning balance data was prepared, a specific accounting year was required. The year 2000 was used to establish these initial balances. Therefore, as you are solving the problems, you will reference the year 2000 even though the actual year may be before or after 2000. The payroll problems are an exception to this arrangement in that the payroll transactions must be processed with a date in the year 1998. This is because the payroll tax tables utilized by the Peachtree software are for the year 1998. If a date later than 1998 is used, the software will be unable to calculate the payroll taxes.

CHAPTER 2 DEMONSTRATION PROBLEM (02-DEMO)

The Chapter 2 Demonstration Problem involves recording accounting transactions in the accounting equation and preparing financial statements for the company Home and Away Inspections. Because the Peachtree software does not have the capability of entering transactions into an accounting equation, you will instead utilize the software to create a chart of accounts, enter the account balances directly, and then display financial statements. The step-by-step instructions for solving the problem utilizing the Peachtree software are listed below:

STEP 1: Start up the Peachtree software.

Choose Peachtree Accounting from the Start button.

STEP 2: Open the data file for the Chapter 2 Demonstration Problem.

If the Startup Screen shown in Figure 2.1 appears on your screen, click on the Open button. If the screen shown in Figure 2.1 does not appear, click on the File menu and choose the Open Company menu option.

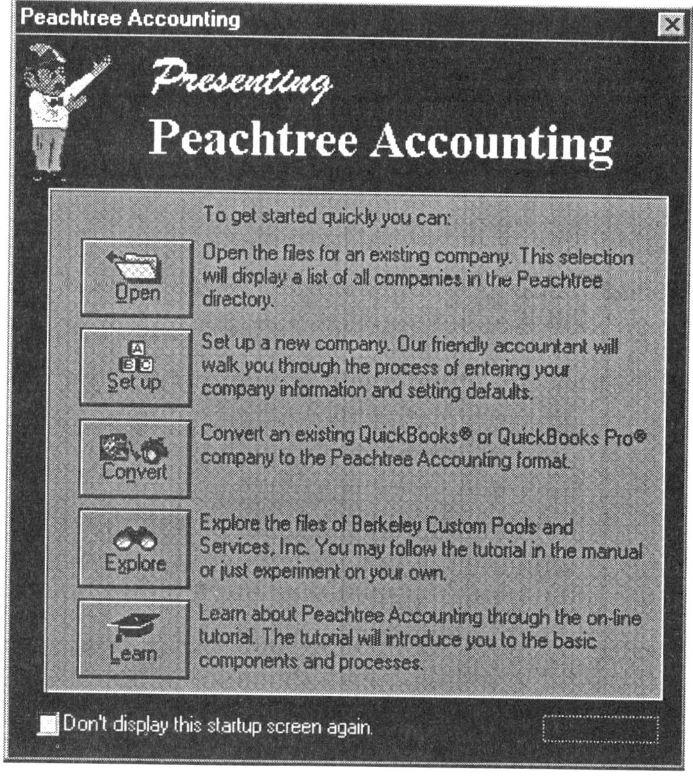

FIGURE 2.1 Peachtree Startup Dialog Box

When the Open Company dialog box shown in Figure 2.2 appears, select the directory in which you installed the Peachtree data files then choose the company named "02-Demo Home and Away."

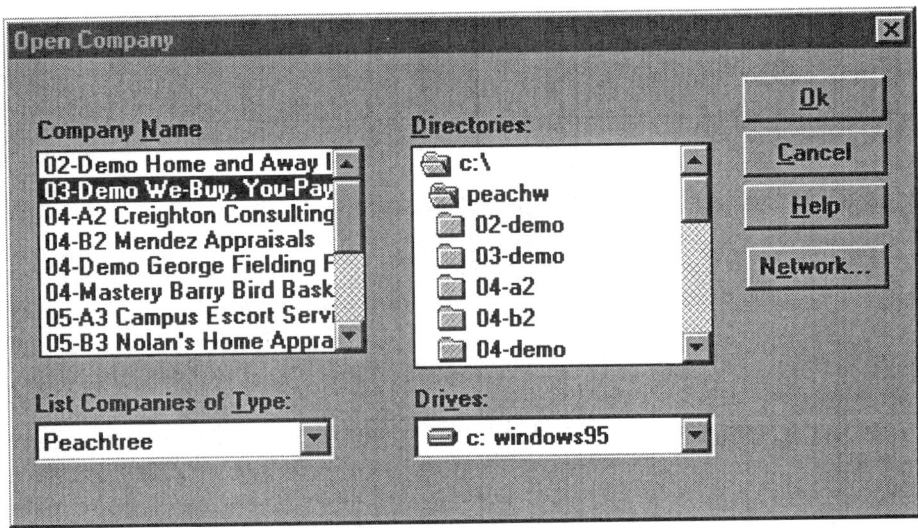

FIGURE 2.2 Open Company Dialog Box

STEP 3: Enter the chart of accounts entries shown below.

▶ **From the Maintain menu, choose the Chart of Accounts option.**

The Maintain Chart of Accounts window, with the first chart of accounts entry complete, is shown in Figure 2.3.

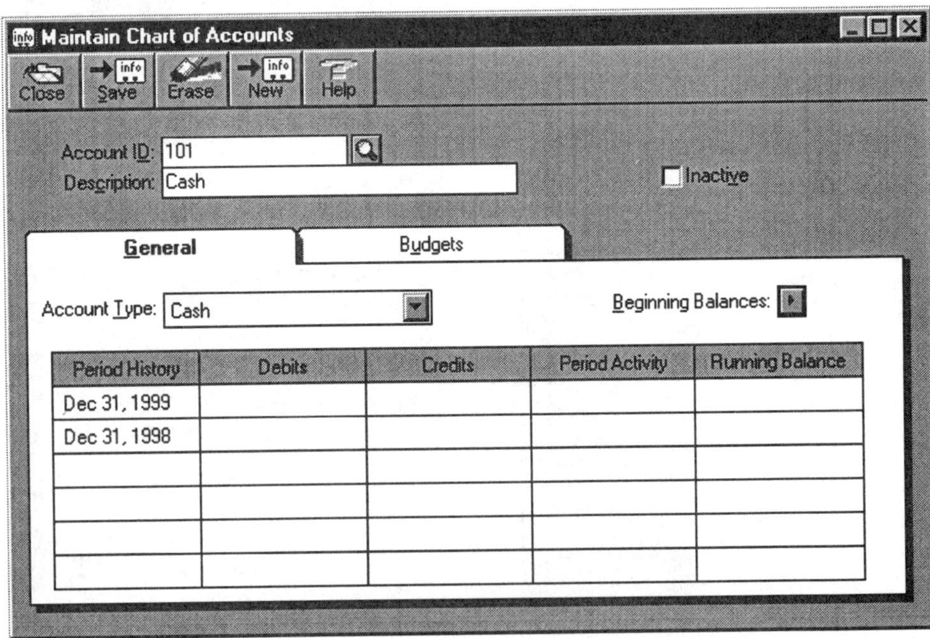

FIGURE 2.3 Maintain Chart of Accounts Window

▶ Enter the Account Number in the Account ID field.

▶ Enter the Account Title in the Description field.

▶ Select the Account Type from the drop-down list.

▶ Click on the Save button to record the account.

Account Number	Account Title	Account Type
101	Cash	Cash
102	Accounts Receivable	Accounts Receivable
103	Supplies	Other Current Asset
104	Prepaid Insurance	Other Current Asset
105	Tools	Fixed Asset
106	Truck	Fixed Asset
201	Accounts Payable	Accounts Payable
301	Damon Young, Capital	Equity-Retained Earnings
303	Damon Young, Drawing	Equity-Gets Closed
401	Inspection Fees	Income
501	Wages Expense	Expense
503	Rent Expense	Expense
505	Telephone Expense	Expense
507	Utilities Expense	Expense

STEP 4: Enter the account balances shown on the following page.

▶ Click on the right-arrow button labeled "Beginning Balances" on the Maintain Chart of Accounts window. The button is located near the center of the screen just to the right of the Account Type field.

▶ When the Select Period window shown in Figure 2.4 appears, choose "From 12/1/00 through 12/31/00" and click on Ok.

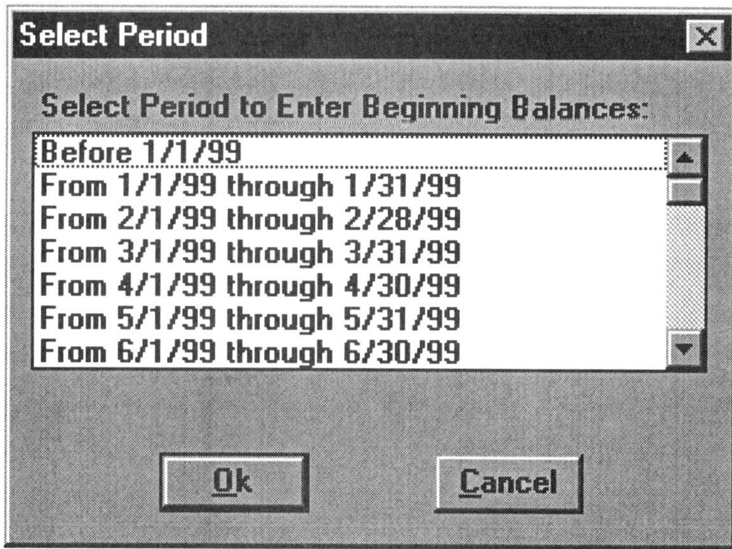

FIGURE 2.4 Select Period Window

▶ **When the Chart of Accounts Beginning Balances window shown in Figure 2.5 appears, enter the account balances. Make sure that you enter the decimal point. After entering each account balance, press Tab to move to the next account.**

▶ **After all balances are entered, click on the Ok button.**

Account Title	Account Balance	
Cash	7665.00	
Accounts Receivable	1300.00	
Supplies	300.00	
Prepaid Insurance	600.00	
Tools	3000.00	
Truck	8000.00	
Accounts Payable	2200.00	
Damon Young, Capital	15000.00	
Damon Young, Drawing	–500.00	(You must include the minus (–) sign.)
Inspection Fees	5000.00	
Wages Expense	450.00	
Rent Expense	300.00	
Telephone Expense	35.00	
Utilities Expense	50.00	

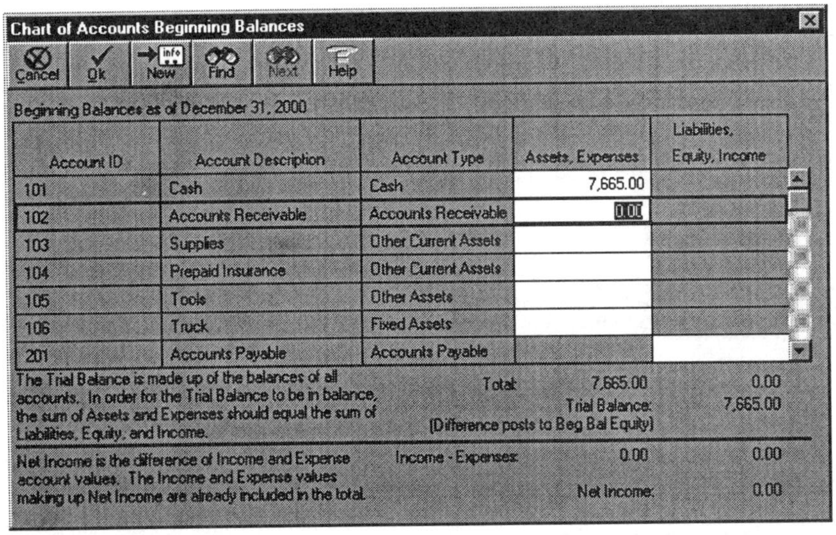

Chart of Accounts Beginning Balances

Cancel | Ok | New | Find | Next | Help

Beginning Balances as of December 31, 2000

Account ID	Account Description	Account Type	Assets, Expenses	Liabilities, Equity, Income
101	Cash	Cash	7,665.00	
102	Accounts Receivable	Accounts Receivable	0.00	
103	Supplies	Other Current Assets		
104	Prepaid Insurance	Other Current Assets		
105	Tools	Other Assets		
106	Truck	Fixed Assets		
201	Accounts Payable	Accounts Payable		

The Trial Balance is made up of the balances of all accounts. In order for the Trial Balance to be in balance, the sum of Assets and Expenses should equal the sum of Liabilities, Equity, and Income.

Total: 7,665.00 0.00

Trial Balance: 7,665.00

(Difference posts to Beg Bal Equity)

Net Income is the difference of Income and Expense account values. The Income and Expense values making up Net Income are already included in the total.

Income - Expenses: 0.00 0.00

Net Income: 0.00

FIGURE 2.5 Chart of Accounts Beginning Balances

Notice that as you enter the account balances two totals are updated near the bottom of the window. The first is the total of Assets and Expenses and the second is the total of Liabilities, Equity, and Income. After all balances have been entered, the two totals must be equal. If they are not, you must find and fix any errors or the software will not allow you to proceed. Also, notice that the balance for drawing is negative and must be entered with a preceding minus sign (–500.00).

STEP 5: Close the Maintain Chart of Accounts window by clicking on the Close button.

STEP 6: Display a Chart of Accounts Report.

Click on the Reports menu and choose the General Ledger option.

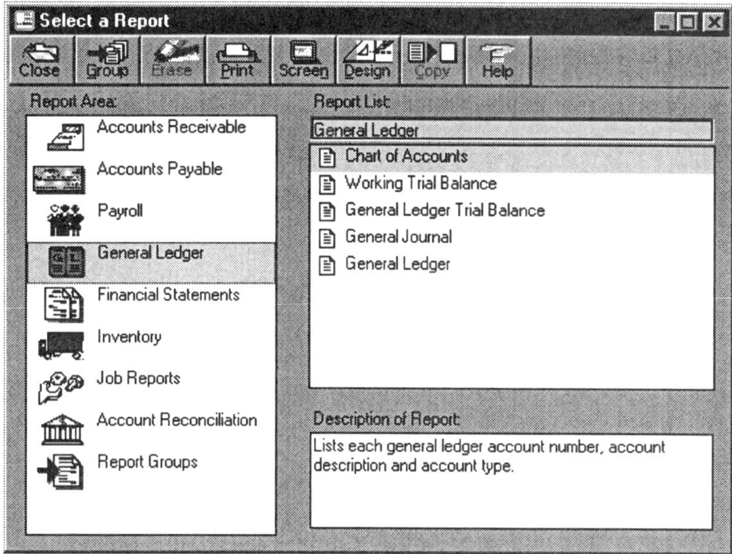

FIGURE 2.6 Select a Report Window

- ▶ **When the In the Report List shown in Figure 2.6 appears, click on Chart of Accounts under Report List.**
- ▶ **Click on the Screen button to display the report on the screen.**
- ▶ **When the Chart of Accounts filter shown in Figure 2.7 appears, click on Ok to display the chart of accounts report.**

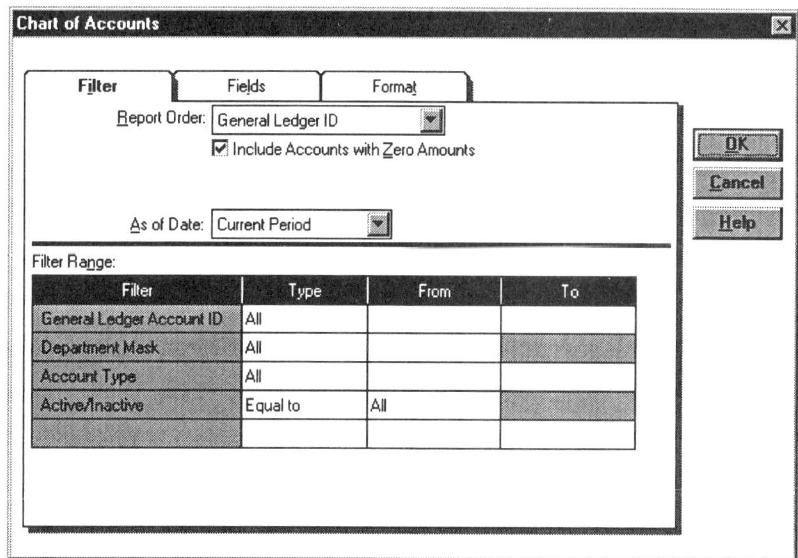

FIGURE 2.7 Chart of Accounts Report Filter

- ▶ **When the Chart of Accounts Report shown in Figure 2.8 appears, click on Print to obtain a hard copy of the report.**
- ▶ **When the Print window appears, just click Ok to print the hard copy report.**
- ▶ **Click the Close button to dismiss the Chart of Accounts Report screen.**

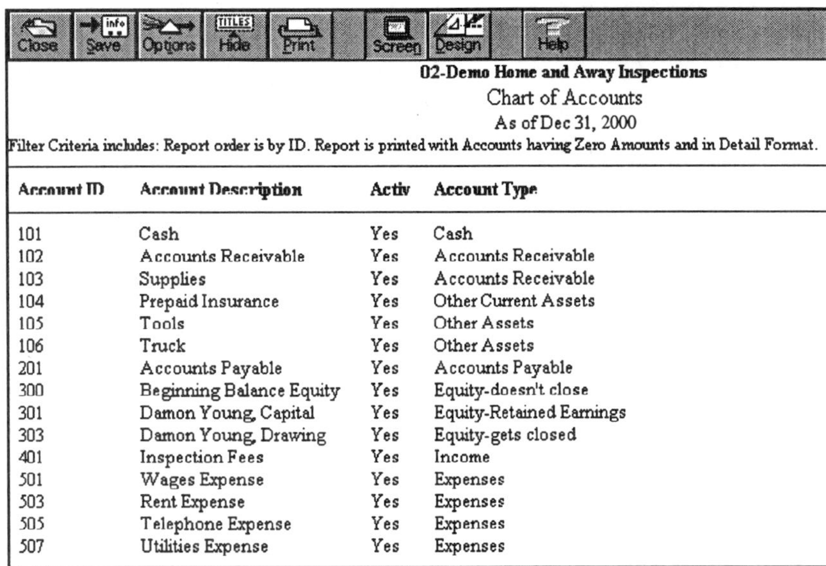

02-Demo Home and Away Inspections
Chart of Accounts
As of Dec 31, 2000
Filter Criteria includes: Report order is by ID. Report is printed with Accounts having Zero Amounts and in Detail Format.

Account ID	Account Description	Activ	Account Type
101	Cash	Yes	Cash
102	Accounts Receivable	Yes	Accounts Receivable
103	Supplies	Yes	Accounts Receivable
104	Prepaid Insurance	Yes	Other Current Assets
105	Tools	Yes	Other Assets
106	Truck	Yes	Other Assets
201	Accounts Payable	Yes	Accounts Payable
300	Beginning Balance Equity	Yes	Equity-doesn't close
301	Damon Young, Capital	Yes	Equity-Retained Earnings
303	Damon Young, Drawing	Yes	Equity-gets closed
401	Inspection Fees	Yes	Income
501	Wages Expense	Yes	Expenses
503	Rent Expense	Yes	Expenses
505	Telephone Expense	Yes	Expenses
507	Utilities Expense	Yes	Expenses

FIGURE 2.8 Chart of Accounts Report

STEP 7: Print the Financial Statements.

- ▶ **Click on Financial Statements in the Report Area of the Select a Report window shown above in Figure 2.6.**
- ▶ **Display the Basic Balance Sheet and compare it to the one shown in Figure 2.9.**

02-Demo Home and Away Inspections
Balance Sheet
December 31, 2000

Assets				
Cash	$	7,665.00		
Accounts Receivable		1,300.00		
Supplies		300.00		
Prepaid Insurance		600.00		
Tools		3,000.00		
Truck		8,000.00		
Total Assets			$	20,865.00

LIABILITIES AND CAPITAL

Liabilities				
Accounts Payable	$	2,200.00		
Total Liabilities				2,200.00
Capital				
Damon Young, Capital		15,000.00		
Damon Young, Drawing		<500.00>		
Net Income		4,165.00		
Total Capital				18,665.00
Total Liabilities & Capital			$	20,865.00

FIGURE 2.9 Balance Sheet Report

▶ **Display the Basic Income Statement, and compare it to the one shown in Figure 2.10.**

	02-Demo Home and Away Inspections Income Statement For the One Month Ending December 31, 2000	
		Year to Date
Revenues		
Inspection Fees	$	5,000.00
Total Revenues		5,000.00
Expenses		
Wages Expense		450.00
Rent Expense		300.00
Telephone Expense		35.00
Utilities Expense		50.00
Total Expenses		835.00
Net Income	$	4,165.00

FIGURE 2.10 Income Statement Report

▶ **Display the Statement of Owner's Equity, and compare it to the one shown in Figure 2.11.**

	02-Demo Home and Away Inspections Statement of Owner's Equity December 31, 2000	
Capital, Beginning of Period		15,000.00
Net Income for the Period	4,165.00	
Less Withdrawals for Period	500.00	
Capital, End of Period		18,665.00

FIGURE 2.11 Statement of Owner's Equity

CHAPTER 3 DEMONSTRATION PROBLEM (03-DEMO)

Celia Pints opened We-Buy, You-Pay Shopping Services. For a fee that is based on the amount of research and shopping time required, Pints and her associates will shop for almost anything from groceries to home furnishings. Business is particularly heavy around Christmas and in early summer. The business operates from a rented store front. The associates receive a commission based on the revenues they produce and a mileage reimbursement for the use of their personal automobiles for shopping trips. Pints decided to use the following accounts to record transactions:

Assets
- Cash
- Accounts Receivable
- Office Equipment
- Computer Equipment

Owner's Equity
- Celia Pints, Capital
- Celia Pints, Drawing

Revenue
- Shopping Fees

Liabilities	Expenses
Accounts Payable	Rent Expense
Notes Payable	Telephone Expense
	Commissions Expense
	Utilities Expense
	Travel Expense

The following transactions are for the month of December 20--.

(a) Pints invested cash in the business, $30,000.

(b) Bought office equipment for $10,000. Paid $2,000 in cash, and promised to pay the balance over the next four months.

(c) Paid rent for December, $500.

(d) Provided shopping services for customers on account, $5,200.

(e) Paid telephone bill, $90.

(f) Borrowed cash from the bank by signing a note payable, $5,000.

(g) Bought a computer and printer, $4,800.

(h) Collected cash from customers for services performed on account, $4,000.

(i) Paid commissions to associates for revenues generated during the first half of the month, $3,500.

(j) Paid utility bill, $600.

(k) Paid cash on account for the office equipment purchased in transaction (b), $2,000.

(l) Earned shopping fees of $13,200: $6,000 in cash and $7,200 on account.

(m) Paid commissions to associates for last half of month, $7,000.

(n) Paid mileage reimbursements for the month, $1,500.

(o) Paid cash on note payable to bank, $1,000.

(p) Pints withdrew cash for personal use, $2,000.

REQUIRED

1. Enter the transactions for December in T accounts. Use the accounting equation as a guide for setting up the T accounts.
2. Foot the T accounts, and determine their balances as necessary.
3. Prepare a trial balance of the accounts as of December 31 of the current year.
4. Prepare an income statement for the month ended December 31 of the current year.
5. Prepare a statement of owner's equity for the month ended December 31 of the current year.
6. Prepare a balance sheet as of December 31 of the current year.

The Chapter 3 Demonstration Problem involves recording accounting transactions in T accounts and preparing financial statements. Because the Peachtree software does not have the capability of entering transactions into T accounts, you will utilize the software to enter the account balances directly and then display the financial statements. The step-by-step instructions for solving the problem utilizing the Peachtree software are listed as follows.

STEP 1: Start up the Peachtree software.

Choose Peachtree Accounting from the Start button.

STEP 2: Open the data file for the Chapter 3 Demonstration Problem.

STEP 3: Enter the account balances shown below.

- **From the Maintain menu, choose the Chart of Accounts option.**
- **Click on the Beginning Balances on the Maintain Chart of Accounts window.**
- **When the Select Period Dialog appears, choose "From 12/1/00 through 12/31/00" and click on Ok. Be sure to select December of 2000 and not December of 1999.**
- **When the Chart of Accounts Beginning Balances window appears, enter the account balances. Make sure that you enter the decimal point. After entering each account balance, press Tab to move to the next account.**
- **After all balances are entered, click on the Ok button.**

Account Title	Account Balance
Cash	20,010.00
Accounts Receivable	8,400.00
Office Equipment	10,000.00
Computer Equipment	4,800.00
Accounts Payable	6,000.00
Notes Payable	4,000.00
Celia Pints, Capital	30,000.00
Celia Pints, Drawing	–2,000.00
Shopping Fees	18,400.00
Rent Expense	500.00
Telephone Expense	90.00
Commissions Expense	10,500.00
Utilities Expense	600.00
Travel Expense	1,500.00

Notice that as you enter the account balances two totals are updated near the bottom of the window. The first is the total of Assets and Expenses and the second is the total of Liabilities, Equity, and Income. After all balances have been entered, the two totals must be equal. If they are not, you must find and fix any errors or the software will not allow you to proceed. Also, notice that the balance for drawing is negative and must be entered with a preceding minus sign (–2000.00).

STEP 4: Close the Maintain Chart of Accounts window by clicking on the Close button.

STEP 5: Display the Financial Statements.

- **Click on Financial Statements in the Report Area of the Select a Report window.**
- **Display the Basic Balance Sheet, and compare it to the one shown in Figure 2.12.**

03-Demo We-Buy, You-Pay Shopping Serv.
Balance Sheet
December 31, 2000

Assets				
Cash	$	20,010.00		
Accounts Receivable		8,400.00		
Office Equipment		10,000.00		
Computer Equipment		4,800.00		
Total Assets			$	43,210.00

LIABILITIES AND CAPITAL

Liabilities				
Accounts Payable	$	6,000.00		
Notes Payable		4,000.00		
Total Liabilities				10,000.00
Capital				
Celia Pints, Capital		30,000.00		
Celia Pints, Drawing		<2,000.00>		
Net Income		5,210.00		
Total Capital				33,210.00
Total Liabilities & Capital			$	43,210.00

FIGURE 2.12 Balance Sheet Report

▶ **Display the Basic Income Statement. Compare it to the report shown in Figure 2.13.**

03-Demo We-Buy, You-Pay Shopping Serv.
Income Statement
For the Month Ending December 31, 2000

		Year to Date
Revenues		
Shopping Fees	$	18,400.00
Total Revenues		18,400.00
Expenses		
Rent Expense		500.00
Telephone Expense		90.00
Commissions Expense		10,500.00
Utilities Expense		600.00
Travel Expense		1,500.00
Total Expenses		13,190.00
Net Income	$	5,210.00

FIGURE 2.13 Income Statement Report

▶ **Display the Statement of Owner's Equity, and compare it to the one shown in Figure 2.14.**

03-Demo We-Buy, You-Pay Shopping Serv. Statement of Owner's Equity December 31, 2000		
Capital, Beginning of Period		30,000.00
Net Income for the Period	5,210.00	
Less Withdrawals for Period	2,000.00	
Capital, End of Period		33,210.00

FIGURE 2.14 Statement of Owner's Equity

CHAPTER 4 DEMONSTRATION PROBLEM (04-DEMO)

George Fielding is a financial planning consultant. He provides budgeting, estate planning, tax planning, and investing advice for professional golfers. He developed the following chart of accounts for his business.

Assets
101 Cash
142 Office Supplies

Liabilities
202 Accounts Payable

Owner's Equity
311 George Fielding, Capital
312 George Fielding, Drawing

Revenues
401 Professional Fees

Expenses
511 Wages Expense
521 Rent Expense
525 Telephone Expense
533 Utilities Expense
534 Charitable Contributions Expense
538 Automobile Expense

The following transactions took place during the month of December of the current year.

Dec. 1 Fielding invested cash to start the business, $20,000.

3 Paid Bollhorst Real Estate for December office rent, $1,000.

4 Received cash from Aaron Patton, a client, for services, $2,500.

6 Paid T. Z. Anderson Electric for December heating and light, $75.

7 Received cash from Andrew Conder, a client, for services, $2,000.

12 Paid Fichter's Super Service for gasoline and oil purchases for the company car, $60.

14 Paid Hillenburg Staffing for temporary secretarial services during the past two weeks, $600.

17 Bought office supplies from Bowers Office Supply on account, $280.

20 Paid Mitchell Telephone Co. for business calls during the past month, $100.

21 Fielding withdrew cash for personal use, $1,100.

24 Made donation to the National Multiple Sclerosis Society, $100.

27 Received cash from Billy Walters, a client, for services, $2,000.

28 Paid Hillenburg Staffing for temporary secretarial services during the past two weeks, $600.

29 Made payment on account to Bowers Office Supply, $100.

REQUIRED 1. Record the preceding transactions in a general journal.

2. Post the entries to the general ledger.

3. Prepare a trial balance.

The Chapter 4 Demonstration Problem involves entering general journal entries into the computer, displaying a general journal report, and displaying a general ledger trial balance report. Follow the step-by-step instructions below to complete the Chapter 4 Demonstration Problem.

STEP 1: Start up the Peachtree software.

Choose Peachtree Accounting from the Start button.

STEP 2: Open the data file for the Chapter 4 Demonstration Problem.

STEP 3: Enter the December transactions into the General Journal window.

From the Tasks menu, choose the General Journal Entry option. The first journal entry is illustrated in the General Journal Entry window shown in Figure 2.15.

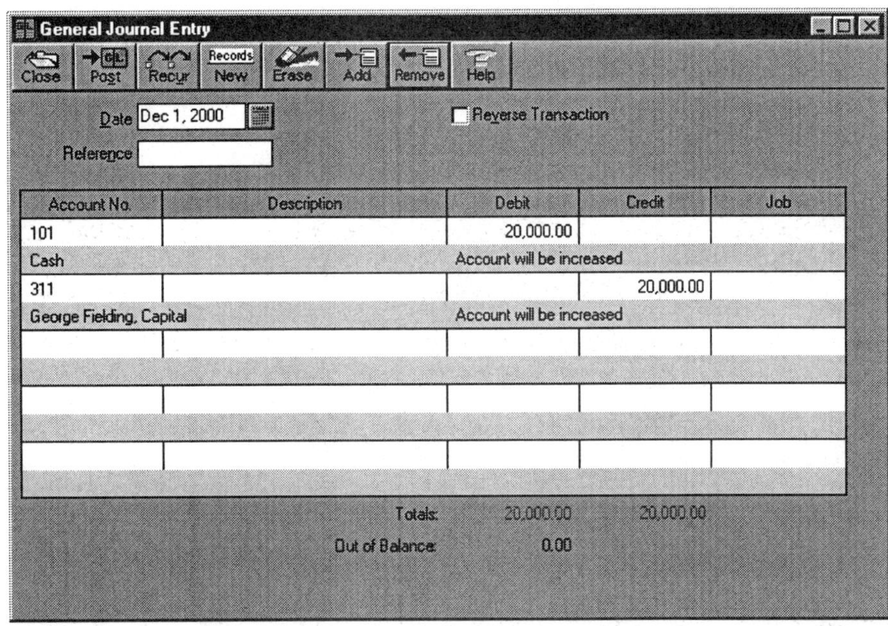

FIGURE 2.15 General Journal Entry Window

- **Enter the transaction date.**
- **Since reference numbers are not provided in this problem, leave the Reference field blank.**
- **For each leg of the transaction, enter the appropriate account number or select it from the drop-down Chart of Accounts list.**
- **Enter a description of the transaction.**
- **For each leg of the transaction, enter the debit or credit amount.**
- **When the transaction is complete, click on the Post button.**

STEP 4: Display a General Journal Report.

- **Click on the Reports menu, and choose the General Ledger option.**
- **In the Report List, click on General Journal with Titles and click on Screen.**

STEP 5: If errors are detected on the General Journal Report, return to the General Journal window and make corrections.

- **Click on the Edit Icon Bar button.**
- **Highlight the entry you wish to correct and click on Ok.**
- **Make corrections and click on Post.**
- **After all corrections are made, display another General Journal with Titles Report.**

STEP 6: Display a General Ledger Trial Balance Report.

- **Display a trial balance report by double-clicking on the General Ledger Trial Balance in the Report List section of the Select a Report window.**

STEP 7: Display a General Ledger Report.

- **Double-click on General Ledger in the Report List section of the Select a Report window. Compare your report to the General Ledger Accounts shown in the Demonstration Problem.**

  See the solution section of this workbook for the solution to the demonstration problem.

PROBLEM 4A2

Annette Creighton opened Creighton Consulting. She rented a small office and paid a part-time worker to answer the telephone and make deliveries. Her chart of accounts is as follows:

Chart of Accounts

Assets
101 Cash
142 Office Supplies
181 Office Equipment

Liabilities
202 Accounts Payable

Owner's Equity
311 Annette Creighton, Capital
312 Annette Creighton, Drawing

Revenues
401 Consulting Fees

Expenses
511 Wages Expense
512 Advertising Expense
521 Rent Expense
525 Telephone Expense
526 Transportation Expense
533 Utilities Expense
549 Miscellaneous Expense

Creighton's transactions for the first month of business are as follows:

Jan. 1 Creighton invested cash in the business, $10,000.

1 Paid rent, $500.

2 Purchased office supplies on account, $300.

4 Purchased office equipment on account, $1,500.

6 Received cash for services rendered, $580.

7 Paid telephone bill, $42.

8 Paid utilities bill, $38.

10 Received cash for services rendered, $360.

12 Made payment on account, $50.

13 Paid for car rental while visiting an out-of-town client (transportation expense), $150.

15 Paid part-time worker, $360.

17 Received cash for services rendered, $420.

18 Creighton withdrew cash for personal use, $100.

20 Paid for a newspaper ad, $26.

22 Reimbursed part-time employee for cab fare incurred delivering materials to clients (transportation expense), $35.

24 Paid for books on consulting practices (miscellaneous expense), $28.

25 Received cash for services rendered, $320.

27 Made payment on account for office equipment purchased, $150.

29 Paid part-time worker, $360.

30 Received cash for services rendered, $180.

REQUIRED

1. Set up four-column general ledger accounts from the chart of accounts.
2. Journalize the transactions for January in a two-column general journal.
3. Post the transactions from the general journal.
4. Prepare a trial balance.
5. Prepare an income statement and a statement of owner's equity for the month of January, and a balance sheet as of January 31, 20--.

In Problem 4A2, you will enter the general journal entries for the month of January for the year 2000, display a general journal report, display a general ledger trial balance, and display financial statements. Follow the step-by-step instructions below to complete Problem 4A2.

STEP 1: Start up the Peachtree software.

Choose Peachtree Accounting from the Start button.

STEP 2: Open the data file for the Problem 4A2 (Creighton Consulting).

STEP 3: Enter the January transactions into the General Journal window.

STEP 4: Display a General Journal with Titles Report.

STEP 5: Display a General Ledger Trial Balance Report.

STEP 6: Display a Basic Income Statement.

STEP 7: Display a Statement of Owner's Equity.

STEP 8: Display a Basic Balance Sheet.

PROBLEM 4B2

Benito Mendez opened Mendez Appraisals. He rented office space and has a part-time secretary to answer the telephone and make appraisal appointments. His chart of accounts is as follows:

Chart of Accounts

Assets
101 Cash
122 Accounts Receivable
142 Office Supplies
181 Office Equipment

Liabilities
202 Accounts Payable

Owner's Equity
311 Benito Mendez, Capital
312 Benito Mendez, Drawing

Revenues
401 Appraisal Fees

Expenses
511 Wages Expense
512 Advertising Expense
521 Rent Expense
525 Telephone Expense
526 Transportation Expense
533 Electricity Expense
549 Miscellaneous Expense

Mendez's transactions for the first month of business are as follows:

May 1 Mendez invested cash in the business, $5,000.
2 Paid rent, $500.
3 Purchased office supplies, $100.
4 Purchased office equipment on account, $2,000.
5 Received cash for services rendered, $280.
8 Paid telephone bill, $38.
9 Paid electric bill, $42.
10 Received cash for services rendered, $310.
13 Paid part-time employee, $500.
14 Paid car rental for out-of-town trip, $200.
15 Paid for newspaper ad, $30.
18 Received cash for services rendered, $620.
19 Paid mileage reimbursement for part-time employee's use of personal car for business deliveries (transportation expense), $22.
21 Mendez withdrew cash for personal use, $50.
23 Made payment on account for office equipment purchased earlier, $200.
24 Earned appraisal fee, which will be paid in a week, $500.
26 Paid for newspaper ad, $30.
27 Paid for local softball team sponsorship (miscellaneous expense), $15.
28 Paid part-time employee, $500.
29 Received cash on account, $250.
30 Received cash for services rendered, $280.
31 Paid cab fare (transportation expense), $13.

REQUIRED

1. Set up four-column general ledger accounts from the chart of accounts.
2. Journalize the transactions for May in a two-column general journal.
3. Post the transactions from the general journal.
4. Prepare a trial balance.
5. Prepare an income statement and a statement of owner's equity for the month of May, and a balance sheet as of May 31, 20--.

Problem 4B2 involves entering general journal entries for the month of May, displaying a general journal report, general ledger trial balance, and financial statements. Follow the step-by-step instructions below to complete the Problem 4B2.

STEP 1: Start up the Peachtree software.

STEP 2: Open the data file for the Problem 4B2 (Mendez Appraisals).

STEP 3: Enter the May transactions into the General Journal window.

STEP 4: Display the General Journal with Titles Report.

STEP 5: Display a General Ledger Trial Balance Report.

STEP 6: Display a Basic Income Statement.

STEP 7: Display a Statement of Owner's Equity.

STEP 8: Display a Basic Balance Sheet.

CHAPTER 4 MASTERY PROBLEM

Barry Bird opened the Barry Bird Basketball Camp for children ages 10 through 18. Campers typically register for one week in June or July, arriving on Sunday and returning home the following Saturday. College players serve as cabin counselors and assist the local college and high school coaches who run the practice sessions. The registration fee includes a room, meals at a nearby restaurant, and basketball instruction. In the off-season, the facilities are used for weekend retreats and coaching clinics. Bird developed the following chart of accounts for his service business.

Chart of Accounts

Assets
101 Cash
142 Office Supplies
183 Athletic Equipment
184 Basketball Facilities

Liabilities
202 Accounts Payable

Owner's Equity
311 Barry Bird, Capital
312 Barry Bird, Drawing

Revenues
401 Registration Fees

Expenses
511 Wages Expense
512 Advertising Expense
524 Food Expense
525 Telephone Expense
533 Utilities Expense
536 Postage Expense

The following transactions took place during the month of June.

June 1	Bird invested cash in the business, $10,000.
1	Purchased basketballs and other athletic equipment, $3,000.
2	Paid Hite Advertising for fliers that had been mailed to prospective campers, $5,000.
2	Collected registration fees, $15,000.
2	Rogers Construction completed work on a new basketball court that cost $12,000. Arrangements were made to pay the bill in July.
5	Purchased office supplies on account from Gordon Office Supplies, $300.
6	Received bill from Magic's Restaurant for meals served to campers on account, $5,800.
7	Collected registration fees, $16,200.
10	Paid wages to camp counselors, $500.
14	Collected registration fees, $13,500.
14	Received bill from Magic's Restaurant for meals served to campers on account, $6,200.
17	Paid wages to camp counselors, $500.
18	Paid postage, $85.
21	Collected registration fees, $15,200.
22	Received bill from Magic's Restaurant for meals served to campers on account, $6,500.
24	Paid wages to camp counselors, $500.
28	Collected registration fees, $14,000.
30	Received bill from Magic's Restaurant for meals served to campers on account, $7,200.
30	Paid wages to camp counselors, $500.
30	Paid Magic's Restaurant on account, $25,700.
30	Paid utility bill, $500.
30	Paid telephone bill, $120.
30	Bird withdrew cash for personal use, $2,000.

REQUIRED
1. Enter the above transactions in a general journal.
2. Post the entries to the general ledger.
3. Prepare a trial balance.

The Chapter 4 Mastery Problem involves entering general journal entries for the month of June, displaying a general journal report and a general ledger trial balance. Follow the step-by-step instructions below to complete the Chapter 4 Mastery Problem.

STEP 1: Start up the Peachtree software.

STEP 2: Open the data file for the Chapter 4 Mastery Problem.

STEP 3: Enter the June transactions into the General Journal window.

STEP 4: Display the General Journal with Titles Report.

STEP 5: Display a General Ledger Trial Balance Report.

CHAPTER 5 DEMONSTRATION PROBLEM (05-DEMO)

Justin Park is a lawyer specializing in corporate tax law. He began his practice on January 1. A chart of accounts and trial balance taken on December 31, 20--, are provided below and on the next page. Information for year-end adjustments is as follows:

(a) Office supplies on hand at year end amounted to $300.

(b) On January 1, 20--, Park purchased office equipment costing $15,000 with an expected life of five years and no salvage value.

(c) Computer equipment costing $6,000 with an expected life of three years and no salvage value was purchased on July 1, 20--. Assume that Park computes depreciation to the nearest full month.

(d) A premium of $1,200 for a one-year insurance policy was paid on December 1, 20--.

(e) Wages earned by Park's part-time secretary, which have not yet been paid, amount to $300.

REQUIRED 1. Prepare the work sheet for the year ended December 31, 20--.

2. Prepare adjusting entries in a general journal.

JUSTIN PARK LEGAL SERVICES CHART OF ACCOUNTS			
Assets		**Revenue**	
101	Cash	401	Client Fees
142	Office Supplies		
145	Prepaid Insurance	**Expenses**	
181	Office Equipment	511	Wages Expense
181.1	Accumulated Depr.—	521	Rent Expense
	Office Equipment	523	Office Supplies Expense
187	Computer Equipment	525	Telephone Expense
187.1	Accumulated Depr.—	533	Utilities Expense
	Computer Equipment	535	Insurance Expense
Liabilities		541	Depr. Expense—
201	Notes Payable		Office Equipment
202	Accounts Payable	542	Depr. Expense—
219	Wages Payable		Computer Equipment
Owner's Equity			
311	Justin Park, Capital		
312	Justin Park, Drawing		

In the Chapter 5 Demonstration Problem, you will enter the adjusting entries, display the adjusting entries, and display the financial statements. A worksheet is not necessary in Peachtree. Follow the step-by-step instructions below to complete the Chapter 5 Demonstration Problem.

STEP 1: **Start up the Peachtree software.**

STEP 2: **Open the data file for the Chapter 5 Demonstration Problem.**

STEP 3: **Enter the adjusting entries into the General Journal window.**

Justin Park Legal Services
Trial Balance
December 31, 20 - -

ACCOUNT TITLE	ACCOUNT NO.	DEBIT BALANCE	CREDIT BALANCE
Cash	101	7 0 0 0 00	
Office Supplies	142	8 0 0 00	
Prepaid Insurance	145	1 2 0 0 00	
Office Equipment	181	15 0 0 0 00	
Computer Equipment	187	6 0 0 0 00	
Notes Payable	201		5 0 0 0 00
Accounts Payable	202		5 0 0 00
Justin Park, Capital	311		11 4 0 0 00
Justin Park, Drawing	312	5 0 0 0 00	
Client Fees	401		40 0 0 0 00
Wages Expense	511	12 0 0 0 00	
Rent Expense	521	5 0 0 0 00	
Telephone Expense	525	1 0 0 0 00	
Utilities Expense	533	3 9 0 0 00	
		56 9 0 0 00	56 9 0 0 00

Enter each entry with a date of December 31, 2000, and enter "Adjusting Entry" as the description.

STEP 4: **Display the adjusting entries using the General Journal with Titles Report.**

STEP 5: **Display a Basic Income Statement.**

STEP 6: **Display a Statement of Owner's Equity.**

STEP 7: **Display a Basic Balance Sheet.**

See the solution section of this workbook for the solution to the demonstration problem.

PROBLEM 5A3

Jason Armstrong started a business called Campus Escort Service. After the first month of operations, the trial balance as of November 30, 20--, is as shown on the next page.

Information needed to make month-end adjustments follows:

(a) Ending inventory of supplies on November 30, $185.

(b) Unexpired (remaining) insurance as of November 30, $800.

(c) Depreciation expense on van, $300.

(d) Wages earned, but not paid as of November 30, $190.

Campus Escort Service
Work Sheet
For Month Ended November 30, 20 - -

	ACCOUNT TITLE	TRIAL BALANCE DEBIT	TRIAL BALANCE CREDIT	ADJUSTMENTS DEBIT	ADJUSTMENTS CREDIT	
1	Cash	980 00				1
2	Accounts Receivable	590 00				2
3	Supplies	575 00				3
4	Prepaid Insurance	1300 00				4
5	Van	5800 00				5
6	Accum. Depr.—Van					6
7	Accounts Payable		960 00			7
8	Wages Payable					8
9	Jason Armstrong, Capital		10000 00			9
10	Jason Armstrong, Drawing	600 00				10
11	Escort Fees		2600 00			11
12	Wages Expense	1800 00				12
13	Advertising Expense	380 00				13
14	Rent Expense	900 00				14
15	Supplies Expense					15
16	Telephone Expense	220 00				16
17	Insurance Expense					17
18	Repair Expense	315 00				18
19	Oil and Gas Expense	100 00				19
20	Depr. Expense—Van					20
21		13560 00	13560 00			21

Account Name	Account Number	Balance in Account Before Adjusting Entry
Supplies	141	$ 575
Prepaid Insurance	145	1,300
Accum. Depr.—Van	185.1	0
Wages Payable	219	0
Wages Expense	511	1,800
Supplies Expense	523	0
Insurance Expense	535	0
Depr. Expense—Van	541	0

REQUIRED 1. Journalize the adjusting entries.
2. Post the adjusting entries to the general ledger.

In Problem 5A3, you will enter the adjusting entries, display adjusting entries, display a trial balance, and display the financial statements. Follow the step-by-step instructions below to complete Problem 5A3.

STEP 1: Start up the Peachtree software.

STEP 2: Open the data file for Problem 5A3.

STEP 3: Enter the adjusting entries into the General Journal window.

STEP 4: Display the adjusting entries using the General Journal with Titles Report.

STEP 5: **Display the General Ledger Trial Balance Report.**

STEP 6: **Display a Basic Income Statement.**

STEP 7: **Display a Statement of Owner's Equity.**

STEP 8: **Display a Basic Balance Sheet.**

PROBLEM 5B3

Val Nolan started a business called Nolan's Home Appraisals. The trial balance as of October 31, after the first month of operations, is shown below.

Nolan's Home Appraisals
Work Sheet
For Month Ended October 31, 20 - -

	ACCOUNT TITLE	TRIAL BALANCE		ADJUSTMENTS		
		DEBIT	CREDIT	DEBIT	CREDIT	
1	Cash	830 00				1
2	Accounts Receivable	760 00				2
3	Supplies	625 00				3
4	Prepaid Insurance	950 00				4
5	Automobile	6500 00				5
6	Accum. Depr.—Automobile					6
7	Accounts Payable		1500 00			7
8	Wages Payable					8
9	Val Nolan, Capital		9900 00			9
10	Val Nolan, Drawing	1100 00				10
11	Appraisal Fees		3000 00			11
12	Wages Expense	1560 00				12
13	Advertising Expense	420 00				13
14	Rent Expense	1050 00				14
15	Supplies Expense					15
16	Telephone Expense	255 00				16
17	Insurance Expense					17
18	Repair Expense	270 00				18
19	Oil and Gas Expense	80 00				19
20	Depr. Expense—Automobile					20
21		14400 00	14400 00			21

Information needed to make month-end adjustments follows:

(a) Supplies inventory as of October 31, $210.

(b) Unexpired (remaining) insurance as of October 31, $800.

(c) Depreciation of automobile, $250.

(d) Wages earned, but not paid as of October 31, $175.

Account Name	Account Number	Balance in Account Before Adjusting Entry
Supplies	141	$ 625
Prepaid Insurance	145	950
Accum. Depr.—Automobile	185.1	0
Wages Payable	219	0
Wages Expense	511	1,560
Supplies Expense	523	0
Insurance Expense	535	0
Depr. Expense—Automobile	541	0

REQUIRED

1. Journalize the adjusting entries.
2. Post the adjusting entries to the general ledger.

In Problem 5B3, you will enter the adjusting entries, display a trial balance, and display the financial statements. Follow the step-by-step instructions below to complete Problem 5B3.

STEP 1: Start up the Peachtree software.

STEP 2: Open the data file for Problem 5B3.

STEP 3: Enter the adjusting entries into the General Journal window.

STEP 4: Display the adjusting entries using the General Journal with Titles Report.

STEP 5: Display the General Ledger Trial Balance Report.

STEP 6: Display a Basic Income Statement.

STEP 7: Display a Statement of Owner's Equity.

STEP 8: Display a Basic Balance Sheet.

CHAPTER 5 MASTERY PROBLEM

Kristi Williams offers family counseling services specializing in financial and marital problems. A chart of accounts and a trial balance taken on December 31, 20-1, are provided on the next page.

Information for year-end adjustments:

(a) Office supplies on hand at year end amounted to $100.

(b) On January 1, 20-1, Williams purchased office equipment that cost $18,000. It has an expected useful life of ten years and no salvage value.

(c) On July 1, 20-1, Williams purchased computer equipment costing $6,000. It has an expected useful life of four years and no salvage value. Assume that Williams computes depreciation to the nearest full month.

(d) On December 1, 20-1, Williams paid a premium of $600 for a six-month insurance policy.

REQUIRED

1. Prepare the worksheet for the year ended December 31, 20-1.
2. Prepare adjusting entries in a general journal.

KRISTI WILLIAMS FAMILY COUNSELING SERVICES
CHART OF ACCOUNTS

Assets		Revenue	
101	Cash	401	Client Fees
142	Office Supplies		
145	Prepaid Insurance	**Expenses**	
181	Office Equipment	511	Wages Expense
181.1	Accumulated Depr.—	521	Rent Expense
	Office Equipment	523	Office Supplies Expense
187	Computer Equipment	533	Utilities Expense
187.1	Accumulated Depr.—	535	Insurance Expense
	Computer Equipment	541	Depr. Expense—
			Office Equipment
Liabilities		542	Depr. Expense—
201	Notes Payable		Computer Equipment
202	Accounts Payable	549	Miscellaneous Expense
Owner's Equity			
311	Kristi Williams, Capital		
312	Kristi Williams, Drawing		

Kristi Williams Family Counseling Services
Trial Balance
December 31, 20 - 1

ACCOUNT TITLE	ACCOUNT NO.	DEBIT BALANCE	CREDIT BALANCE
Cash	101	8 7 3 0 00	
Office Supplies	142	7 0 0 00	
Prepaid Insurance	145	6 0 0 00	
Office Equipment	181	18 0 0 0 00	
Computer Equipment	187	6 0 0 0 00	
Notes Payable	201		8 0 0 0 00
Accounts Payable	202		5 0 0 00
Kristi Williams, Capital	311		11 4 0 0 00
Kristi Williams, Drawing	312	3 0 0 0 00	
Client Fees	401		35 8 0 0 00
Wages Expense	511	9 5 0 0 00	
Rent Expense	521	6 0 0 0 00	
Utilities Expense	533	2 1 7 0 00	
Miscellaneous Expense	549	1 0 0 0 00	
		55 7 0 0 00	55 7 0 0 00

In the Chapter 5 Mastery Problem, you will enter the adjusting entries, display a trial balance, and display the financial statements. Follow the step-by-step instructions below to complete the Chapter 5 Mastery Problem.

STEP 1: **Start up the Peachtree software.**

STEP 2: **Open the data file for the Chapter 5 Mastery Problem. For this Peachtree project, the 2000 date on your data disk is correct.**

STEP 3: **Enter the adjusting entries into the General Journal window.**

STEP 4: **Display the adjusting entries using the General Journal with Titles Report.**

STEP 5: **Display the General Ledger Trial Balance Report.**

STEP 6: **Display a Basic Income Statement.**

STEP 7: **Display a Statement of Owner's Equity.**

STEP 8: **Display a Basic Balance Sheet.**

CHAPTER 6 DEMONSTRATION PROBLEM (06-DEMO)

Timothy Chang owns and operates Hard Copy Printers. A worksheet for the year ended December 31, 20--, is provided on the next page. Chang made no additional investments during the year.

REQUIRED 1. Prepare financial statements.

2. Prepare closing entries.

In the Chapter 6 Demonstration Problem, you will display the financial statements and close the accounting period. Follow the step-by-step instructions below to complete the Chapter 6 Demonstration Problem.

STEP 1: **Start up the Peachtree software.**

STEP 2: **Open the data file for the Chapter 6 Demonstration Problem.**

STEP 3: **Enter the adjusting entries from the adjustment column of the worksheet.**

STEP 4: **Display a Statement of Owner's Equity.**

STEP 5: **Display a Basic Balance Sheet.**

STEP 6: **Display a Basic Income Statement.**

STEP 7: **Change the accounting period to January 1 of 2001.**

- ▶ **From the Tasks menu, select System, then select Change Accounting Periods from the submenu.**
- ▶ **When the Change Accounting Period window appears, select January 1, 2001, to January 31, 2001, and click on Ok.**
- ▶ **A message box appears, asking if you would like to print reports before continuing. Since you just printed reports in the above steps, respond No.**

Changing the accounting period to the next fiscal year will change the processing cycle from the year 2000 to the year 2001, in effect closing the year 2000. It is really a temporary closing. A permanent closing doesn't occur until the fiscal year is actually closed via the Close Fiscal Year option.

STEP 8: **Display a trial balance report.**

Because you changed to a new fiscal accounting year, the trial balance report should reflect the closing of the year 2000. If you should discover an error and wish to edit transactions from the previous period, simply change the accounting period back to December of 2000, make the corrections, display your reports, and again change the accounting period to January of 2001.

See the solution section of this workbook for the solution to the demonstration problem.

Hard Copy Printers
Work Sheet
For Year Ended December 31, 20 - -

	ACCOUNT TITLE	TRIAL BALANCE		ADJUSTMENTS		ADJUSTED TRIAL BALANCE		INCOME STATEMENT		BALANCE SHEET		
		DEBIT	CREDIT	DEBIT	CREDIT	DEBIT	CREDIT	DEBIT	CREDIT	DEBIT	CREDIT	
1	Cash	1,180 00				1,180 00				1,180 00		1
2	Paper Supplies	3,600 00			(a) 3,550 00	50 00				50 00		2
3	Prepaid Insurance	1,000 00			(b) 505 00	495 00				495 00		3
4	Printing Equipment	5,800 00				5,800 00				5,800 00		4
5	Accum. Depr.—Printing Equipment				(d) 1,200 00		1,200 00				1,200 00	5
6	Accounts Payable		500 00				500 00				500 00	6
7	Wages Payable				(c) 30 00		30 00				30 00	7
8	Timothy Chang, Capital		10,000 00				10,000 00				10,000 00	8
9	Timothy Chang, Drawing	13,000 00				13,000 00				13,000 00		9
10	Printing Fees		35,100 00				35,100 00		35,100 00			10
11	Wages Expense	11,970 00		(c) 30 00		12,000 00		12,000 00				11
12	Rent Expense	7,500 00				7,500 00		7,500 00				12
13	Paper Supplies Expense			(a) 3,550 00		3,550 00		3,550 00				13
14	Telephone Expense	550 00				550 00		550 00				14
15	Utilities Expense	1,000 00				1,000 00		1,000 00				15
16	Insurance Expense			(b) 505 00		505 00		505 00				16
17	Depr. Expense—Printing Equipment			(d) 1,200 00		1,200 00		1,200 00				17
18		45,600 00	45,600 00	5,285 00	5,285 00	46,830 00	46,830 00	26,305 00	35,100 00	20,525 00	11,730 00	18
19	Net Income							8,795 00			8,795 00	19
20								35,100 00	35,100 00	20,525 00	20,525 00	20
21												21
22												22
23												23
24												24
25												25
26												26
27												27
28												28
29												29
30												30

PROBLEM 6A3

A chart of accounts for Monte's Repairs is provided below.

Monte's Repairs
Chart of Accounts

Assets	**Revenues**
101 Cash	401 Repair Fees
122 Accounts Receivable	
141 Supplies	**Expenses**
145 Prepaid Insurance	511 Wages Expense
185 Delivery Equipment	512 Advertising Expense
185.1 Accum. Depr.—Delivery Equip.	521 Rent Expense
	523 Supplies Expense
Liabilities	525 Telephone Expense
202 Accounts Payable	535 Insurance Expense
219 Wages Payable	538 Gas and Oil Expense
	541 Depr. Exp.—Delivery Equip.
Owner's Equity	549 Miscellaneous Expense
311 Monte Eli, Capital	
312 Monte Eli, Drawing	
313 Income Summary	

Refer to the worksheet on the next page.

REQUIRED 1. Journalize and post the adjusting entries.

2. Journalize and post the closing entries.

3. Prepare a post-closing trial balance.

In Problem 6A3, you will enter the adjusting entries for Monte's Repairs, display reports, and enter closing entries. The processing for Problem 6A3 is somewhat different from the Chapter 6 Demonstration Problem because of a difference in the accounting period. The Demonstration Problem had a fiscal period of one year, whereas this problem has a fiscal period of one month. The Peachtree software assumes a fiscal period of one year. It allows for monthly accounting periods, but does not close until the end of the fiscal period. All this means is that, in order to close the accounting period at the end of a month, you must manually enter the closing journal entries. Follow the step-by-step procedures below to complete the processing for Problem 6A3.

STEP 1: Open the data file for Problem 6A3.

STEP 2: Enter the adjusting entries from the adjustment column of the worksheet.

STEP 3: Display the adjusting entries with the General Journal with Titles Report.

STEP 4: Display a Basic Income Statement.

STEP 5: Display a Statement of Owner's Equity.

STEP 6: Display a Basic Balance Sheet.

STEP 7: Display a Trial Balance Report.

STEP 8: Enter the closing entries into the General Journal window. Enter a transaction date of January 31, 2000, and a description of "Closing Entry."

STEP 9: Display the journal entries. Your report will include both adjusting and closing entries.

STEP 10: Display a post-closing trial balance, which is really just the normal trial balance report. It becomes post-closing because it was printed after closing entries were processed.

Monte's Repairs
Work Sheet
For Month Ended January 31, 20 - -

	ACCOUNT TITLE	TRIAL BALANCE		ADJUSTMENTS		ADJUSTED TRIAL BALANCE		INCOME STATEMENT		BALANCE SHEET		
		DEBIT	CREDIT	DEBIT	CREDIT	DEBIT	CREDIT	DEBIT	CREDIT	DEBIT	CREDIT	
1	Cash	3,080.00				3,080.00				3,080.00		1
2	Accounts Receivable	1,200.00				1,200.00				1,200.00		2
3	Supplies	800.00			(a) 200.00	600.00				600.00		3
4	Prepaid Insurance	900.00			(b) 100.00	800.00				800.00		4
5	Delivery Equipment	3,000.00				3,000.00				3,000.00		5
6	Accum. Depr.—Delivery Equipment				(d) 30.00		30.00				30.00	6
7	Accounts Payable		1,100.00				1,100.00				1,100.00	7
8	Wages Payable				(c) 150.00		150.00				150.00	8
9	Monte Eli, Capital		7,000.00				7,000.00				7,000.00	9
10	Monte Eli, Drawing	1,000.00				1,000.00				1,000.00		10
11	Repair Fees		4,230.00				4,230.00		4,230.00			11
12	Wages Expense	1,650.00		(c) 150.00		1,800.00		1,800.00				12
13	Advertising Expense	170.00				170.00		170.00				13
14	Rent Expense	420.00				420.00		420.00				14
15	Supplies Expense			(a) 200.00		200.00		200.00				15
16	Telephone Expense	49.00				49.00		49.00				16
17	Insurance Expense			(b) 100.00		100.00		100.00				17
18	Gas and Oil Expense	33.00				33.00		33.00				18
19	Depr. Expense—Delivery Equipment			(d) 30.00		30.00		30.00				19
20	Miscellaneous Expense	28.00				28.00		28.00				20
21		12,330.00	12,330.00	480.00	480.00	12,510.00	12,510.00	2,830.00	4,230.00	9,680.00	8,280.00	21
22	Net Income							1,400.00			1,400.00	22
23								4,230.00	4,230.00	9,680.00	9,680.00	23
24												24
25												25
26												26
27												27
28												28
29												29
30												30

PROBLEM 6B3

A chart of accounts for Juanita's Consulting is provided below.

Juanita's Consulting
Chart of Accounts

Assets		Revenues	
101	Cash	401	Consulting Fees
122	Accounts Receivable		
141	Supplies		Expenses
145	Prepaid Insurance	511	Wages Expense
181	Office Equipment	512	Advertising Expense
181.1	Accum. Depr.—Office Equip.	521	Rent Expense
		523	Supplies Expense
Liabilities		525	Telephone Expense
202	Accounts Payable	533	Electricity Expense
219	Wages Payable	535	Insurance Expense
		538	Gas and Oil Expense
Owner's Equity		541	Depr. Exp.—Office Equip.
311	Juanita Alvarez, Capital	549	Miscellaneous Expense
312	Juanita Alvarez, Drawing		
313	Income Summary		

Refer to the worksheet on the following page.

REQUIRED
1. Journalize and post the adjusting entries.
2. Journalize and post the closing entries.
3. Prepare a post-closing trial balance.

In Problem 6B3, you will enter the adjusting entries for Juanita's Consulting, display reports, and enter closing entries. This problem is similar to 6A3 in that the fiscal period is one month in duration, which means that you must close the period by actually entering the closing entries. Follow the step-by-step procedures below to complete the processing for Problem 6B3.

STEP 1: Open the data file for Problem 6B3.

STEP 2: Enter the adjusting entries from the adjustment column of the worksheet.

STEP 3: Display the adjusting entries with the General Journal with Titles Report.

STEP 4: Display a Basic Income Statement.

STEP 5: Display a Statement of Owner's Equity.

STEP 6: Display a Basic Balance Sheet.

STEP 7: Display a Trial Balance Report.

STEP 8: Enter the closing entries into the General Journal window. Enter a transaction date of June 30, 2000, and a description of "Closing Entry."

STEP 9: Display the journal entries. Your report will include both adjusting and closing entries.

STEP 10: Display a post-closing trial balance, which is really just the normal trial balance report. It becomes post-closing because it was printed after closing entries were processed.

Juanita's Consulting
Work Sheet
For Month Ended June 30, 20 - -

	ACCOUNT TITLE	TRIAL BALANCE		ADJUSTMENTS		ADJUSTED TRIAL BALANCE		INCOME STATEMENT		BALANCE SHEET		
		DEBIT	CREDIT	DEBIT	CREDIT	DEBIT	CREDIT	DEBIT	CREDIT	DEBIT	CREDIT	
1	Cash	5,285.00				5,285.00				5,285.00		1
2	Accounts Receivable	1,075.00				1,075.00				1,075.00		2
3	Supplies	750.00			(a) 250.00	500.00				500.00		3
4	Prepaid Insurance	500.00			(b) 100.00	400.00				400.00		4
5	Office Equipment	2,200.00				2,200.00				2,200.00		5
6	Accum. Depr.—Office Equipment				(d) 110.00		110.00				110.00	6
7	Accounts Payable		1,500.00				1,500.00				1,500.00	7
8	Wages Payable				(c) 200.00		200.00				200.00	8
9	Juanita Alvarez, Capital		7,000.00				7,000.00				7,000.00	9
10	Juanita Alvarez, Drawing	800.00				800.00				800.00		10
11	Consulting Fees		4,204.00				4,204.00		4,204.00			11
12	Wages Expense	1,400.00		(c) 200.00		1,600.00		1,600.00				12
13	Advertising Expense	60.00				60.00		60.00				13
14	Rent Expense	500.00				500.00		500.00				14
15	Supplies Expense			(a) 250.00		250.00		250.00				15
16	Telephone Expense	46.00				46.00		46.00				16
17	Electricity Expense	39.00				39.00		39.00				17
18	Insurance Expense			(b) 100.00		100.00		100.00				18
19	Gas and Oil Expense	28.00				28.00		28.00				19
20	Depr. Expense—Office Equipment			(d) 110.00		110.00		110.00				20
21	Miscellaneous Expense	21.00				21.00		21.00				21
22		12,704.00	12,704.00	660.00	660.00	13,014.00	13,014.00	2,754.00	4,204.00	10,260.00	8,810.00	22
23	Net Income							1,450.00			1,450.00	23
24								4,204.00	4,204.00	10,260.00	10,260.00	24
25												25
26												26
27												27
28												28
29												29
30												30

CHAPTER 6 MASTERY PROBLEM

Elizabeth Soltis owns and operates Aunt Ibby's Styling Salon. A year-end worksheet is provided on the next page. Using this information, prepare financial statements and closing entries. Soltis made no additional investments during the year.

In the Chapter 6 Mastery Problem, you will display the financial statements and close out the accounting period. Follow the step-by-step instructions below to complete the Chapter 6 Mastery Problem.

STEP 1: **Start up the Peachtree software.**

STEP 2: **Open the data file for the Chapter 6 Mastery Problem.**

STEP 3: **Enter the adjusting entries from the adjustment column of the worksheet.**

STEP 4: **Display the adjusting entries with a General Journal with Titles Report.**

STEP 5: **Display a Statement of Owner's Equity.**

STEP 6: **Display a Basic Balance Sheet.**

STEP 7: **Display an Income Statement.**

STEP 8: **Change the accounting period to January 1 of 2001.**

- **From the Tasks menu, select System, then select Change Accounting Periods from the submenu.**
- **When the Change Accounting Period window appears, select January 1, 2001, to January 31, 2001, and click on Ok.**
- **A message box appears, asking if you would like to print reports before continuing. Since you just printed reports in the above steps, respond No.**

Changing the accounting period to the next fiscal year will change the processing cycle from the year 2000 to the year 2001, in effect closing the year 2000.

STEP 9: **Display a General Ledger Trial Balance Report.**

Because you changed to a new fiscal accounting year, the General Ledger Trial Balance Report should reflect the closing of the year 2000. If you should discover an error and wish to edit transactions from the previous period, simply change the accounting period back to December of 2000, make the corrections, display your reports, and again change the accounting period to January of 2001.

COMPREHENSIVE PROBLEM 1

Bob Night opened The General's Favorite Fishing Hole. The fishing camp is open from April through September and attracts many famous college basketball coaches during the off-season. Guests typically register for one week, arriving on Sunday afternoon and returning home the following Saturday afternoon. The registration fee includes room and board, the use of fishing boats, and professional instruction in fishing techniques. The chart of accounts for the camping operation is provided on page 62.

Aunt Ibby's Styling Salon
Work Sheet
For Year Ended December 31, 20 - -

	ACCOUNT TITLE	TRIAL BALANCE		ADJUSTMENTS		ADJUSTED TRIAL BALANCE		INCOME STATEMENT		BALANCE SHEET		
		DEBIT	CREDIT	DEBIT	CREDIT	DEBIT	CREDIT	DEBIT	CREDIT	DEBIT	CREDIT	
1	Cash	940 00				940 00				940 00		1
2	Styling Supplies	1 500 00			(a) 1 450 00	50 00				50 00		2
3	Prepaid Insurance	800 00			(b) 650 00	150 00				150 00		3
4	Salon Equipment	4 500 00				4 500 00				4 500 00		4
5	Accum. Depr.—Salon Equipment				(d) 900 00		900 00				900 00	5
6	Accounts Payable		225 00				225 00				225 00	6
7	Wages Payable				(c) 40 00		40 00				40 00	7
8	Elizabeth Soltis, Capital		2 765 00				2 765 00				2 765 00	8
9	Elizabeth Soltis, Drawing	12 000 00				12 000 00				12 000 00		9
10	Styling Fees		32 000 00				32 000 00		32 000 00			10
11	Wages Expense	8 000 00		(c) 40 00		8 040 00		8 040 00				11
12	Rent Expense	6 000 00				6 000 00		6 000 00				12
13	Styling Supplies Expense			(a) 1 450 00		1 450 00		1 450 00				13
14	Telephone Expense	450 00				450 00		450 00				14
15	Utilities Expense	800 00				800 00		800 00				15
16	Insurance Expense			(b) 650 00		650 00		650 00				16
17	Depr. Expense—Salon Equipment			(d) 900 00		900 00		900 00				17
18		34 990 00	34 990 00	3 040 00	3 040 00	35 930 00	35 930 00	18 290 00	32 000 00	17 640 00	3 930 00	18
19	Net Income							13 710 00			13 710 00	19
20								32 000 00	32 000 00	17 640 00	17 640 00	20
21												21
22												22
23												23
24												24
25												25
26												26
27												27
28												28
29												29
30												30

The General's Favorite Fishing Hole
Chart of Accounts

Assets
101 Cash
142 Office Supplies
144 Food Supplies
145 Prepaid Insurance
181 Fishing Boats
181.1 Accum. Depr.—Fishing Boats

Liabilities
202 Accounts Payable
219 Wages Payable

Owner's Equity
311 Bob Night, Capital
312 Bob Night, Drawing
313 Income Summary

Revenues
401 Registration Fees

Expenses
511 Wages Expense
521 Rent Expense
523 Office Supplies Expense
524 Food Supplies Expense
525 Telephone Expense
533 Utilities Expense
535 Insurance Expense
536 Postage Expense
542 Depr. Exp.—Fishing Boats

The following transactions took place during April 20--.

Apr. 1 Night invested cash in business, $90,000.

1 Paid insurance premium for camping season, $9,000.

2 Paid rent for lodge and campgrounds for the month of April, $40,000.

2 Deposited registration fees, $35,000.

2 Purchased ten fishing boats on account for $60,000. The boats have estimated useful lives of five years, at which time they will be donated to a local day camp. Arrangements were made to pay for the boats in July.

3 Purchased food supplies from Acme Super Market on account, $7,000.

5 Purchased office supplies from Gordon Office Supplies on account, $500.

7 Deposited registration fees, $38,600.

10 Purchased food supplies from Acme Super Market on account, $8,200.

10 Paid wages to fishing guides, $10,000.

14 Deposited registration fees, $30,500.

16 Purchased food supplies from Acme Super Market on account, $9,000.

17 Paid wages to fishing guides, $10,000.

18 Paid postage, $150.

21 Deposited registration fees, $35,600.

24 Purchased food supplies from Acme Super Market on account, $8,500.

24 Paid wages to fishing guides, $10,000.

28 Deposited registration fees, $32,000.

29 Paid wages to fishing guides, $10,000.

30 Purchased food supplies from Acme Super Market on account, $6,000.

30 Paid Acme Super Market on account, $32,700.

30 Paid utilities bill, $2,000.

30 Paid telephone bill, $1,200.

30 Bob Night withdrew cash for personal use, $6,000.

Adjustment information for the end of April is provided below.

(a) Office supplies remaining on hand, $100.

(b) Food supplies remaining on hand, $8,000.

(c) Insurance expired during the month of April, $1,500.

(d) Depreciation on the fishing boats for the month of April, $1,000.

(e) Wages earned, but not yet paid, at the end of April, $500.

REQUIRED

1. Enter the above transactions in a general journal.
2. Post the entries to the general ledger.
3. Prepare a trial balance on a worksheet.
4. Complete the worksheet.
5. Prepare the income statement.
6. Prepare the statement of owner's equity.
7. Prepare the balance sheet.
8. Journalize the adjusting entries.
9. Post the adjusting entries to the general ledger.
10. Journalize the closing entries.
11. Post the closing entries to the general ledger.
12. Prepare a post-closing trial balance.

Comprehensive Problem 1 involves processing the April transactions for The General's Favorite Fishing Hole, processing adjusting entries, generating financial statements, and changing the accounting period.

STEP 1: Open the data file for Comprehensive Problem 1.

STEP 2: Enter the April transactions into the General Journal window.

STEP 3: Display the April transactions with the General Journal with Titles Report.

STEP 4: Display the a General Ledger Trial Balance Report.

STEP 5: Based on the trial balance created in Step 6, enter the adjusting entries.

STEP 6: Display the journal entries. Your report will include the monthly transactions plus the adjusting entries.

STEP 7: Display a Basic Income Statement.

STEP 8: Display a Statement of Owner's Equity.

STEP 9: Display a Basic Balance Sheet.

STEP 10: Display a General Ledger Trial Balance Report.

STEP 11: Change the accounting period to May 1, 2000, to May 31, 2000.

- **From the Tasks menu, choose the System option, then, from the submenu, select the Change Accounting Period option.**
- **When the Change Accounting Period window appears, choose the May 1, 2000 to May 31, 2000 accounting period and click on Ok.**
- **When the message box appears asking if you wish to print reports, respond No.**

STEP 12: Display a post-closing trial balance which is really just the normal General Ledger Trial Balance report. It becomes post-closing because it was printed after the accounting period was changed which, in effect, closes the period.

If you should discover an error and wish to edit transactions from the previous period, simply change the accounting period back to April 1, 2000, to April 30, 2000, then make the corrections, display your reports, and again change the accounting period to May 1, 2000, to May 31, 2000.

CHAPTER 7 DEMONSTRATION PROBLEM (07-DEMO)

Maria Vietor is a financial planning consultant. She developed the following chart of accounts for her business.

Vietor Financial Planning
Chart of Accounts

Assets
101 Cash
142 Office Supplies

Liabilities
202 Accounts Payable

Owner's Equity
311 Maria Vietor, Capital
312 Maria Vietor, Drawing
313 Income Summary

Revenues
401 Professional Fees

Expenses
511 Wages Expense
521 Rent Expense
523 Office Supplies Expense
525 Telephone Expense
526 Automobile Expense
533 Utilities Expense
534 Charitable Contributions Expense

Vietor completed the following transactions during the month of December of the current year:

Dec. 1 Vietor invested cash to start a consulting business, $20,000.

3 Paid December office rent, $1,000.

4 Received a check from Aaron Bisno, a client, for services, $2,500.

6 Paid Union Electric for December heating and light, $75.

7 Received a check from Will Carter, a client, for services, $2,000.

12 Paid Smith's Super Service for gasoline and oil purchases, $60.

14 Paid Comphelp for temporary secretarial services obtained through them during the past two weeks, $600.

17 Purchased office supplies on account from Cleat Office Supply, $280.

20 Paid Cress Telephone Co. for local and long-distance business calls during the past month, $100.

21 Vietor withdrew cash for personal use, $1,100.

24 Made donation to the National Multiple Sclerosis Society, $100.

27 Received a check from Ellen Thaler, a client, for services, $2,000.

28 Paid Comphelp for temporary secretarial services obtained through them during the past two weeks, $600.

29 Made payment on account to Cleat Office Supply, $100.

REQUIRED

1. Enter the transactions in a combination journal. Establish special columns for Professional Fees, Wages Expense, and Automobile Expense. Vietor uses the modified cash basis of accounting.
2. Prove the combination journal.
3. Post these transactions to a general ledger.
4. Prepare a trial balance.

When solved manually, the Chapter 7 Demonstration Problem involves entering transactions in a combination journal. Since the Peachtree Accounting software does not support a combination journal, you will enter the transactions in the general journal. In addition, you will display a journal report and a trial balance report. Follow the step-by-step instructions below to complete the problem.

STEP 1: **Open the data file for the Chapter 7 Demonstration Problem.**

STEP 2: **Enter the December transactions into the General Journal window.**

STEP 3: **Display a General Journal with Titles Report.**

STEP 4: **Display a trial balance report.**

See the solution section of this workbook for the solution to the demonstration problem.

PROBLEM 7A2

Sue Reyton owns a suit tailoring shop. She opened her business in September. She rents a small work space and has an assistant to receive job orders and process claim tickets. Her trial balance on the next page shows her account balances for the first two months of business (September and October). No adjustments were made in September or October.

Reyton's transactions for November are as follows:

Nov. 1 Paid November rent, $300.

2 Purchased tailoring supplies on account from Sew Easy Supplies, $150.

3 Purchased a new buttonhole machine on account from Seam's Sewing Machines, $3,000.

5 Earned first week's revenue: $400 in cash.

8 Paid for newspaper advertising, $13.

9 Paid telephone bill, $28.

Sue Reyton Tailors
Trial Balance
October 31, 20--

ACCOUNT TITLE	ACCOUNT NO.	DEBIT BALANCE	CREDIT BALANCE
Cash	101	5711 00	
Tailoring Supplies	141	1000 00	
Office Supplies	142	485 00	
Prepaid Insurance	145	100 00	
Tailoring Equipment	188	3800 00	
Accumulated Depreciation—Tailoring Equipment	188.1		
Accounts Payable	202		4125 00
Sue Reyton, Capital	311		5430 00
Sue Reyton, Drawing	312	500 00	
Tailoring Fees	401		3600 00
Wages Expense	511	800 00	
Advertising Expense	512	33 00	
Rent Expense	521	600 00	
Telephone Expense	525	60 00	
Utilities Expense	533	44 00	
Miscellaneous Expense	549	22 00	
		13155 00	13155 00

10 Paid electricity bill, $21.

12 Earned second week's revenue: $200 in cash, $300 on account.

15 Paid part-time worker, $400.

16 Made payment on account for tailoring supplies, $100.

17 Paid for magazine subscription (miscellaneous expense), $12.

19 Earned third week's revenue: $450 in cash.

21 Paid for prepaid insurance for the year, $500.

23 Received cash from customers (previously owed), $300.

24 Paid for newspaper advertising, $13.

26 Paid for special delivery fee (miscellaneous expense), $12.

29 Earned fourth week's revenue: $600 in cash.

Additional accounts needed are as follows:

313 Income Summary
523 Office Supplies Expense
524 Tailoring Supplies Expense
535 Insurance Expense
542 Depreciation Expense—Tailoring Equipment

Nov. 30 Adjustments:

(a) Tailoring supplies on hand, $450.

(b) Office supplies on hand, $285.

(c) Prepaid insurance expired over past three months, $150.

(d) Depreciation on tailoring equipment for the last three months, $300.

REQUIRED

1. Journalize the transactions for November using the modified cash basis and the combination journal. Set up special columns for Tailoring Fees (credit), Wages Expense (debit), and Advertising Expense (debit).
2. Determine the cash balance as of November 12.
3. Prove the combination journal.
4. Set up four-column general ledger accounts, including the additional accounts listed above, entering the balances as of November 1, 20--. Post the entries from the combination journal.
5. Prepare a worksheet for the three months ended November 30, 20--.
6. Prepare an income statement and statement of owner's equity for the three months ended November 30 and a balance sheet as of November 30, 20--. (Assume that Reyton made an investment of $5,430 on September 1, 20--.)
7. Record the adjusting and closing entries in the combination journal, and post to the general ledger accounts.

Problem 7A2 involves entering the November transactions for Sue Reyton Tailors in the general journal, processing adjusting entries, generating financial statements, and changing the accounting period.

STEP 1: Open the data file for Problem 7A2.

STEP 2: Since the Peachtree Accounting software does not support the combination journal, enter the November transactions into the General Journal window.

STEP 3: Display the General Journal with Titles Report.

STEP 4: Display a General Ledger Trial Balance Report.

STEP 5: Based on the trial balance created in Step 4, enter the adjusting entries.

STEP 6: Display the journal entries. Your report will include the monthly transactions plus the adjusting entries.

STEP 7: Display a Basic Income Statement.

STEP 8: Display a Statement of Owner's Equity.

STEP 9: Display a Basic Balance Sheet.

STEP 10: Display a General Ledger Trial Balance Report.

STEP 11: Change the accounting period to be December 1, 2000, to December 31, 2000.

- ▶ **From the Tasks menu, choose the System option, then, from the submenu, select the Change Accounting Period option.**
- ▶ **When the Change Accounting Period window appears, choose the December 1, 2000 to December 31, 2000 accounting period and click on Ok.**
- ▶ **When the dialog box appears asking if you wish to print reports, respond No.**

STEP 12: Display a post-closing trial balance, which is really just the normal General Ledger Trial Balance Report. It becomes post-closing because it was printed after the accounting period was changed which, in effect, closes the period.

If you should discover an error and wish to edit transactions from the previous period, simply change the accounting period back to December of 2000, make the corrections, display your reports, and again change the accounting period to January of 2001.

PROBLEM 7B2

Molly Claussen owns a lawn care business. She opened her business in April. She rents a small shop area where she stores her equipment and has an assistant to receive orders and process accounts. Her trial balance shows her account balances for the first two months of business (April and May). No adjustments were made at the end of April or May.

Molly Claussen's Green Thumb
Trial Balance
May 31, 20--

ACCOUNT TITLE	ACCOUNT NO.	DEBIT BALANCE	CREDIT BALANCE
Cash	101	4 604 00	
Lawn Care Supplies	141	588 00	
Office Supplies	142	243 00	
Prepaid Insurance	145	150 00	
Lawn Care Equipment	189	2 408 00	
Accumulated Depreciation—Lawn Care Equipment	189.1		
Accounts Payable	202		1 080 00
Molly Claussen, Capital	311		5 000 00
Molly Claussen, Drawing	312	800 00	
Lawn Care Fees	401		4 033 00
Wages Expense	511	600 00	
Rent Expense	521	400 00	
Telephone Expense	525	88 00	
Electricity Expense	533	62 00	
Repair Expense	537	50 00	
Gas and Oil Expense	538	120 00	
		10 113 00	10 113 00

Transactions for June are as follows:

June 1 Paid shop rent, $200.

2 Purchased office supplies, $230.

3 Purchased new landscaping equipment on account from Earth Care, Inc., $1,000.

5 Paid telephone bill, $31.

6 Received cash for lawn care fees, $640.

8 Paid electricity bill, $31.

10 Paid part-time worker, $300.

11 Received cash for lawn care fees, $580.

12 Paid for a one-year insurance policy, $200.

14 Made payment on account for landscaping equipment previously purchased, $100.

15 Paid for gas and oil, $40.

19 Paid for mower repairs, $25.

21 Received $310 cash for lawn care fees and earned $480 on account.

24 Withdrew cash for personal use, $100.

26 Paid for edging equipment repairs, $20.

28 Received cash from customers (previously owed), $480.

29 Paid part-time worker, $300.

Additional accounts needed are as follows:

313 Income Summary
523 Office Supplies Expense
524 Lawn Care Supplies Expense
535 Insurance Expense
542 Depreciation Expense—Lawn Care Equipment

June 30 Adjustments:

(a) Office supplies on hand, $273.

(b) Lawn care supplies on hand, $300.

(c) Prepaid insurance expired over past three months, $100.

(d) Depreciation on lawn care equipment for past three months, $260.

REQUIRED

1. Journalize the transactions for June using the modified cash basis and the combination journal. Set up special columns for Lawn Care Fees (credit), Repair Expense (debit), and Wages Expense (debit).
2. Determine the cash balance as of June 12.
3. Prove the combination journal.
4. Set up four-column general ledger accounts, including the additional accounts listed above, entering balances as of June 1, 20--. Post the entries from the combination journal.
5. Prepare a worksheet for the three months ended June 30, 20--.
6. Prepare an income statement and statement of owner's equity for the three months ended June 30 and a balance sheet as of June 30, 20--. Assume that Claussen invested $5,000 on April 1, 20--.
7. Record the adjusting and closing entries in the combination journal, and post to the general ledger accounts.

Problem 7B2 involves entering the June transactions for Claussen's Green Thumb in the general journal, processing adjusting entries, generating financial statements, and changing the accounting period.

STEP 1: Open the data file for Problem 7B2.

STEP 2: Since the Peachtree Accounting software does not support the combination journal, enter the November transactions into the General Journal window.

STEP 3: Display the General Journal with Titles Report.

STEP 4: Display a General Ledger Trial Balance Report.

STEP 5: Based on the trial balance created in Step 4, enter the adjusting entries.

STEP 6: Display the journal entries. Your report will include the monthly transactions plus the adjusting entries.

STEP 7: Display a Basic Income Statement.

STEP 8: Display a Statement of Owner's Equity.

STEP 9: Display a Basic Balance Sheet.

STEP 10: Display a General Ledger Trial Balance Report.

STEP 11: Change the accounting period to July 1, 2000 to July 31, 2000.

- ▶ **From the Tasks menu, choose the System option, then, from the submenu, select the Change Accounting Period option.**
- ▶ **When the Change Accounting Period window appears, choose the July 1, 2000 to July 31, 2000 accounting period and click on Ok.**
- ▶ **When the dialog box appears asking if you wish to print reports, respond No.**

STEP 12: Display a post-closing trial balance, which is really just the normal General Ledger Trial Balance Report. It becomes post-closing because it was printed after the accounting period was changed which, in effect, closes the period.

CHAPTER 7 MASTERY PROBLEM

John McRoe opened a tennis resort in June 20--. Most guests register for one week, arriving on Sunday afternoon and returning home the following Saturday afternoon. Guests stay at an adjacent hotel. The tennis resort provides lunch and dinner. Dining and exercise facilities are provided in a building rented by McRoe. A dietitian, masseuse, physical therapist, and athletic trainers are on call to assure the proper combination of diet and exercise. The chart of accounts and transactions for the month of June are provided below. McRoe uses the modified cash basis of accounting.

McRoe Tennis Resort
Chart of Accounts

Assets		Revenue	
101	Cash	401	Registration Fees
142	Office Supplies		
144	Food Supplies	Expenses	
184	Tennis Facilities	511	Wages Expense
184.1	Accum. Depr.—Tennis Facilities	521	Rent Expense
186	Exercise Equipment	523	Office Supplies Expense
186.1	Accum. Depr.—Exercise Equip.	524	Food Supplies Expense
		525	Telephone Expense
Liabilities		533	Utilities Expense
202	Accounts Payable	535	Insurance Expense
		536	Postage Expense
Owner's Equity		541	Depr. Exp.—Tennis Facilities
311	John McRoe, Capital	542	Depr. Exp.—Exercise Equip.
312	John McRoe, Drawing		
313	Income Summary		

June 1	McRoe invested cash in the business, $90,000.
1	Paid for new exercise equipment, $9,000.
2	Deposited registration fees in the bank, $15,000.
2	Paid rent for month of June on building and land, $2,500.
2	Rogers Construction completed work on new tennis courts that cost $70,000. The estimated useful life of the facility is five years, at which time the courts will have to be resurfaced. Arrangements were made to pay the bill in July.
3	Purchased food supplies on account from Au Naturel Foods, $5,000.
5	Purchased office supplies on account from Gordon Office Supplies, $300.
7	Deposited registration fees in the bank, $16,200.
10	Purchased food supplies on account from Au Naturel Foods, $6,200.
10	Paid wages to staff, $500.
14	Deposited registration fees in the bank, $13,500.
16	Purchased food supplies on account from Au Naturel Foods, $4,000.
17	Paid wages to staff, $500.
18	Paid postage, $85.
21	Deposited registration fees in the bank, $15,200.
24	Purchased food supplies on account from Au Naturel Foods, $5,500.
24	Paid wages to staff, $500.
28	Deposited registration fees in the bank, $14,000.
30	Purchased food supplies on account from Au Naturel Foods, $6,000.
30	Paid wages to staff, $500.
30	Paid Au Naturel Foods on account, $28,700.
30	Paid utility bill, $500.
30	Paid telephone bill, $120.
30	McRoe withdrew cash for personal use, $1,500.

REQUIRED

1. Enter the transactions in a combination journal. Establish special columns for Registration Fees (credit), Wages Expense (debit), and Food Supplies (debit).
2. Prove the combination journal.
3. Post these transactions to a general ledger.
4. Prepare a trial balance as of June 30.

The Chapter 7 Mastery Problem involves entering transactions in the general journal, displaying a journal report, and displaying a trial balance report. Follow the step-by-step instructions below to complete the problem.

STEP 1: Open the data file for the Chapter 7 Demonstration Problem.

STEP 2: Enter the June transactions into the General Journal window.

STEP 3: Display a General Journal with Titles Report.

STEP 4: Display a Trial Balance Report.

CHAPTER 8 DEMONSTRATION PROBLEM (08-DEMO)

Jason Kuhn's check stubs indicated a balance of $4,673.12 on March 31. This included a record of a deposit of $926.10 mailed to the bank on March 30 but not credited to Kuhn's account until April 1. In addition, the following checks were outstanding on March 31:

No. 462	$524.26
No. 465	$213.41
No. 473	$543.58
No. 476	$351.38
No. 477	$197.45

The bank statement showed a balance of $5,419.00 as of March 31. The bank statement included a service charge of $4.10 with the date of March 29. In matching the cancelled checks and record of deposits with the stubs, it was discovered that check no. 456, to Office Suppliers, Inc., for $93.00 was erroneously recorded on the stub for $39.00. This caused the bank balance on that stub and those following to be $54.00 too large. It was also discovered that an ATM withdrawal of $100.00 for personal use was not recorded on the books.

Kuhn maintains a $200.00 petty cash fund. His petty cash payments record showed the following totals at the end of March of the current year.

Automobile expense	$ 32.40
Postage expense	27.50
Charitable contributions expense	35.00
Telephone expense	6.20
Travel and entertainment expense	38.60
Miscellaneous expense	17.75
Jason Kuhn, Drawing	40.00
Total	$197.45

This left a balance of $2.55 in the petty cash fund.

REQUIRED

1. Prepare a bank reconciliation for Jason Kuhn as of March 31, 20--.
2. Journalize the entries that should be made by Kuhn on his books as of March 31, 20--, (a) as a result of the bank reconciliation and (b) to replenish the petty cash fund.
3. Show proof that, after these entries, the total of the cash and petty cash account balances equals $4,715.02.

In the Chapter 8 Demonstration Problem, you will reconcile the bank statement for Jason Kuhn as of March 31, 2000. When the problem is solved manually, the journal entry to record the replenishment of petty cash is recorded after reconciliation. In a computerized system, the entry to record the replenishment of petty cash must be made before reconciliation because it is one of the checks that must be stored in the computer so it can be included in the reconciliation. Therefore, in the opening balance data, the check has already been recorded and will appear in the list of checks in the Account Reconciliation window. In the manual problem, you are provided with a list of outstanding checks. The Peachtree Accounting software requires that you enter *cleared* checks; therefore, a list of cleared checks is provided below:

463	213.11
464	2,500.00
466	45.80
467	400.00
468	65.40

469	89.50
470	34.89
471	450.00
472	39.00
474	85.00
475	57.00

STEP 1: **Open the data file for the Chapter 8 Demonstration Problem.**

STEP 2: **Enter the account reconciliation data.**

- **From the Tasks menu, choose the Account Reconciliation option.**
- **When the Account Reconciliation window shown in Figure 2.16 appears, enter or select the cash account number 101 in the Account to Reconcile field.**
- **Enter a Statement Date of March 31, 2000.**
- **Enter the Statement Ending Balance in the lower right corner of the window.**
- **Click on the Adjust Icon Bar button, and enter the adjustments as shown in the Additional Transactions window in Figure 2.17. Enter a date of March 31, 2000, for each entry. When completed, click on Ok.**

  Note: The computer will automatically generate the journal entries resulting from these adjustments. If you discover an error in your adjustments after you have clicked on Ok to record the entry, you must make corrections via the General Journal Entry window. To make corrections, select General Journal Entry from the Tasks menu, click on the Edit Icon Bar button, select the entry in error, make corrections, and click on Post to record the changes.

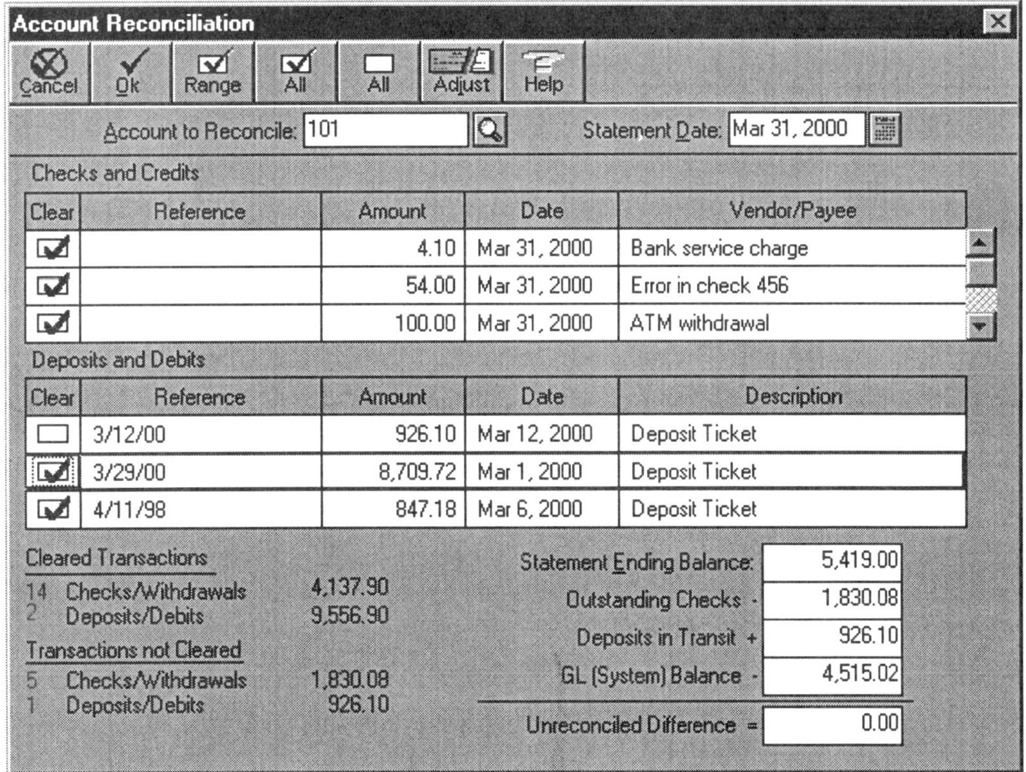

FIGURE 2.16 Account Reconciliation Window

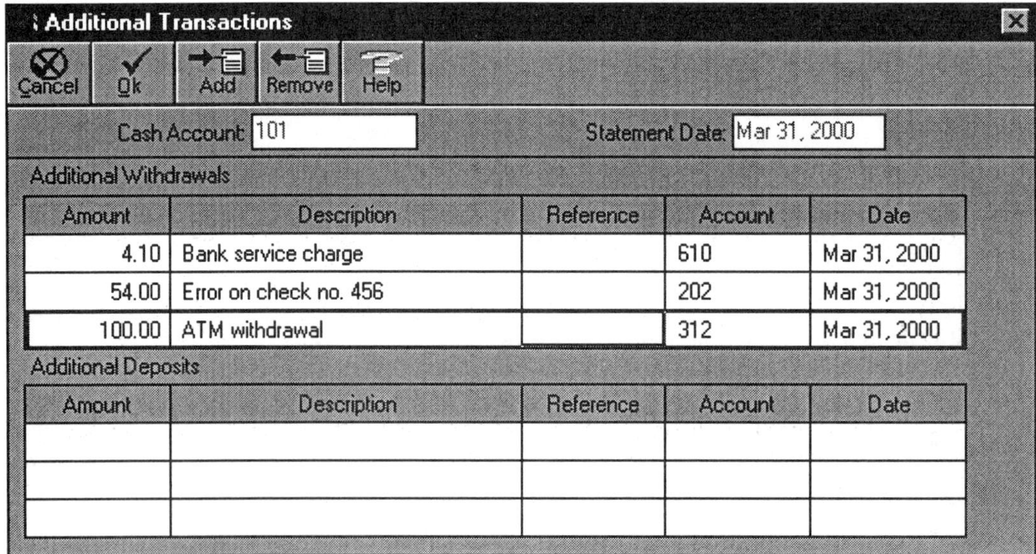

FIGURE 2.17 Additional Transactions Window

- ▶ **In the Checks and Credits section of Account Reconciliation, mark the checks that have cleared by clicking on the rectangular boxes under the Clear column. In the problem, you are provided with a list of outstanding checks. In the software, you need to identify cleared checks. Therefore, you can assume that all checks not listed in the problem as outstanding have cleared.**
- ▶ **In the Deposits and Credits section, mark as cleared all deposits that are no longer outstanding as illustrated in the completed Account Reconciliation window in Figure 2.16.**

STEP 3: From the Reports menu, select the Account Reconciliation option. Display the Account Register and Account Reconciliation Reports.

See the solution section of this workbook for the solution to the demonstration problem.

PROBLEM 8A2

The balance in the checking account of Lyle's Salon as of November 30 is $3,282.95. The bank statement shows an ending balance of $2,127.00. By examining last month's bank reconciliation, comparing the checks deposited and written per books and per bank in November, and noting the service charges and other debit and credit memos shown on the bank statement, the following were found:

a. An ATM withdrawal of $150.00 on November 18 by Lyle for personal use was not recorded on the books.

b. A bank debit memo issued for an NSF check from a customer of $19.50.

c. A bank credit memo issued for interest of $19.00 earned during the month.

d. On November 30, a deposit of $1,177.00 was made, which is not shown on the bank statement.

e. A bank debit memo issued for $17.50 for bank service charges.

f. Checks for the amounts of $185.00, $21.00, and $9.40 were written during November but have not yet been received by the bank.

g. The reconciliation from the previous month showed outstanding checks of $271.95. One of those checks, for $18.65, has not yet been received by the bank.

h. Check No. 523, written to a creditor in the amount of $372.90, was recorded in the books as $327.90.

REQUIRED 1. Prepare a bank reconciliation as of November 30.

2. Prepare the required journal entries.

In Problem 8A2, you will reconcile the bank statement for Lyle's Salon as of November 30, 2000. Follow the step-by-step instructions provided. In the manual problem, you are provided with a list of outstanding checks. The Peachtree Accounting software requires that you enter *cleared* checks; therefore, a list of cleared checks is provided below:

523	327.90
524	32.00
525	2,300.00
526	56.00
527	400.00

STEP 1: **Open the data file for Problem 8A2.**

STEP 2: **From the Tasks menu, choose the Account Reconciliation option.**

- **Enter the cash account number 101 in the Account to Reconcile field.**
- **Enter a Statement Date of November 30, 2000.**
- **Enter the Statement Ending Balance.**
- **Click on the Adjust Icon Bar button and enter the adjustments. When completed, click on Ok. If you discover an error in your adjustments after you have clicked on Ok to record the entry, you must make corrections via the General Journal Entry window. To make corrections, select General Journal Entry from the Tasks menu, click on the Edit Icon Bar button, select the entry in error, make corrections, and click on Post to record the changes.**
- **In the Checks and Credits section of Account Reconciliation, mark the checks that have cleared by clicking on the rectangular boxes under the Clear column. In the problem, you are provided with a list of outstanding checks. In the software, you need to identify cleared checks. Therefore, you can assume that all checks not listed in the problem as outstanding have cleared.**
- **In the Deposits and Credits section, mark as cleared all deposits that are no longer outstanding.**

STEP 3: **From the Reports menu, select the Account Reconciliation option. Display the Account Register and Account Reconciliation Reports.**

PROBLEM 8B2

The balance in the checking account of Tori's Health Center as of April 30 is $4,690.30. The bank statement shows an ending balance of $3,275.60. By examining last month's bank reconciliation, comparing the checks deposited and written per books and per bank in April, and noting the service charges and other debit and credit memos shown on the bank statement, the following were found:

a. An ATM withdrawal of $200.00 on April 20 by Tori for personal use was not recorded on the books.

b. A bank debit memo issued for an NSF check from a customer of $29.10.

c. A bank credit memo issued for interest of $28.00 earned during the month.

d. On April 30, a deposit of $1,592.00 was made, which is not shown on the bank statement.

e. A bank debit memo issued for $24.50 for bank service charges.

f. Checks for the amounts of $215.00, $71.00, and $24.30 were written during April but have not yet been received by the bank.

g. The reconciliation from the previous month showed outstanding checks of $418.25. One of these checks for $38.60 has not yet been received by the bank.

h. Check No. 422, written to a creditor in the amount of $217.90, was recorded in the books as $271.90.

REQUIRED 1. Prepare a bank reconciliation as of April 30.

2. Prepare the required journal entries.

In Problem 8B2, you will reconcile the bank statement for Tori's Health Center as of April 30, 2000. Follow the step-by-step instructions provided. In the manual problem, you are provided with a list of outstanding checks. The Peachtree Accounting software requires that you enter *cleared* checks; therefore, a list of cleared checks is provided below:

422	271.90
425	540.00
427	71.20
429	870.00

STEP 1: Open the data file for Problem 8B2.

STEP 2: From the Tasks menu, choose the Account Reconciliation option.

- **Enter the cash account number 101 in the Account to Reconcile field.**
- **Enter a Statement Date of April 30, 2000.**
- **Enter the Statement Ending Balance.**
- **Click on the Adjust Icon Bar button, and enter the adjustments. Leave the Reference field blank. Enter a date of April 30, 2000, for all adjustments. If you discover an error in your adjustments after you have clicked on Ok to record the entry, you must make corrections via the General Journal Entry window. To make corrections, select General Journal Entry from the Tasks menu, click on the Edit Icon Bar button, select the entry in error, make corrections, and click on Post to record the changes.**
- **In the Checks and Credits section of Account Reconciliation, mark the checks that have cleared by clicking on the rectangular boxes under the Clear column. In the problem, you are provided with a list of outstanding checks. In the software, you need to identify cleared checks. Therefore, you can assume that all checks not listed in the problem as outstanding have cleared.**
- **In the Deposits and Credits section, mark as cleared all deposits that are no longer outstanding.**

STEP 3: From the Reports menu, select the Account Reconciliation option. Display the Account Register and Account Reconciliation Reports.

CHAPTER 9 DEMONSTRATION PROBLEM (09-DEMO)

Carole Vohsen operates a pet grooming salon called Canine Coiffures. She has five employees, all of whom are paid on a weekly basis. Canine Coiffures uses a payroll register, individual employee earnings records, a journal, and a general ledger.

The payroll data for each employee for the week ended January 21, 19--, are given below. Employees are paid 1½ times the regular rate for work over 40 hours a week and double-time for work on Sunday.

Name	Employee No.	No. of Allowances	Marital Status	Total Hours Worked Jan. 15–21	Rate	Total Earnings Jan. 1–14
DeNourie, Katie	1	2	S	44	$11.50	$1,058.00
Garriott, Pete	2	1	M	40	12.00	1,032.00
Martinez, Sheila	3	3	M	39	12.50	987.50
Parker, Nancy	4	4	M	42	11.00	957.00
Shapiro, John	5	2	S	40	11.50	931.50

Sheila Martinez is the manager of the Shampooing Department. Her Social Security number is 500-88-4189, and she was born April 12, 1969. She lives at 46 Darling Crossing; Norwich, CT 06360. Martinez was hired September 1 of last year.

Canine Coiffures uses a federal income tax withholding table. A portion of this weekly table is provided in Figure 9.4 on the following pages. Social Security tax is withheld at the rate of 6.2% of the first $68,400 earned. Medicare tax is withheld at the rate of 1.45%, and city earnings tax at the rate of 1%, both applied to gross pay. Garriott and Parker each have $14.00 and Denourie and Martinez each have $4.00 withheld for health insurance. DeNourie, Martinez, and Shapiro each have $15.00 withheld to be invested in the groomers' credit union. Garriott and Shapiro each have $18.75 withheld under a savings bond purchase plan.

Canine Coiffures' payroll is met by drawing checks on its regular bank account. This week, the checks were issued in sequence, beginning with no. 811.

REQUIRED

1. Prepare a payroll register for Canine Coiffures for the week ended January 21, 19--. Total the column amounts, verify the totals, and rule with single and double lines.
2. Prepare an employee earnings record for Sheila Martinez for the week ended January 21, 19--.
3. Assuming that the wages for the week ended January 21 were paid on January 23, prepare the journal entry for the payment of this payroll.
4. Post the entry in Requirement 3 to the affected accounts in the ledger of Canine Coiffures. Do not enter any amounts in the Balance columns. Use account numbers as follows: Cash—101; Employee Income Tax Payable—211; Social Security Tax Payable—212; Medicare Tax Payable—213; City Earnings Tax Payable—215; Health Insurance Premiums Payable—216; Credit Union Payable—217; Savings Bond Deductions Payable—218; Wages and Salaries Expense—511.

In the Chapter 9 Demonstration Problem, you will process the payroll for the week of January 21, 1998, for Canine Coiffures. The Peachtree Accounting software selects the tax table to use based on the year. At the time these materials were prepared, the Peachtree tax table available was for the year 1998. In order for the computer to calculate taxes correctly, it is imperative that a date in the year 1998 be used for the payroll problems. The step-by-step instructions for completing the Chapter 9 Demonstration Problem are listed below.

Note: The Peachtree Accounting software uses the percentage method of calculating the federal income tax withheld rather than a wage-bracket tax table.

STEP 1: Open the data file for the Chapter 9 Demonstration Problem.

STEP 2: From the Options menu, select the Change System Date option and set the system date to January 21, 1998.

STEP 3: Enter the weekly payroll transactions.

FIGURE 9-4 Federal Withholding Tax Table: Single Persons

SINGLE Persons—WEEKLY Payroll Period

(For Wages Paid in 1998)

If the wages are–		And the number of withholding allowances claimed is—										
At least	But less than	0	1	2	3	4	5	6	7	8	9	10
		The amount of income tax to be withheld is—										
$300	$310	38	30	23	15	7	0	0	0	0	0	0
310	320	40	32	24	16	8	1	0	0	0	0	0
320	330	41	33	26	18	10	2	0	0	0	0	0
330	340	43	35	27	19	11	4	0	0	0	0	0
340	350	44	36	29	21	13	5	0	0	0	0	0
350	360	46	38	30	22	14	7	0	0	0	0	0
360	370	47	39	32	24	16	8	0	0	0	0	0
370	380	49	41	33	25	17	10	2	0	0	0	0
380	390	50	42	35	27	19	11	3	0	0	0	0
390	400	52	44	36	28	20	13	5	0	0	0	0
400	410	53	45	38	30	22	14	6	0	0	0	0
410	420	55	47	39	31	23	16	8	0	0	0	0
420	430	56	48	41	33	25	17	9	2	0	0	0
430	440	58	50	42	34	26	19	11	3	0	0	0
440	450	59	51	44	36	28	20	12	5	0	0	0
450	460	61	53	45	37	29	22	14	6	0	0	0
460	470	62	54	47	39	31	23	15	8	0	0	0
470	480	64	56	48	40	32	25	17	9	1	0	0
480	490	65	57	50	42	34	26	18	11	3	0	0
490	500	67	59	51	43	35	28	20	12	4	0	0
500	510	68	60	53	45	37	29	21	14	6	0	0
510	520	70	62	54	46	38	31	23	15	7	0	0
520	530	72	63	56	48	40	32	24	17	9	1	0
530	540	75	65	57	49	41	34	26	18	10	3	0
540	550	78	66	59	51	43	35	27	20	12	4	0
550	560	81	68	60	52	44	37	29	21	13	6	0
560	570	83	69	62	54	46	38	30	23	15	7	0
570	580	86	72	63	55	47	40	32	24	16	9	1
580	590	89	74	65	57	49	41	33	26	18	10	2
590	600	92	77	66	58	50	43	35	27	19	12	4
600	610	95	80	68	60	52	44	36	29	21	13	5
610	620	97	83	69	61	53	46	38	30	22	15	7
620	630	100	86	71	63	55	47	39	32	24	16	8
630	640	103	88	74	64	56	49	41	33	25	18	10
640	650	106	91	77	66	58	50	42	35	27	19	11
650	660	109	94	79	67	59	52	44	36	28	21	13
660	670	111	97	82	69	61	53	45	38	30	22	14
670	680	114	100	85	70	62	55	47	39	31	24	16
680	690	117	102	88	73	64	56	48	41	33	25	17
690	700	120	105	91	76	65	58	50	42	34	27	19
700	710	123	108	93	79	67	59	51	44	36	28	20
710	720	125	111	96	82	68	61	53	45	37	30	22
720	730	128	114	99	84	70	62	54	47	39	31	23
730	740	131	116	102	87	73	64	56	48	40	33	25
740	750	134	119	105	90	76	65	57	50	42	34	26
750	760	137	122	107	93	78	67	59	51	43	36	28
760	770	139	125	110	96	81	68	60	53	45	37	29
770	780	142	128	113	98	84	70	62	54	46	39	31
780	790	145	130	116	101	87	72	63	56	48	40	32
790	800	148	133	119	104	90	75	65	57	49	42	34
800	810	151	136	121	107	92	78	66	59	51	43	35
810	820	153	139	124	110	95	81	68	60	52	45	37
820	830	156	142	127	112	98	83	69	62	54	46	38
830	840	159	144	130	115	101	86	72	63	55	48	40
840	850	162	147	133	118	104	89	74	65	57	49	41
850	860	165	150	135	121	106	92	77	66	58	51	43
860	870	167	153	138	124	109	95	80	68	60	52	44
870	880	170	156	141	126	112	97	83	69	61	54	46
880	890	173	158	144	129	115	100	86	71	63	55	47
890	900	176	161	147	132	118	103	88	74	64	57	49
900	910	179	164	149	135	120	106	91	77	66	58	50
910	920	181	167	152	138	123	109	94	80	67	60	52
920	930	184	170	155	140	126	111	97	82	69	61	53
930	940	187	172	158	143	129	114	100	85	71	63	55
940	950	190	175	161	146	132	117	102	88	73	64	56
950	960	193	178	163	149	134	120	105	91	76	66	58
960	970	195	181	166	152	137	123	108	94	79	67	59
970	980	198	184	169	154	140	125	111	96	82	69	61
980	990	201	186	172	157	143	128	114	99	85	70	62
990	1,000	204	189	175	160	146	131	116	102	87	73	64
1,000	1,010	207	192	177	163	148	134	119	105	90	76	65
1,010	1,020	209	195	180	166	151	137	122	108	93	78	67
1,020	1,030	212	198	183	168	154	139	125	110	96	81	68
1,030	1,040	215	200	186	171	157	142	128	113	99	84	70
1,040	1,050	218	203	189	174	160	145	130	116	101	87	72
1,050	1,060	221	206	191	177	162	148	133	119	104	90	75
1,060	1,070	223	209	194	180	165	151	136	122	107	92	78
1,070	1,080	226	212	197	182	168	153	139	124	110	95	81
1,080	1,090	229	214	200	185	171	156	142	127	113	98	84
1,090	1,100	232	217	203	188	174	159	144	130	115	101	86
1,100	1,110	235	220	205	191	176	162	147	133	118	104	89
1,110	1,120	238	223	208	194	179	165	150	136	121	106	92
1,120	1,130	241	226	211	196	182	167	153	138	124	109	95
1,130	1,140	244	228	214	199	185	170	156	141	127	112	98
1,140	1,150	247	231	217	202	188	173	158	144	129	115	100
1,150	1,160	250	234	219	205	190	176	161	147	132	118	103
1,160	1,170	253	237	222	208	193	179	164	150	135	120	106
1,170	1,180	256	240	225	210	196	181	167	152	138	123	109
1,180	1,190	259	243	228	213	199	184	170	155	141	126	112
1,190	1,200	262	246	231	216	202	187	172	158	143	129	114
1,200	1,210	266	249	233	219	204	190	175	161	146	132	117
1,210	1,220	269	253	236	222	207	193	178	164	149	134	120
1,220	1,230	272	256	240	224	210	195	181	166	152	137	123
1,230	1,240	275	259	243	227	213	198	184	169	155	140	126
1,240	1,250	278	262	246	230	216	201	186	172	157	143	128

FIGURE 9-4 Federal Withholding Tax Table: *(continued)* Married Persons

MARRIED Persons—**WEEKLY** Payroll Period

(For Wages Paid in 1998)

If the wages are–		And the number of withholding allowances claimed is—										
At least	But less than	0	1	2	3	4	5	6	7	8	9	10
		The amount of income tax to be withheld is—										
$290	$300	26	18	10	2	0	0	0	0	0	0	0
300	310	27	19	12	4	0	0	0	0	0	0	0
310	320	29	21	13	5	0	0	0	0	0	0	0
320	330	30	22	15	7	0	0	0	0	0	0	0
330	340	32	24	16	8	0	0	0	0	0	0	0
340	350	33	25	18	10	2	0	0	0	0	0	0
350	360	35	27	19	11	3	0	0	0	0	0	0
360	370	36	28	21	13	5	0	0	0	0	0	0
370	380	38	30	22	14	6	0	0	0	0	0	0
380	390	39	31	24	16	8	0	0	0	0	0	0
390	400	41	33	25	17	9	2	0	0	0	0	0
400	410	42	34	27	19	11	3	0	0	0	0	0
410	420	44	36	28	20	12	5	0	0	0	0	0
420	430	45	37	30	22	14	6	0	0	0	0	0
430	440	47	39	31	23	15	8	0	0	0	0	0
440	450	48	40	33	25	17	9	1	0	0	0	0
450	460	50	42	34	26	18	11	3	0	0	0	0
460	470	51	43	36	28	20	12	4	0	0	0	0
470	480	53	45	37	29	21	14	6	0	0	0	0
480	490	54	46	39	31	23	15	7	0	0	0	0
490	500	56	48	40	32	24	17	9	1	0	0	0
500	510	57	49	42	34	26	18	10	3	0	0	0
510	520	59	51	43	35	27	20	12	4	0	0	0
520	530	60	52	45	37	29	21	13	6	0	0	0
530	540	62	54	46	38	30	23	15	7	0	0	0
540	550	63	55	48	40	32	24	16	9	1	0	0
550	560	65	57	49	41	33	26	18	10	2	0	0
560	570	66	58	51	43	35	27	19	12	4	0	0
570	580	68	60	52	44	36	29	21	13	5	0	0
580	590	69	61	54	46	38	30	22	15	7	0	0
590	600	71	63	55	47	39	32	24	16	8	1	0
600	610	72	64	57	49	41	33	25	18	10	2	0
610	620	74	66	58	50	42	35	27	19	11	4	0
620	630	75	67	60	52	44	36	28	21	13	5	0
630	640	77	69	61	53	45	38	30	22	14	7	0
640	650	78	70	63	55	47	39	31	24	16	8	0
650	660	80	72	64	56	48	41	33	25	17	10	2
660	670	81	73	66	58	50	42	34	27	19	11	3
670	680	83	75	67	59	51	44	36	28	20	13	5
680	690	84	76	69	61	53	45	37	30	22	14	6
690	700	86	78	70	62	54	47	39	31	23	16	8
700	710	87	79	72	64	56	48	40	33	25	17	9
710	720	89	81	73	65	57	50	42	34	26	19	11
720	730	90	82	75	67	59	51	43	36	28	20	12
730	740	92	84	76	68	60	53	45	37	29	22	14
740	750	93	85	78	70	62	54	46	39	31	23	15
750	760	95	87	79	71	63	56	48	40	32	25	17
760	770	96	88	81	73	65	57	49	42	34	26	18
770	780	98	90	82	74	66	59	51	43	35	28	20
780	790	99	91	84	76	68	60	52	45	37	29	21
790	800	101	93	85	77	69	62	54	46	38	31	23
800	810	102	94	87	79	71	63	55	48	40	32	24
810	820	104	96	88	80	72	65	57	49	41	34	26
820	830	105	97	90	82	74	66	58	51	43	35	27
830	840	107	99	91	83	75	68	60	52	44	37	29
840	850	108	100	93	85	77	69	61	54	46	38	30
850	860	110	102	94	86	78	71	63	55	47	40	32
860	870	111	103	96	88	80	72	64	57	49	41	33
870	880	113	105	97	89	81	74	66	58	50	43	35
880	890	114	106	99	91	83	75	67	60	52	44	36
890	900	116	108	100	92	84	77	69	61	63	46	38
900	910	118	109	102	94	86	78	70	63	55	47	39
910	920	121	111	103	95	87	80	72	64	56	49	41
920	930	124	112	105	97	89	81	73	66	58	50	42
930	940	126	114	106	98	90	83	75	67	59	52	44
940	950	129	115	108	100	92	84	76	69	61	53	45
950	960	132	117	109	101	93	86	78	70	62	55	47
960	970	135	120	111	103	95	87	79	72	64	56	48
970	980	138	123	112	104	96	89	81	73	65	58	50
980	990	140	126	114	106	98	90	82	75	67	59	51
990	1,000	143	129	115	107	99	92	84	76	68	61	53
1,000	1,010	146	131	117	109	101	93	85	78	70	62	54
1,010	1,020	149	134	120	110	102	95	87	79	71	64	56
1,020	1,030	152	137	122	112	104	96	88	81	73	65	57
1,030	1,040	154	140	125	113	105	98	90	82	74	67	59
1,040	1,050	157	143	128	115	107	99	91	84	76	68	60
1,050	1,060	160	145	131	116	108	101	93	85	77	70	62
1,060	1,070	163	148	134	119	110	102	94	87	79	71	63
1,070	1,080	166	151	136	122	111	104	96	88	80	73	65
1,080	1,090	168	154	139	125	113	105	97	90	82	74	66
1,090	1,100	171	157	142	128	114	107	99	91	83	76	68
1,100	1,110	174	159	145	130	116	108	100	93	85	77	69
1,110	1,120	177	162	148	133	119	110	102	94	86	79	71
1,120	1,130	180	165	150	136	121	111	103	96	88	80	72
1,130	1,140	182	168	153	139	124	113	105	97	89	82	74
1,140	1,150	185	171	156	142	127	114	106	99	91	83	75
1,150	1,160	188	173	159	144	130	116	108	100	92	85	77
1,160	1,170	191	176	162	147	133	118	109	102	94	86	78
1,170	1,180	194	179	164	150	135	121	111	103	95	88	80
1,180	1,190	196	182	167	153	138	124	112	105	97	89	81
1,190	1,200	199	185	170	156	141	126	114	106	98	91	83
1,200	1,210	202	187	173	158	144	129	115	108	100	92	84
1,210	1,220	205	190	176	161	147	132	117	109	101	94	86
1,220	1,230	208	193	178	164	149	135	120	111	103	95	87
1,230	1,240	210	196	181	167	152	138	123	112	104	97	89
1,240	1,250	213	199	184	170	155	140	126	114	106	98	90
1,250	1,260	216	201	187	172	158	143	129	115	107	100	92
1,260	1,270	219	204	190	175	161	146	131	117	109	101	93
1,270	1,280	222	207	192	178	163	149	134	120	110	103	95
1,280	1,290	224	210	195	181	166	152	137	123	112	104	96

- From the Tasks menu, select the Payroll Entry option.
- Enter the Employee ID code of the employee you wish to pay (or click on the magnifying glass button and select the employee to pay from the list).
- For the first employee, enter a check number of 811. Thereafter, the computer will increment by 1 for each employee.
- Enter a Check Date of January 21, 1998.
- Enter the hours worked. Any hours worked in excess of 40 should be recorded as overtime.
- Enter the health insurance, credit union, and savings bond deductions. The deductions must be entered with a preceding minus sign (e.g., –4.00).
- You may click on the Journal Icon Bar button to view the journal entry that will be generated as a result of this entry.
- Click on the Post Icon Bar button to save the transaction.

A Payroll Entry window with the first entry completed is illustrated in Figure 2.18.

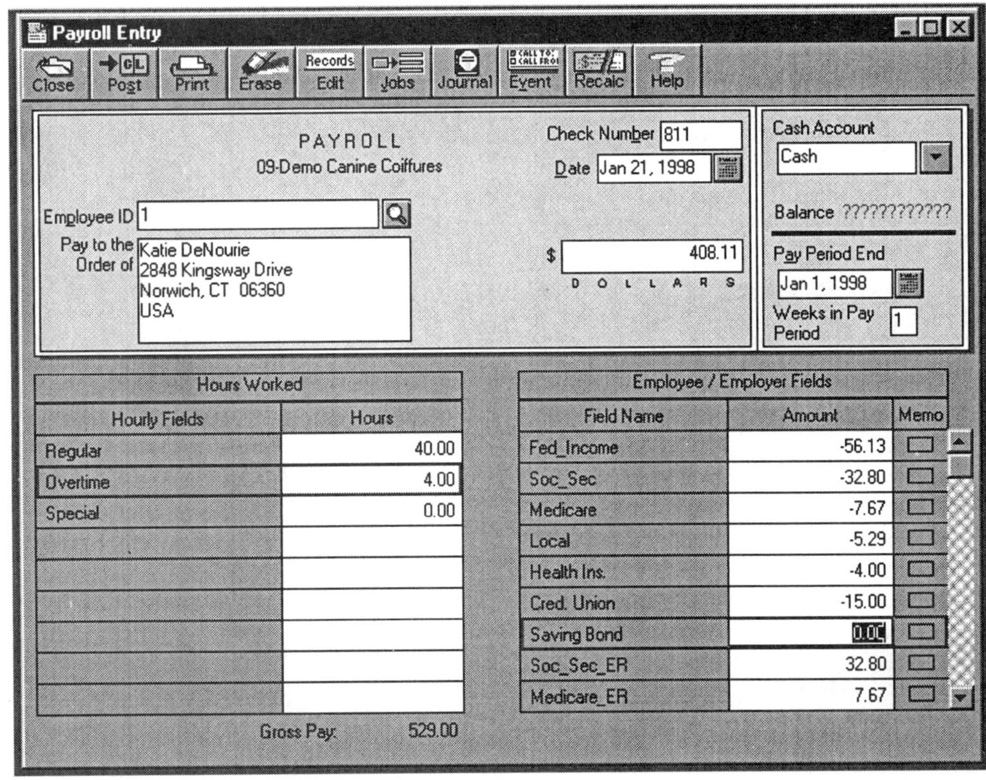

FIGURE 2.18 Payroll Entry Window

STEP 4: Display the payroll reports.

- From the Reports menu, select the Payroll option and click on Check Register.
- When the Check Register filter window appears, choose a date range of January 15, 1998, to January 21, 1998.
- Click on Payroll Journal (choose a date range of January 15, 1998, to January 21, 1998).
- Click on Payroll Register (choose a date range of January 15, 1998, to January 21, 1998).

See the solution section of this workbook for the solution to the demonstration problem.

PROBLEM 9A2

Don McCullum operates a travel agency called Don's Luxury Travel. He has five employees, all of whom are paid on a weekly basis. The travel agency uses a payroll register, individual employee earnings records, and a general journal.

Don's Luxury Travel uses a weekly federal income tax withholding table. The payroll data for each employee for the week ended March 22, 19--, are given below. Employees are paid 1½ times the regular rate for working over 40 hours per week.

Name	No. of Allowances	Marital Status	Total Hours Worked Mar. 16–22	Rate	Total Earnings Jan. 1–Mar. 15
Ali, Loren	4	M	45	$11.00	$5,280.00
Carson, Judy	1	S	40	12.00	5,760.00
Hernandez, Maria	3	M	43	9.50	4,560.00
Knox, Wayne	1	S	39	11.00	5,125.50
Paglione, Jim	2	M	40	10.50	4,720.50

Social Security tax is withheld from the first $68,400 of earnings at the rate of 6.2%. Medicare tax is withheld at the rate of 1.45%, and city earnings tax at the rate of 1%, both applied to gross pay. Ali and Knox have $15.00 withheld and Carson and Hernandez have $5.00 withheld for health insurance. Ali and Knox have $20.00 withheld to be invested in the travel agencies' credit union. Carson has $38.75 withheld and Hernandez has $18.75 withheld under a savings bond purchase plan.

Don's Luxury Travel's payroll is met by drawing checks on its regular bank account. The checks were issued in sequence, beginning with check no. 423.

REQUIRED

1. Prepare a payroll register for Don's Luxury Travel for the week ended March 22, 19--. Total the column amounts, verify the totals, and rule with single and double lines.
2. Assuming that the wages for the week ended March 22 were paid on March 24, prepare the journal entry for the payment of the payroll.

In Problem 9A2, you will process the payroll for the week ended March 22, 1998, for Don's Luxury Travel. The Peachtree Accounting software selects the tax table to use based on the year. At the time these materials were prepared, the tax table available was for the year 1998. Therefore, it is imperative that a date in the year 1998 be used for the payroll problems. The step-by-step instructions for completing Problem 9A2 are listed below.

STEP 1: Open the data file for Problem 9A2.

STEP 2: From the Options menu, select the Change System Date option and set the system date to March 22, 1998.

STEP 3: Enter the weekly payroll transactions.

- **From the Tasks menu, select the Payroll Entry option.**
- **Enter the Employee ID code for the employee you wish to pay.**
- **For the first employee, enter a check number of 423. Thereafter, the computer will increment by 1 for each employee.**
- **Enter a Check Date of March 22, 1998.**
- **Enter the hours worked. Any hours worked in excess of 40 should be recorded as overtime.**
- **Enter the health insurance, credit union, and savings bond deductions. The deductions must be entered with a preceding minus sign (e.g., –4.00).**

- ▶ You may click on the Journal Icon Bar button to view the journal entry that will be generated as a result of this entry.
- ▶ Click on the Post Icon Bar button to save the transaction.

STEP 4: Display the payroll reports.

- ▶ From the Reports menu, select the Payroll option and click on Check Register.
- ▶ When the Check Register filter window appears, choose a date range of March 16, 1998, to March 22, 1998.
- ▶ Click on Payroll Journal (choose a date range March 16, 1998, to March 22, 1998). The computer-generated journal entries appear somewhat different from those prepared manually. This is because the computer generates a journal entry for each employee, whereas manually one journal entry is prepared to record the entire payroll. In addition, the computer generates the entries to record the employer's share of payroll as well.
- ▶ Click on Payroll Register (choose a date range of March 16, 1998 to March 22, 1998).

  Note: The Peachtree Accounting software uses the percentage method of calculating the federal income tax withheld rather than a wage-bracket tax table.

PROBLEM 9B2

Karen Jolly operates a bakery called Karen's Cupcakes. She has five employees, all of whom are paid on a weekly basis. Karen's Cupcakes uses a payroll register, individual employee earnings records, and a general journal.

Karen's Cupcakes uses a weekly federal income tax withholding table. The payroll data for each employee for the week ended February 15, 19--, are given below. Employees are paid 1½ times the regular rate for working over 40 hours per week.

Name	No. of Allowances	Marital Status	Total Hours Worked Feb. 9–15	Rate	Total Earnings Jan. 1–Feb. 15
Barone, William	1	S	40	$10.00	$2,400.00
Hastings, Gene	4	M	45	12.00	3,360.00
Nitobe, Isako	3	M	46	8.75	2,935.00
Smith, Judy	4	M	42	11.00	2,745.00
Tarshis, Dolores	1	S	39	10.50	2,650.75

Social Security tax is withheld from the first $68,400 of earnings at the rate of 6.2%. Medicare tax is withheld at the rate of 1.45%, and city earnings tax at the rate of 1%, both applied to gross pay. Hastings and Smith have $35.00 withheld and Nitobe and Tarshis have $15.00 withheld for health insurance. Nitobe and Tarshis have $25.00 withheld to be invested in the bakers' credit union. Hastings has $18.75 withheld and Smith has $43.75 withheld under a savings bond purchase plan.

Karen's Cupcakes' payroll is met by drawing checks on its regular bank account. The checks were issued in sequence, beginning with no. 365.

REQUIRED

1. Prepare a payroll register for Karen's Cupcakes for the week ended February 15, 19--. Total the amount columns, verify the totals, and rule with single and double lines.
2. Assuming that the wages for the week ended February 15 were paid on February 17, prepare the journal entry for the payment of this payroll.

In Problem 9B2, you will process the payroll for the week ended February 15, 1998, for Karen's Cupcakes. The Peachtree Accounting software selects the tax table to use based on the year. At the time these materials were prepared, the tax table available was for the year 1998. Therefore, it is imperative that a date in the year 1998 be used for the payroll problems. The step-by-step instructions for completing Problem 9B2 are listed below.

STEP 1: Open the data file for Problem 9B2.

STEP 2: From the Options menu, select the Change System Date option and set the system date to February 15, 1998.

STEP 3: Enter the weekly payroll transactions.

- **From the Tasks menu, select the Payroll Entry option.**
- **Enter the Employee ID code for the employee you wish to pay.**
- **For the first employee, enter a check number of 365. Thereafter, the computer will increment by 1 for each employee.**
- **Enter a Check Date of February 15, 1998.**
- **Enter the hours worked. Any hours worked in excess of 40 should be recorded as overtime.**
- **Enter the health insurance, credit union, and savings bond deductions. The deductions must be entered with a preceding minus sign (e.g., –4.00).**
- **You may click on the Journal Icon Bar button to view the journal entry that will be generated as a result of this entry.**
- **Click on the Post Icon Bar button to save the transaction.**

STEP 4: Display the payroll reports.

- **From the Reports menu, select the Payroll option and click on Check Register.**
- **When the Check Register filter window appears, choose a date range of February 8, 1998, to February 15, 1998.**
- **Click on Payroll Journal (choose a date range of February 8, 1998, to February 15, 1998)**
- **Click on Payroll Register (choose a date range of February 8, 1998, to February 15, 1998).**

  Note: The Peachtree Accounting software uses the percentage method of calculating the federal income tax withheld rather than a wage-bracket tax table.

CHAPTER 9 MASTERY PROBLEM

Abigail Trenkamp owns and operates the Trenkamp Collection Agency. Listed below are the name, number of allowances claimed, marital status, information from time cards on hours worked each day, and the hourly rate of each employee. All hours worked in excess of 40 hours for Monday through Friday are paid at 1½ times the regular rate. All weekend hours are paid at double the regular rate.

Trenkamp uses a weekly federal income tax withholding table (see Figure 9.4 on pages 78 and 79). Social Security tax is withheld at the rate of 6.2% for the first $68,400 earned. Medicare tax is withheld at 1.45% and state income tax at 3.5%. Each employee has $5.00 withheld for health insurance. All employees use payroll deduction to the credit union for varying amounts as listed on the next page.

Trenkamp Collection Agency
Payroll Information for the Week Ended November 18, 19--

Name	Employee No.	No. of Allow.	Marital Status	Regular Hours Worked S	S	M	T	W	T	F	Hourly Rate	Credit Union Deposit	Total Earnings 1/1–11/11
Berling, James	1	3	M	2	2	9	8	8	9	10	$12.00	$149.60	$24,525.00
Merz, Linda	2	4	M	4	3	8	8	8	8	11	10.00	117.00	20,480.00
Goetz, Ken	3	5	M	0	0	6	7	8	9	10	11.00	91.30	21,500.00
Menick, Judd	4	2	M	8	8	0	0	8	8	9	11.00	126.50	22,625.00
Morales, Eva	5	3	M	0	0	8	8	8	6	8	13.00	117.05	24,730.00
Heimbrock, Jacob	6	2	S	0	0	8	8	8	8	8	30.00	154.25	67,600.00
Townsley, Sarah	7	2	M	4	0	6	6	6	6	4	9.00	83.05	21,425.00
Salzman, Ben	8	4	M	6	2	8	8	6	6	6	11.00	130.00	6,635.00
Layton, Esther	9	4	M	0	0	8	8	8	8	8	11.00	88.00	5,635.00
Thompson, David	10	5	M	0	2	10	9	7	7	10	11.00	128.90	21,635.00
Vadillo, Carmen	11	2	S	8	0	4	8	8	8	9	13.00	139.11	24,115.00

The Trenkamp Collection Agency follows the practice of drawing a single check for the net amount of the payroll and depositing the check in a special payroll account at the bank. Individual checks issued were numbered consecutively, beginning with no. 331.

REQUIRED

1. Prepare a payroll register for Trenkamp Collection Agency for the week ended November 18, 19--. (In the Taxable Earnings/Unemployment Compensation column, enter $365 for Salzman and $440 for Layton. Leave this column blank for all other employees.) Total the column amounts, verify the totals, and rule with single and double lines.
2. Assuming that the wages for the week ended November 18 were paid on November 21, prepare the journal entry for the payment of this payroll.
3. Update Salzman's earnings record to reflect the November 18 payroll. Although this information should have been entered earlier, complete the required information on the earnings record. The necessary information is provided below.

Name	Ben F. Salzman
Address	12 Windmill Lane Trumbull, CT 06611
Employee No.	8
Gender	Male
Department	Administration
Occupation	Office Manager
Social Security No.	446-46-6321
Marital Status	Married
Allowances	4
Pay Rate	$11.00 per hour
Date of Birth	4/5/64
Date Hired	7/22/--

In the Chapter 9 Mastery Problem, you will process the payroll for the week ended November 18, 1998, for Trenkamp Collection. The step-by-step instructions for completing the Problem are listed below.

STEP 1: Open the data file for Chapter 9 Mastery Problem.

STEP 2: From the Options menu, select the Change System Date option and set the system date to November 18, 1998.

STEP 3: Enter the weekly payroll transactions.

- ▶ From the Tasks menu, select the Payroll Entry option.
- ▶ Enter the Employee ID code.
- ▶ For the first employee, enter a check number of 331. Thereafter, the computer will increment by 1 for each employee.
- ▶ Enter a Check Date of November 18, 1998.
- ▶ Enter the hours worked. Any hours worked in excess of 40 during the workweek should be recorded as overtime. All weekend hours are recorded as special hours and are paid double the regular rate.
- ▶ Enter the health insurance and credit union deductions. The deductions must be entered with a preceding minus sign (e.g., –4.00).
- ▶ You may click on the Journal Icon Bar button to view the journal entry that will be generated as a result of this entry.
- ▶ Click on the Post Icon Bar button to save the transaction.

STEP 4: Display the payroll reports.

- ▶ From the Reports menu, select the Payroll option, click on Check Register and then click on the Screen Icon Bar button.
- ▶ When the Check Register filter window appears, choose a date range of November 12, 1998, to November 18, 1998.
- ▶ Click on Payroll Journal (choose a date range of November 12, 1998, to November 18, 1998).
- ▶ Click on Payroll Register (choose a date range of November 12, 1998, to November 18, 1998).

  Note: The Peachtree Accounting software uses the percentage method of calculating the federal income tax withheld rather than a wage-bracket tax table.

CHAPTER 10 DEMONSTRATION PROBLEM (10-DEMO)

The totals line from Hart Company's payroll register for the week ended December 31, 19--, is as follows:

(left side)

PAYROLL

	NAME	EMPLOYEE NUMBER	ALLOWANCES	MARITAL STATUS	EARNINGS				TAXABLE EARNINGS		
					REGULAR	OVERTIME	TOTAL	CUMULATIVE TOTAL	UNEMPLOYMENT COMPENSATION	SOCIAL SECURITY	
21	Totals				3500 00	300 00	3800 00	197600 00	400 00	3800 00	21

REGISTER—PERIOD ENDED December 31,19--

(right side)

	DEDUCTIONS							NET PAY	CHECK NO.	
	FEDERAL INCOME TAX	SOCIAL SECURITY TAX	MEDICARE TAX	HEALTH INSURANCE	UNITED WAY	OTHER	TOTAL			
21	380 00	235 60	55 10	50 00	100 00		820 70	2979 30		21

Payroll taxes are imposed as follows: Social Security, 6.2%; Medicare, 1.45%; FUTA, 0.8%; and SUTA, 5.4%.

REQUIRED 1. a. Prepare the journal entry for payment of this payroll on December 31, 19--.

b. Prepare the journal entry for the employer's payroll taxes for the period ended December 31, 19--.

2. Hart Company had the following balances in its general ledger after the entries for Requirement 1 were made:

Employee Income Tax Payable	$1,520.00
Social Security Tax Payable	1,847.00
Medicare Tax Payable	433.00
FUTA Tax Payable	27.20
SUTA Tax Payable	183.60

a. Prepare the journal entry for payment of the liabilities for employee federal income taxes and Social Security and Medicare taxes on January 15, 19--.

b. Prepare the journal entry for payment of the liability for FUTA tax on January 31, 19--.

c. Prepare the journal entry for payment of the liability for SUTA tax on January 31, 19--.

3. Hart Company paid a premium of $280 for workers' compensation insurance based on estimated payroll as of the beginning of the year. Based on actual payroll as of the end of the year, the premium is $298. Prepare the adjusting entry to reflect the underpayment of the insurance premium.

In the Chapter 10 Demonstration Problem you will enter the journal entries to record the payroll, the employer's payroll taxes, and the payment of payroll withholding liabilities. Follow the steps listed to complete the Chapter 10 Demonstration Problem.

STEP 1: Open the data file for the Chapter 10 Demonstration Problem.

STEP 2: Enter the December general journal entries. December journal entries include Requirement 1 parts (a) and (b) as well as the workers' compensation adjustment in Requirement 3.

STEP 3: Select the General Journal with Titles Report to display the December journal entries.

STEP 4: Change the accounting period to be January 1, 2001, to January 31, 2001.

- ▶ **From the Tasks menu, choose the System option, then select Change Accounting Period from the submenu.**
- ▶ **When the Change Accounting Period window appears, select January 1, 2001, to January 31, 2001.**
- ▶ **Click on the Ok button.**

STEP 5: Enter the January journal entries.

STEP 6: Use the General Journal with Titles Report to display the January journal entries.

STEP 7: Display a General Ledger Trial Balance Report.

Note: If you need to make corrections to your journal entries using the Edit option, you will need to change the Period in the upper right portion of the Select Journal Entry window to reflect the correct period. The Select Journal Entry window appears when you click on the Edit Icon Bar button to make corrections from the General Journal window. If you want to change a December transaction, change it to December. If you want to change a January transaction, change the period to January.

See the solution section of this workbook for the solution to the demonstration problem.

PROBLEM 10A2

The Cascade Company has four employees. All are paid on a monthly basis. The fiscal year of the business is July 1 to June 30. Payroll taxes are imposed as follows:

1. Social Security tax of 6.2% withheld from employees' wages on the first $68,400 of earnings and Medicare tax withheld at 1.45% of gross earnings.
2. Social Security tax of 6.2% imposed on the employer on the first $68,400 of earnings and Medicare tax of 1.45% on gross earnings.
3. SUTA tax of 5.4% imposed on the employer on the first $7,000 of earnings.
4. FUTA tax of 0.8% imposed on the employer on the first $7,000 of earnings.

The accounts kept by Cascade include the following:

Account Number	Title	Balance on July 1
101	Cash	$50,200
211	Employee Income Tax Payable	1,015
212	Social Security Tax Payable	1,458
213	Medicare Tax Payable	342
218	Savings Bond Deductions Payable	350
221	FUTA Tax Payable	164
222	SUTA Tax Payable	810
511	Wages and Salaries Expense	0
530	Payroll Taxes Expense	0

The following transactions relating to payrolls and payroll taxes occurred during July and August.

July 15	Paid $2,815 covering the following June taxes:		
	Social Security tax		$ 1,458
	Medicare tax		342
	Employee income tax withheld		1,015
	Total		$ 2,815
31	July payroll:		
	Total wages and salaries expense		$12,000
	Less amounts withheld:		
	Social Security tax	$ 744	
	Medicare tax	174	
	Employee income tax	1,020	
	Savings bond deductions	350	2,288
	Net amount paid		$ 9,712
31	Purchased savings bonds for employees, $700		
31	Data for completing employer's payroll taxes expense for July:		
	Social Security taxable wages		$12,000
	Unemployment taxable wages		3,000
Aug. 15	Paid $2,856 covering the following July taxes:		
	Social Security tax		$ 1,488
	Medicare tax		348
	Employee income tax withheld		1,020
	Total		$ 2,856
15	Paid SUTA tax for the quarter, $972		
15	Paid FUTA tax, $188		

REQUIRED

1. Journalize the preceding transactions using a general journal.
2. Open T accounts for the payroll expenses and liabilities. Enter the beginning balances, and post the transactions recorded in the journal.

In Problem 10A2, you will enter the journal entries to record the payroll, the employer's payroll taxes, and the payment of payroll withholding liabilities. Follow the steps listed to complete the Chapter 10 Demonstration Problem.

STEP 1: Open the data file for the Problem 10A2.

STEP 2: Enter the July general journal entries.

STEP 3: Use the General Journal with Titles Report to display the July journal entries.

STEP 4: Change the accounting period to August.

- ▶ **From the Tasks menu, choose the System option, then select Change Accounting Period from the submenu.**
- ▶ **When the Change Accounting Period window appears, select August 1, 2000, to August 31, 2000.**
- ▶ **Click on the Ok button.**

STEP 5: Enter the August journal entries.

STEP 6: Use the General Journal with Titles Report to display the August journal entries.

STEP 7: Display the General Ledger Report. Make sure that you change the filter date to include both July and August, or the report will only list August transactions.

STEP 8: Display a General Ledger Trial Balance Report.

Note: If you need to make corrections to your journal entries using the Edit option, you will need to change the Period in the upper right portion of the Select Journal Entry screen to reflect the correct period. If you want to change a July transaction, change it to July. If you want to change an August transaction, change the period to August.

PROBLEM 10B2

The Oxford Company has five employees. All are paid on a monthly basis. The fiscal year of the business is June 1 to May 31. Payroll taxes are imposed as follows:

1. Social Security tax of 6.2% to be withheld from employees' wages on the first $68,400 of earnings and Medicare tax of 1.45% on gross earnings.
2. Social Security tax of 6.2% imposed on the employer on the first $68,400 of earnings and Medicare tax of 1.45% on gross earnings.
3. SUTA tax of 5.4% imposed on the employer on the first $7,000 of earnings.
4. FUTA tax of 0.8% imposed on the employer on the first $7,000 of earnings.

The accounts kept by the Oxford Company include the following:

Account Number	Title	Balance on June 1
101	Cash	$48,650
211	Employee Income Tax Payable	1,345
212	Social Security Tax Payable	1,823
213	Medicare Tax Payable	427
218	Savings Bond Deductions Payable	525
221	FUTA Tax Payable	360
222	SUTA Tax Payable	920
511	Wages and Salaries Expense	0
530	Payroll Taxes Expense	0

The following transactions relating to payrolls and payroll taxes occurred during June and July.

June 15	Paid $3,595.00 covering the following May taxes:		
	Social Security tax		$ 1,823.00
	Medicare tax		427.00
	Employee income tax withheld		1,345.00
	Total		$ 3,595.00
30	June payroll:		
	Total wages and salaries expense		$14,700.00
	Less amounts withheld:		
	Social Security tax	$ 911.40	
	Medicare tax	213.15	
	Employee income tax	1,280.00	
	Savings bond deductions	525.00	2,929.55
	Net amount paid		$11,770.45
30	Purchased savings bonds for employees, $1,050.00		
30	Data for completing employer's payroll taxes expense for June:		
	Social Security taxable wages		$14,700.00
	Unemployment taxable wages		4,500.00
July 15	Paid $3,529.10 covering the following June taxes:		
	Social Security tax		$ 1,822.80
	Medicare tax		426.30
	Employee income tax withheld		1,280.00
	Total		$ 3,529.10
15	Paid SUTA tax for the quarter, $1,163.00		
15	Paid FUTA tax, $396.00		

REQUIRED

1. Journalize the preceding transactions using a general journal.
2. Open T accounts for the payroll expenses and liabilities. Enter the beginning balances, and post the transactions recorded in the journal.

In Problem 10B2, you will enter the journal entries to record the payroll, the employer's payroll taxes, and the payment of payroll withholding liabilities. Follow the steps listed to complete the problem.

STEP 1: Open the data file for Problem 10B2.

STEP 2: Enter the June general journal entries.

STEP 3: Use the General Journal with Titles Report to display the June journal entries.

STEP 4: Change the accounting period to July.

- ▶ From the Tasks menu, choose the System option, then select Change Accounting Period from the submenu.
- ▶ When the Change Accounting Period window appears, select July 1, 2000, to July 31, 2000.
- ▶ Click on the Ok button.

STEP 5: **Enter the July journal entries.**

STEP 6: **Use the General Journal with Titles Report to display the July journal entries.**

STEP 7: **Display the General Ledger Report. Make sure that you change the filter date to include both June and July or the report will only list July transactions.**

STEP 8: **Display a General Ledger Trial Balance Report.**

Note: If you need to make corrections to your journal entries using the Edit option, you will need to change the Period in the upper right portion of the Select Journal Entry screen to reflect the correct period. If you want to change a June transaction, change it to June. If you want to change a July transaction, change the period to July.

CHAPTER 10 MASTERY PROBLEM

The totals line from Nix Company's payroll register for the week ended March 31, 19--, is as follows:

Payroll taxes are imposed as follows: Social Security tax, 6.2%; Medicare tax, 1.45%; FUTA tax, 0.8%; and SUTA tax, 5.4%.

(left side)

PAYROLL

					EARNINGS				TAXABLE EARNINGS		
	NAME	EMPLOYEE NUMBER	ALLOWANCES	MARITAL STATUS	REGULAR	OVERTIME	TOTAL	CUMULATIVE TOTAL	UNEMPLOYMENT COMPENSATION	SOCIAL SECURITY	
21	Totals				5,400 00	100 00	5,500 00	71,500 00	5,000 00	5,500 00	21

(right side)

REGISTER—PERIOD ENDED December 31,19--

	DEDUCTIONS							NET PAY	CHECK NO.	
	FEDERAL INCOME TAX	SOCIAL SECURITY TAX	MEDICARE TAX	HEALTH INSURANCE	LIFE INSURANCE	OTHER	TOTAL			
21	500 00	341 00	79 75	165 00	200 00		1,285 75	4,214 25		21

REQUIRED 1. a. Prepare the journal entry for payment of this payroll on March 31, 19--.

b. Prepare the journal entry for the employer's payroll taxes for the period ended March 31, 19--.

2. Nix Company had the following balances in its general ledger before the entries for Requirement 1 were made:

Employee income tax payable	$2,500
Social Security tax payable	2,008
Medicare tax payable	470
FUTA tax payable	520
SUTA tax payable	3,510

a. Prepare the journal entry for payment of the liabilities for federal income taxes and Social Security and Medicare taxes on April 15, 19--.

b. Prepare the journal entry for payment of the liability for FUTA tax on April 30, 19--.

c. Prepare the journal entry for payment of the liability for SUTA tax on April 30, 19--.

3. Nix Company paid a premium of $420 for workers' compensation insurance based on the estimated payroll as of the beginning of the year. Based on actual payroll as of the end of the year, the premium is only $400. Prepare the adjusting entry to reflect the overpayment of the insurance premium at the end of the year (December 31, 19--).

In the Chapter 10 Mastery Problem, you will enter the journal entries to record the payroll, the employer's payroll taxes, and the payment of payroll withholding liabilities. Follow the steps listed to complete the problem:

STEP 1: Open the data file for the Chapter 10 Mastery Problem.

STEP 2: Enter the March general journal entries.

STEP 3: Use the General Journal with Titles Report to display the March journal entries.

STEP 4: Change the accounting period to be April 1, 2000, to April 30, 2000.

STEP 5: Enter the April journal entries.

STEP 6: Use the General Journal with Titles Report to display the April journal entries.

STEP 7: Change the accounting period to be December 1, 2000, to December 31, 2000.

STEP 8: Enter the December journal entry.

STEP 9: Use the General Journal with Titles Report to display the December journal entry.

STEP 10: Display a General Ledger Trial Balance Report.

Note: If you need to make corrections to your journal entries using the Edit option, you will need to change the Period in the upper right portion of the Select Journal Entry screen to reflect the correct period.

CHAPTER 11 DEMONSTRATION PROBLEM (11-DEMO)

Karen Hunt operates Hunt's Audio-Video Store. The books include a sales journal, a cash receipts journal, and a general journal. The following transactions related to sales on account and cash receipts occurred during April 20--.

April 3 Sold merchandise on account to Susan Haberman, $159.50 plus tax of $11.17. Sale no. 41.

4 Sold merchandise on account to Goro Kimura, $299.95 plus tax of $21.00. Sale no. 42.

6 Received payment from Tera Scherrer on account, $69.50.

7 Issued a credit memo to Kenneth Watt for merchandise returned that had been sold on account, $42.75 including tax of $2.80.

10 Received payment from Kellie Cokley on account, $99.95.

11 Sold merchandise on account to Victor Cardona, $499.95 plus tax of $35.00. Sale no. 43.

14 Received payment from Kenneth Watt in full settlement of account, $157.00.

17 Sold merchandise on account to Susan Haberman, $379.95 plus tax of $26.60. Sale no. 44.

19 Sold merchandise on account to Tera Scherrer, $59.95 plus tax of $4.20. Sale no. 45.

21 Issued a credit memo to Goro Kimura for merchandise returned that had been sold on account, $53.45 including tax of $3.50.

24 Received payment from Victor Cardona on account, $299.95.

25 Sold merchandise on account to Kellie Cokley, $179.50 plus tax of $12.57. Sale no. 46.

26 Received payment from Susan Haberman on account, $250.65.

28 Sold merchandise on account to Kenneth Watt, $49.95 plus tax of $3.50. Sale no. 47.

30 Bank credit card sales for the month, $1,220.00 plus tax of $85.40. Bank credit card expense on these sales, $65.27.

30 Cash sales for the month, $2,000.00 plus tax of $140.00.

Hunt had the following general ledger account balances as of April 1:

Account Title	Account No.	General Ledger Balance on April 1
Cash	101	$5,000.00
Accounts Receivable	122	1,208.63
Sales Tax Payable	231	72.52
Sales	401	8,421.49
Sales Returns and Allowances	401.1	168.43
Bank Credit Card Expense	513	215.00

Hunt also had the following accounts receivable ledger account balances as of April 1:

Customer	Accounts Receivable Balance
Victor Cardona 6300 Washington Blvd. St. Louis, MO 63130-9523	$299.95
Kellie Cokley 4220 Kingsbury Blvd. St. Louis, MO 63130-1645	$99.95
Susan Haberman 9421 Garden Ct. Kirkwood, MO 63122-1878	$79.98
Goro Kimura 6612 Arundel Pl. Clayton, MO 63150-9266	$379.50
Tera Scherrer 315 W. Linden St. Webster Groves, MO 63119-9881	$149.50
Kenneth Watt 11742 Fawnridge Dr. St. Louis, MO 63131-1726	$199.75

REQUIRED

1. Open four-column general ledger accounts and three-column accounts receivable ledger accounts for Hunt's Audio-Video Store as of April 1, 20--. Enter the April 1 balance in each of the accounts.
2. Enter each transaction either in a three-column sales journal, a six-column cash receipts journal, or a general journal.
3. Post directly from each of the three journals to the proper customers' accounts in the accounts receivable ledger. Each subsidiary ledger account should show the initials "S," "CR," or "J," followed by the appropriate journal page number as a posting reference for each transaction.
4. Enter the totals, and rule the sales journal and the cash receipts journal. Complete the summary posting of the cash receipts and sales journals and the individual posting of the general journal to the proper general ledger accounts. Each general ledger account should show the initials "S," "CR," or "J," followed by the appropriate journal page number as a posting reference for each transaction.
5. Prove the balance of the summary accounts receivable account by preparing a schedule of accounts receivable as of April 30, based on the accounts receivable ledger.

In the Chapter 11 Demonstration Problem, you will use the Peachtree Accounting software to process sales, cash receipts, and credit memos. In addition, you will display the invoice register, sales journal, cash receipts journal, and customer accounts receivable ledger. Follow the steps listed to complete the problem.

STEP 1: **Open the data file for the Chapter 11 Demonstration Problem.**

STEP 2: **From the Tasks menu, select the Sales/Invoicing option and enter the sales on account and credit memo transactions.**

Sales on Account Transactions:

- **Enter or select the Customer ID.**
- **Enter the Sale No. into the Invoice Number field.**
- **Enter the Date of the transaction.**
- **In the Description field, enter "Merchandise."**
- **Accept the default GL Account of 401 and Tax Code of 1.**
- **Enter the amount of the credit to Sales.**
- **Verify that the sales tax is calculated correctly. If not, select the correct Sales Tax Code of MO near the lower left corner of the windows.**
- **Click on the Journal Icon Bar button to verify that the correct journal entry is being generated. Click Ok to return to the Sales/Invoicing screen.**
- **Click on Post to record the transaction.**

A completed Sales/Invoicing window is illustrated in Figure 2.19 on the following page.

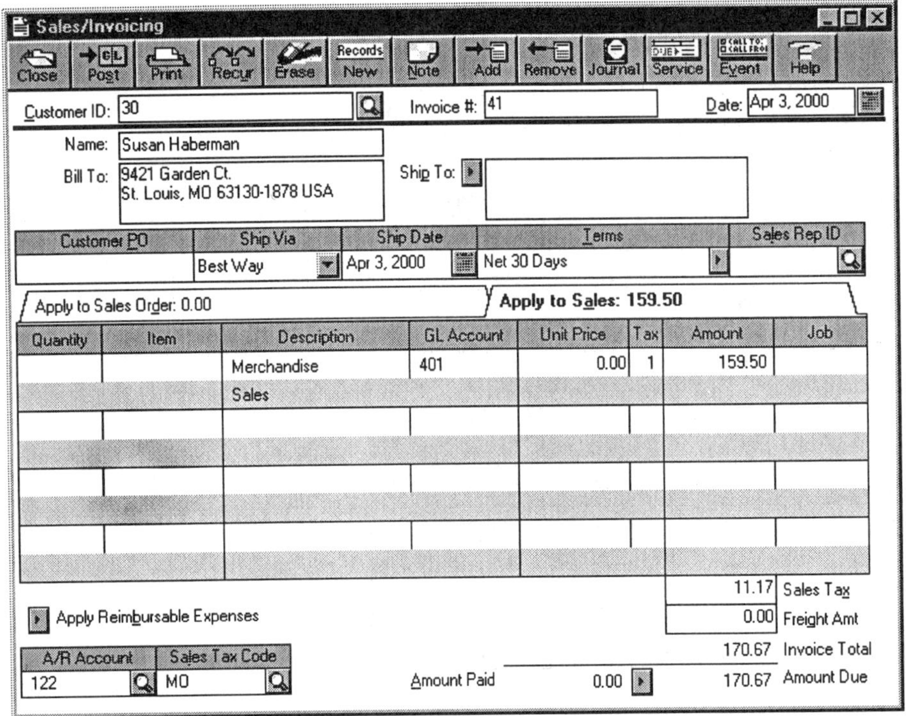

FIGURE 2.19 Sales/Invoicing Window (Sales on Account)

Credit Memo Transactions:

- Enter or select the Customer ID.
- Enter CM followed by a consecutively assigned number beginning with 1 (e.g., CM1).
- Enter the Date of the credit memo.
- In the Description field, enter "Credit Memo."
- Enter the Sales Returns and Allowance account number in the GL Account column.
- Accept the default Tax Code of 1.
- Enter the amount of the sales return or allowance as a negative number.
- Verify that the A/R Account and Sales Tax Code fields in the lower left corner of the screen have been selected.
- Click on the Journal Icon Bar button to verify that the correct journal entry is being generated. Click Ok to return to the Sales/Invoicing screen.
- Click on Post to record the transaction.

The recording of the first credit memo transaction is illustrated in the Sales/Invoicing window shown in Figure 2.20.

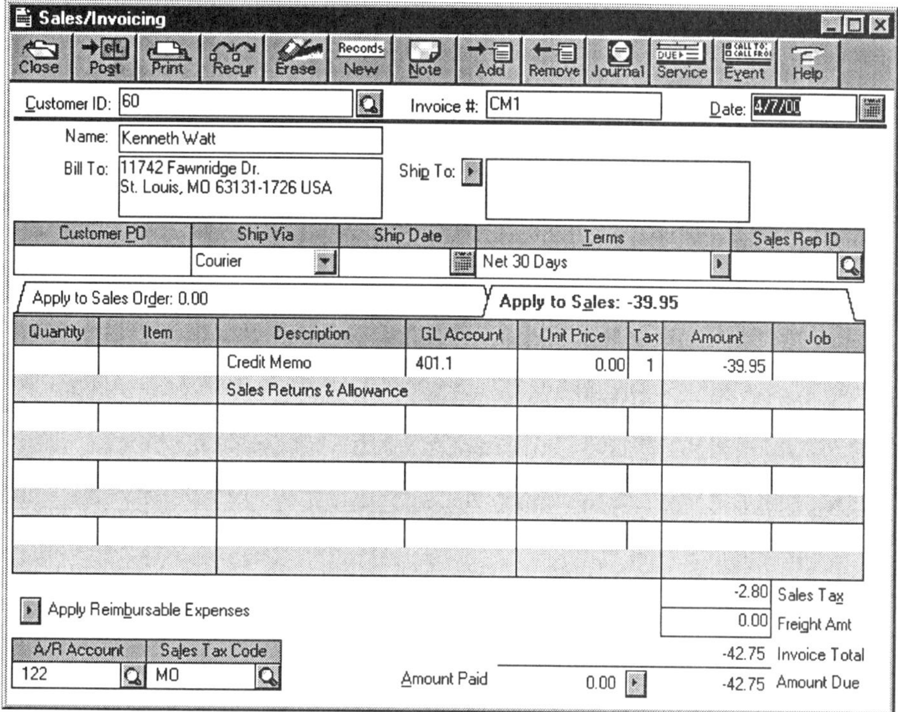

FIGURE 2.20 Sales/Invoicing Window (Credit Memo)

STEP 3: From the Tasks menu, select the Receipts option and enter the cash receipts on account, credit card sales, and cash sales transactions.

Cash Received on Account Transactions:

- Enter 04/30/00 as the Deposit ticket ID. (This provides a deposit ticket reference for bank reconciliation.)
- Enter or select the customer number.
- A Reference number is required. Since none is provided, either number the transactions consecutively beginning with 1 or simply record a reference of "Cash" for each.
- Enter the transaction Date.
- Select a payment method of Cash.
- Select Cash as the G/L Account.
- Click on the Apply to Invoices Tab.
- If more than one invoice is displayed, move the cursor to the Description column for the invoice you wish to pay. Enter "On account" as the description. If the payment covers more than one invoice, you must split it among the applicable invoices or it may be applied to the balance forward. If the entire invoice is being paid, simply click on the Pay box and a red check mark will appear and the amount paid will also appear. If it is a partial payment, enter the amount of cash received into the Amount Paid column that is to be applied to that invoice. If a credit memo applies to an invoice being paid, click on the Pay box for the credit memo to apply it to the invoice being paid.
- Click on Post to record the transaction.

An example of a cash receipt on account transaction with the first cash receipt transaction completed is illustrated in Figure 2.21.

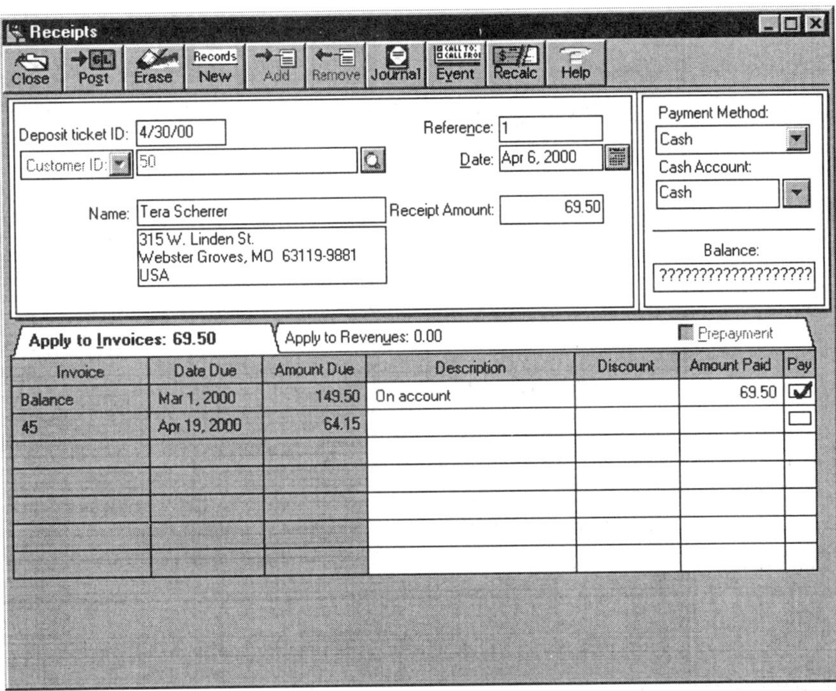

FIGURE 2.21 Receipts Window (Cash Received on Account)

Figure 2.22 illustrates the transaction on April 14th for Kenneth Watt. In this example, cash was received on account where an invoice is paid that has a credit memo applied.

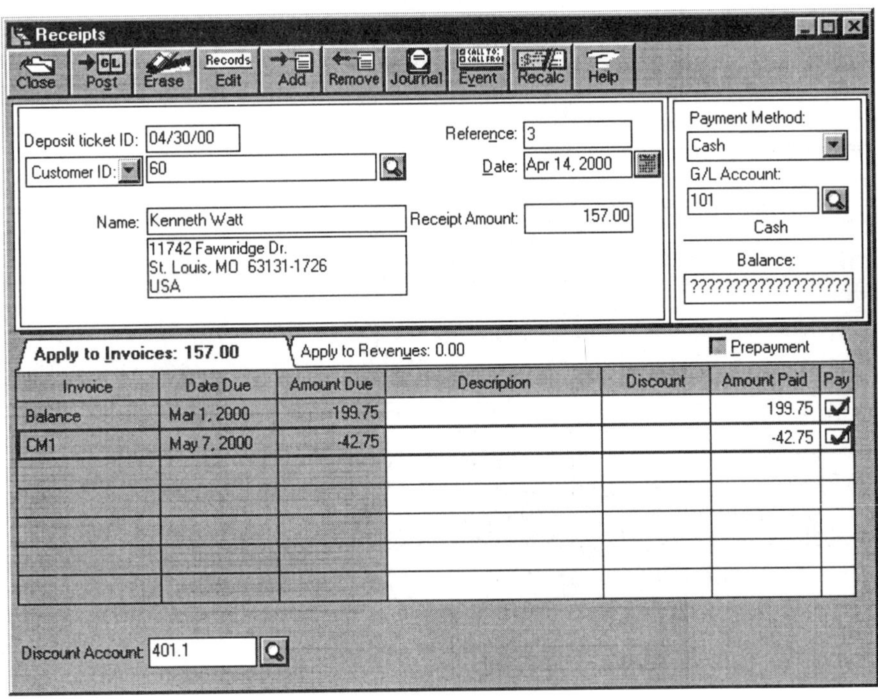

FIGURE 2.22 Receipts Window (Cash on Account for Invoice with Credit Memo Applied)

Credit Card Sales Transactions:

- Enter VISA as the Deposit ticket ID.
- Leave the Customer ID blank.
- Enter "Credit card receipts" in the Name field.
- Enter either the next consecutive number or "Credit card" as the Reference.
- Enter the Date of the transaction.
- Select a payment method of VISA.
- Select Cash as the G/L Account.
- Click on the Apply to Revenues tab.
- Leave the Quantity and Item fields blank.
- On the first line, enter "Credit card receipts" in the Description column, the Sales account number in the GL Account column, 1 as the Tax code and the Sales Credit amount in the Amount Column.
- On the second line, enter "Credit card expense" in the Description column, the Credit Card Expense account number in the GL Account column, 2 as the Tax Code, and the amount of the credit card expense in the Amount column as a negative number.
- Click on Post to record the transaction.

  A completed Receipts window illustrating credit card receipts is illustrated in Figure 2.23.

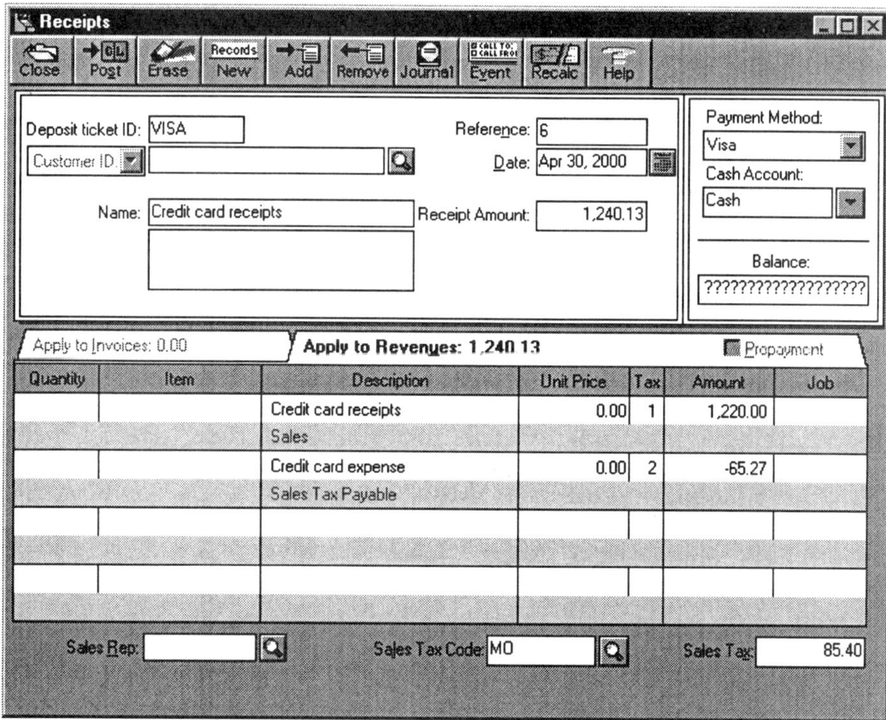

FIGURE 2.23 Receipts Window (Credit Card Receipts)

Cash Sales:

- ▶ Enter 04/30/00 as the Deposit ticket ID.
- ▶ Leave the Customer ID blank.
- ▶ Enter "Cash sales" in the Name field.
- ▶ Enter the day of the month as the Reference.
- ▶ Enter the Date of the transaction.
- ▶ Select a payment method of Cash.
- ▶ Select Cash as the G/L Account.
- ▶ Click on the Apply to Revenues tab.
- ▶ Leave the Quantity and Item fields blank.
- ▶ On the first line, enter "Cash sales" in the Description column, enter the Sales Account number in the GL Account column, enter 1 as the Tax Code, and enter the Sales Credit amount in the Amount Column.
- ▶ Verify that the Sales Tax Code shown near the bottom of the screen contains "MO." If not, select it from the list. The sales tax amount should appear in the Sales Tax field in the lower right corner of the window. If you enter the Sales Tax Code rather than select it from the list, it must be keyed as shown, that is, all upper case.
- ▶ Click on Post to record the transaction.

A completed cash sale transaction is illustrated in Figure 2.24.

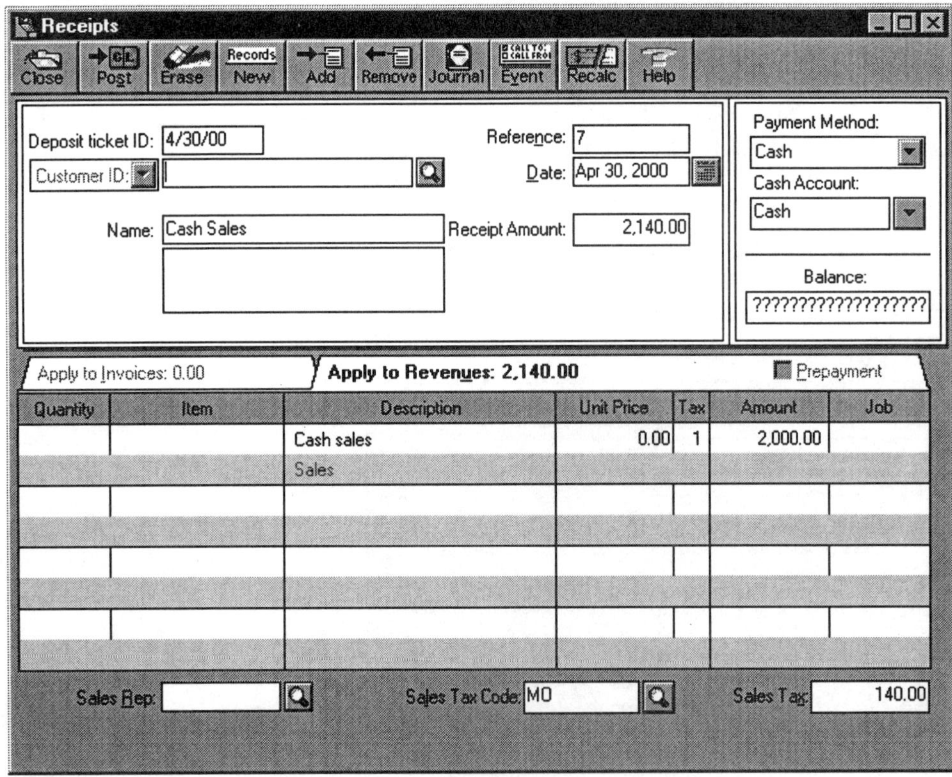

FIGURE 2.24 Receipts Windows (Cash Sales)

STEP 4: Display the accounts receivable reports.

- **From the Reports menu, select the Accounts Receivable option.**
- **Display the Sales Journal with Titles.**
- **Display the Cash Receipts Journal with Titles.**
- **Display the Invoice Register.**
- **Display the Customer Ledgers report.**

STEP 5: If errors are detected on the reports, return to the appropriate data-entry window (Sales/Invoicing or Receipts) and use the Edit Icon Bar button to select the transaction in error and make corrections.

See the solution section of this workbook for the solution to the demonstration problem.

PROBLEM 11A3

Owens Distributors is a retail business. The following sales, returns, and cash receipts occurred during March 20--. There is an 8% sales tax. Beginning general ledger account balances were: Cash, $9,741.00; and Accounts Receivable, $1,058.25. Beginning customer account balances were: Thompson Group, $1,058.25.

March 1	Sale no. 33C to Able & Co., $1,800 plus sales tax.
3	Sale no. 33D to R. J. Kalas, Inc., $2,240 plus sales tax.
5	Able & Co. returned merchandise from sale no. 33C for a credit (credit memo no. 66), $30 plus sales tax.
7	Cash sales for the week, $3,160 plus sales tax.
10	Received payment from Able & Co. for sale no. 33C less credit memo no. 66.
11	Sale no. 33E to Blevins Bakery, $1,210 plus sales tax.
13	Received payment from R. J. Kalas for sale no. 33D.
14	Cash sales for the week, $4,200 plus sales tax.
16	Blevins Bakery returned merchandise from sale no. 33E for a credit (credit memo no. 67), $44 plus sales tax.
18	Sale no. 33F to R. J. Kalas, Inc., $2,620 plus sales tax.
20	Received payment from Blevins Bakery for sale no. 33E less credit memo no. 67.
21	Cash sales for the week, $2,400 plus sales tax.
25	Sale no. 33G to Blevins Bakery, $1,915 plus sales tax.
27	Sale no. 33H to Thompson Group, $2,016 plus sales tax.
28	Cash sales for the week, $3,500 plus sales tax.

REQUIRED

1. Record the transactions in the sales journal, the cash receipts journal, and the general journal. Total, verify, and rule the columns where appropriate at the end of the month.
2. Post from the journals to the general ledger and accounts receivable ledger accounts. Use account numbers as shown in the chapter.

In Problem 11A3, you will use the Peachtree Accounting software to process sales and cash receipts and display the accounts receivable reports. Follow the steps listed to complete the problem.

STEP 1: **Open the data file for the Problem 11A3.**

STEP 2: **From the Tasks Menu, select the Sales/Invoicing option and enter the sales on account transactions into the Sales/Invoicing window.**

- ▶ **Enter "Merchandise" in the Description field.**
- ▶ **Verify that "Indiana" is selected for the Sales Tax Code in the lower left portion of the window.**

STEP 3: **Enter the credit memo transactions into the Sales/Invoicing window.**

- ▶ **Enter CM followed by the credit memo number into the Invoice No. field (e.g., CM66).**
- ▶ **Enter "Credit Memo" in the Description field.**
- ▶ **Enter the account number for Sales Returns and Allowance in the GL Account field.**
- ▶ **Enter the credit memo amount as a negative number.**

STEP 4: **From the Tasks menu, select the Receipts option and enter the cash receipts on account transactions.**

- ▶ **Enter Deposit ticket ID of "03/31/00."**
- ▶ **Enter the invoice number provided as the reference.**
- ▶ **Enter "On account" in the Description Field.**
- ▶ **Be sure to apply in applicable credit memos.**

STEP 5: **Enter the cash sales into the Receipts window.**

- ▶ **Enter "Cash sales" in the Name field; enter "Cash sales" in the Description field.**
- ▶ **Enter the credit to sales in the Amount field.**
- ▶ **Select "Indiana" in the Sales Tax Code field near the bottom of the screen.**

STEP 6: **Display the accounts receivable reports.**

- ▶ **From the Reports menu, select the Accounts Receivable option.**
- ▶ **Display the Sales Journal with Titles.**
- ▶ **Display the Cash Receipts Journal with Titles.**
- ▶ **Display the Invoice Register.**
- ▶ **Display the Customer Ledgers Report.**
- ▶ **Display a Trial Balance Report.**

STEP 7: **If errors are detected on the reports, return to the appropriate data entry window (Sales/Invoicing or Receipts) and use the Edit Icon Bar button to select the transaction in error and make corrections.**

PROBLEM 11B3

Paul Jackson owns a retail business. The following sales, returns, and cash receipts are for April 20--. There is a 7% sales tax.

April 1	Sale no. 111 to O. L. Meyers, $2,100 plus sales tax.
3	Sale no. 112 to Andrew Plaa, $1,000 plus sales tax.
6	O. L. Meyers returned merchandise from sale no. 111 for a credit (credit memo no. 42), $50 plus sales tax.
7	Cash sales for the week, $3,240 plus sales tax.
9	Received payment from O. L. Meyers for sale no. 111 less credit memo no. 42.
12	Sale no. 113 to Melissa Richfield, $980 plus sales tax.
14	Cash sales for the week, $2,180 plus sales tax.
17	Melissa Richfield returned merchandise from sale no. 113 for a credit (credit memo no. 43), $40 plus sales tax.
19	Sale no. 114 to Kelsay Munkres, $1,020 plus sales tax.
21	Cash sales for the week, $2,600 plus sales tax.
24	Sale no. 115 to O. L. Meyers, $920 plus sales tax.
27	Sale no. 116 to Andrew Plaa, $1,320 plus sales tax.
28	Cash sales for the week, $2,800 plus sales tax.

Beginning general ledger account balances:

Cash	$2,864.54
Accounts Receivable	2,726.25

Beginning customer account balances:

O. L. Meyers	$2,186.00
K. Munkres	482.00
M. Richfield	58.25

REQUIRED

1. Record the transactions in the sales journal, the cash receipts journal, and the general journal. Total, verify, and rule the columns where appropriate at the end of the month.
2. Post from the journals to the general ledger and accounts receivable ledger accounts. Use account numbers as shown in the chapter.

In Problem 11B3, you will use the Peachtree Accounting software to process sales and cash receipts and display the accounts receivable reports. Follow the steps listed to complete the problem.

STEP 1: Open the data file for Problem 11B3.

STEP 2: From the Tasks Menu, select the Sales/Invoicing option and enter the sales on account transactions into the Sales/Invoicing window.

- ▶ **Enter "Merchandise" in the Description field.**
- ▶ **Verify that "Indiana" is selected for the Sales Tax Code in the lower left portion of the window.**

STEP 3: Enter the credit memo transactions into the Sales/Invoicing window.

- ▶ **Enter CM followed by the credit memo number into the Invoice No. field (e.g., CM33).**
- ▶ **Enter "Credit Memo" in the Description field.**

- ▶ Enter the account number for Sales Returns and Allowance in the GL Account field.
- ▶ Enter the credit memo amount as a negative number.

STEP 4: From the Tasks menu, select the Receipts option and enter the cash receipts on account transactions.

- ▶ Enter Deposit ticket ID of "04/30/00."
- ▶ Enter the invoice number provided as the reference.
- ▶ Enter "On account" in the Description Field.
- ▶ Be sure to apply in applicable credit memos.

STEP 5: Enter the cash sales into the Receipts window.

- ▶ Enter "Cash sales" in the Name field; enter "Cash sales" in the Description field.
- ▶ Enter the credit to sales in the Amount field.
- ▶ Select "CT" in the Sales Tax Code field near the bottom of the screen.

STEP 6: Display the accounts receivable reports.

- ▶ From the Reports menu, select the Accounts Receivable option.
- ▶ Display the Sales Journal with Titles.
- ▶ Display the Cash Receipts Journal with Titles.
- ▶ Display the Invoice Register.
- ▶ Display the Customer Ledgers Report.
- ▶ Display a Trial Balance Report.

STEP 7: If errors are detected on the reports, return to the appropriate data entry window (Sales/Invoicing or Receipts) and use the Edit Icon Bar button to select the transaction in error and make corrections.

CHAPTER 11 MASTERY PROBLEM

Geoff and Sandy Harland own and operate Wayward Kennel and Pet Supply. Their motto is, "If your pet is not becoming to you, he should be coming to us." The Harlands maintain a sales tax payable account throughout the month to account for the 6% sales tax. They use a sales journal, a cash receipts journal, and a general journal. The following sales and cash collections took place during the month of September.

Sept. 2 Sold a fish aquarium on account to Ken Shank, $125.00 plus tax of $7.50, terms n/30. Sale no. 101.

3 Sold dog food on account to Nancy Truelove, $68.25 plus tax of $4.10, terms n/30. Sale no. 102.

5 Sold a bird cage on account to Jean Warkentin, $43.95 plus tax of $2.64, terms n/30. Sale no. 103.

8 Cash sales for the week, $2,332.45 plus tax of $139.95.

10 Received cash for boarding and grooming services, $625.00 plus tax of $37.50.

11 Jean Warkentin stopped by the store to point out a minor defect in the bird cage purchased in sale no. 103. The Harlands offered a sales allowance of $10.00 plus tax on the price of the cage, which satisfied Warkentin.

12 Sold a cockatoo on account to Tully Shaw, $1,200.00 plus tax of $72.00, terms n/30. Sale no. 104.

14 Received cash on account from Rosa Alanso, $256.00.

15 Rosa Alanso returned merchandise, $93.28 including tax of $5.28.

15 Cash sales for the week, $2,656.85 plus tax of $159.41.

16 Received cash on account from Nancy Truelove, $58.25.

18 Received cash for boarding and grooming services, $535.00 plus tax of $32.10.

19 Received cash on account from Ed Cochran, $63.25.

20 Sold pet supplies on account to Susan Hays, $83.33 plus tax of $5.00, terms n/30. Sale no. 105.

21 Sold three Labrador Retriever puppies to All American Day Camp, $375.00 plus tax of $22.50, terms n/30. Sale no. 106.

22 Cash sales for the week, $3,122.45 plus tax of $187.35.

23 Received cash for boarding and grooming services, $515.00 plus tax of $30.90.

25 Received cash on account from Ken Shank, $132.50.

26 Received cash on account from Nancy Truelove, $72.35.

27 Received cash on account from Joe Gloy, $273.25.

28 Borrowed cash to purchase a pet limousine, $11,000.00.

29 Cash sales for the week, $2,835.45 plus tax of $170.13.

30 Received cash for boarding and grooming services, $488.00 plus tax of $29.28.

Wayward had the following general ledger account balances as of September 1:

Account Title	Account No.	General Ledger Balance on Sept. 1
Cash	101	$23,500.25
Accounts Receivable	122	850.75
Notes Payable	201	2,500.00
Sales Tax Payable	231	909.90
Sales	401	13,050.48
Sales Returns and Allowances	401.1	86.00
Boarding and Grooming Revenue	402	2,115.00

Wayward also had the following accounts receivable ledger balances as of September 1:

Customer	Accounts Receivable Balance
Rosa Alanso 2541 East 2nd Street Bloomington, IN 47401-5356	$456.00

Ed Cochran
2669 Windcrest Drive
Bloomington, IN 47401-5446 $63.25

Joe Gloy
1458 Parnell Avenue
Muncie, IN 47304-2682 $273.25

Nancy Truelove
2300 E. National Road
Cumberland, IN 46229-4824 $58.25

New customers opening accounts during September were:

All American Day Camp
3025 Old Mill Run
Bloomington, IN 47408-1080

Susan Hays
1424 Jackson Creek Road
Nashville, IN 47448-2245

Ken Shank
6422 E. Bender Road
Bloomington, IN 47401-7756

Tully Shaw
3315 Longview Avenue
Bloomington, IN 47401-7223

Jean Warkentin
1813 Deep Well Court
Bloomington, IN 47401-5124

REQUIRED

1. Enter the transactions for the month of September in the proper journals.
2. Enter the totals, and rule the journals where appropriate.
3. Post the entries to the general and subsidiary ledgers. Open new accounts for any customers who did not have a balance as of September 1.
4. Prepare a schedule of accounts receivable.
5. Compute the net sales for the month of September.

In the Chapter 11 Mastery Problem, you will use the Peachtree Accounting software to process sales and cash receipts, and to display the invoice register, sales journal, cash receipts journal, and customer accounts receivable ledger. Follow the steps listed to complete the problem.

STEP 1: Open the data file for the Chapter 11 Mastery Problem.

STEP 2: From the Tasks menu, select the Sales/Invoicing option and enter the sales on account transactions into the Sales/Invoicing window.

- ▶ **Enter a description of the merchandise sold in the Description field.**
- ▶ **Verify that "Indiana" is selected for the Sales Tax Code in the lower left portion of the window.**

STEP 3: Enter the credit memo transactions into the Sales/Invoicing window.

- ▶ **Enter CM followed by the original invoice number into the Invoice No. field (e.g., CM103). If the return applies to the balance forward for that customer, enter "CMBalance."**
- ▶ **Enter "Credit Memo" in the Description field.**
- ▶ **Enter the account number for Sales Returns and Allowance in the GL Account field.**
- ▶ **Enter the credit memo amount as a negative number.**

STEP 4: **From the Tasks menu, select the Receipts option and enter the cash receipts on account transactions.**

- **Enter Deposit ticket ID of "09/30/00."**
- **Enter the invoice number provided as the reference. If a specific invoice does not apply, enter "Balance" to indicate that it applies to the balance forward for that customer.**
- **Enter "On account" in the Description Field.**
- **Be sure to apply in applicable credit memos.**

STEP 5: **Enter the cash sales into the Receipts window.**

- **Enter the day of the month as the Reference.**
- **Enter "Cash sales" in the Name field; enter "Cash sales" in the Description field.**
- **Enter or select the correct revenue account in the GL Account field (either Sales or Board and Groom Revenue).**
- **Enter the credit to sales in the Amount field.**
- **Select "Indiana" in the Sales Tax Code field near the bottom of the screen.**

  Note: When entering the transaction involving borrowed cash, enter "Borrowed Cash" as the Description, enter "Notes Payable" as the GL Account number, and enter a Tax Code of 2 which indicates that there is no sales tax.

STEP 6: **Display the accounts receivable reports.**

- **From the Reports menu, select the Accounts Receivable option.**
- **Display the Sales Journal with Titles.**
- **Display the Cash Receipts Journal with Titles.**
- **Display the Invoice Register.**
- **Display the Customer Ledgers Report.**
- **Display a Trial Balance Report.**

STEP 7: **If errors are detected on the reports, return to the appropriate data entry window (Sales/Invoicing or Receipts) and use the Edit Icon Bar button to select the transaction in error and make corrections.**

CHAPTER 12 DEMONSTRATION PROBLEM (12-DEMO)

Jodi Rutman operates a retail pharmacy called Rutman Pharmacy. The books of original entry include a purchases journal in which purchases of merchandise on account are entered, a cash payments journal in which all cash payments (except petty cash) are entered, and a general journal in which entries such as purchases returns and allowances are made. A subsidiary ledger is used for accounts payable. The following are the transactions related to purchases and cash payments for the month of June 20--.

June 1 Purchased merchandise from Sullivan Co. on account, $234.20. Invoice no. 71 dated June 1, terms 2/10, n/30.

2 Issued check no. 536 for payment of June rent (Rent Expense), $1,000.00.

5 Purchased merchandise from Amfac Drug Supply on account, $562.40. Invoice no. 196 dated June 2, terms 1/15, n/30.

7 Purchased merchandise from University Drug Co. on account, $367.35. Invoice no. 914A dated June 5, terms 3/10 eom, n/30.

9 Issued check no. 537 to Sullivan Co. in payment of invoice no. 71 less 2% discount.

12 Received a credit memo from Amfac Drug Supply for merchandise returned that was purchased on June 5, $46.20.

14 Purchased merchandise from Mutual Drug Co. on account, $479.40. Invoice no. 745 dated June 14, terms 2/10, n/30.

15 Received a credit memo from University Drug Co. for merchandise returned that was purchased on June 7, $53.70.

16 Issued check no. 538 to Amfac Drug Supply in payment of invoice no. 196 less the credit memo of June 12 and less 1% discount.

23 Issued check no. 539 to Mutual Drug Co. in payment of invoice no. 745 less 2% discount.

27 Purchased merchandise from Flites Pharmaceuticals on account, $638.47. Invoice no. 675 dated June 27, terms 2/10 eom, n/30.

29 Issued check no. 540 to Dolgin Candy Co. for a cash purchase of merchandise, $270.20.

30 Issued check no. 541 to Vashon Medical Supply in payment of invoice no. 416, $1,217.69. No discount allowed.

REQUIRED

1. Enter the transactions in a purchases journal, a five-column cash payments journal, and a general journal. Total and rule the purchases and cash payments journals. Prove the cash payments journal.
2. Post from the journals to the general ledger accounts and the accounts payable ledger. Then, update the account balances.
3. Prepare a schedule of accounts payable from the accounts payable ledger in the problem. Verify that the total of accounts payable in the schedule equals the June 30 balance of Accounts Payable in the general ledger.

In the Chapter 12 Demonstration Problem, you will use the Peachtree Accounting software to process purchases and cash payments, and to display a trial balance, schedule of accounts payable, purchases journal, check register, and cash disbursements journal. Follow the steps listed to complete the Chapter 12 Demonstration Problem.

STEP 1: Open the data file for the Chapter 12 Demonstration Problem.

STEP 2: From the Tasks menu, select the Purchases/Receive Inventory option and enter the purchases on account and returns and allowance transactions.

Entering Purchases Transactions:

- **Enter or select the Vendor ID number.**
- **Enter the Invoice Number.**
- **Enter the Date of the transaction.**
- **Verify that the terms of the sale are correctly indicated. If not, click on the right arrow button at the end of the Terms field and a Term Information window will appear allowing you to enter the pertinent discount data.**

- **On the Apply to Purchases tab, enter "Merchandise" in the Description field.**
- **Enter the amount of the purchase in the Amount field.**
- **Click on Post to record the transaction.**

An example of the recording of a purchase of merchandise on account is illustrated in the Purchases/Receive Inventory window shown in Figure 2.25.

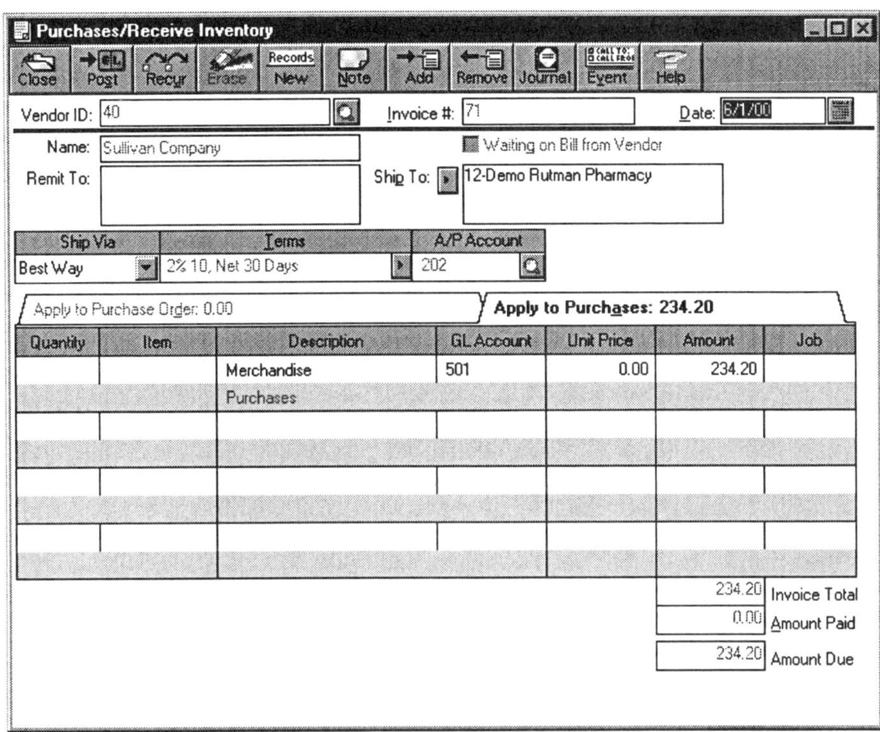

FIGURE 2.25 Purchases/Receive Inventory (Purchase on Account)

Entering Purchases Returns and Allowance Transactions:

- **Enter or select the Vendor ID number.**
- **Enter an Invoice Number consisting of CM plus the original invoice number.**
- **Verify that the terms of the sale are correct; if not, click on the right arrow button in the Terms field and enter correct terms.**
- **Enter "Credit memo" as the Description.**
- **Enter the Purchases Returns and Allowances Account Number in the GL Account field.**
- **Enter the amount of the credit memo received as a negative number.**
- **Click on Post to record the transaction.**

The recording of a Purchase Return transaction is illustrated in the Purchases/Receive Inventory window shown in Figure 2.26.

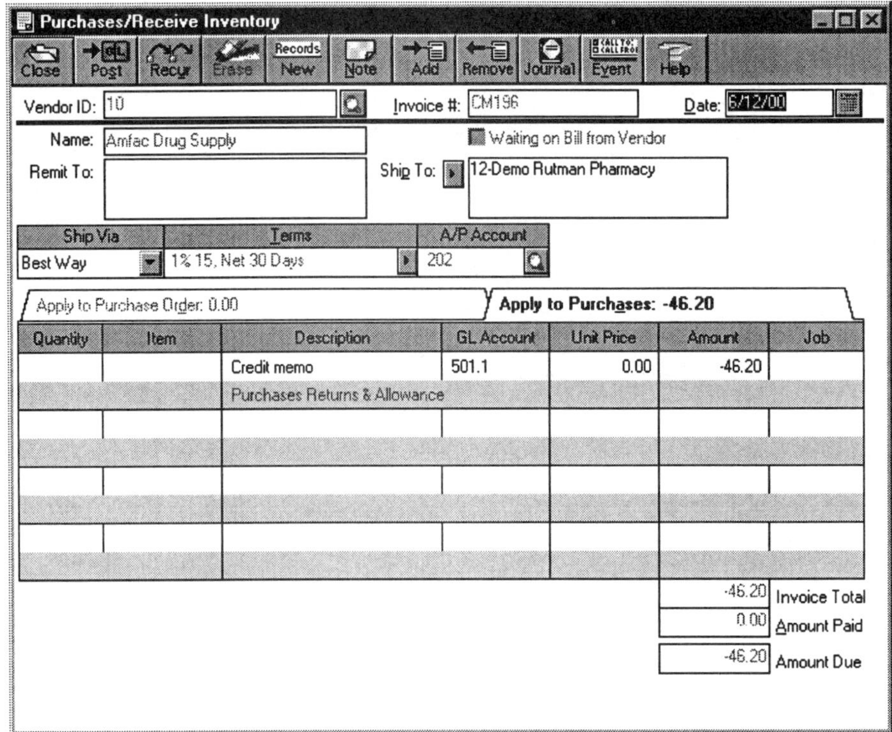

FIGURE 2.26 Purchases/Receive Inventory (Purchases Return)

STEP 3: From the Tasks menu, select the Payments option and enter the cash payment transactions.

There are two types of cash payments: (1) payments on account and (2) direct payments. Payments on account require a vendor number and must be applied to the applicable invoice(s). Direct payments do not require a vendor number and are applied to expenses.

Direct payments require that a name be entered in the Pay to the Order of field. If none is provided in the transaction, you will have to be creative and come up with one as the software will not allow you to proceed without entering a name.

When entering payments on account, you must select the invoices you wish to pay and apply the appropriate credit memos to the invoice(s). An example of a completed Payments window illustrating the payment of an invoice and applying a credit memo is shown in Figure 2.27.

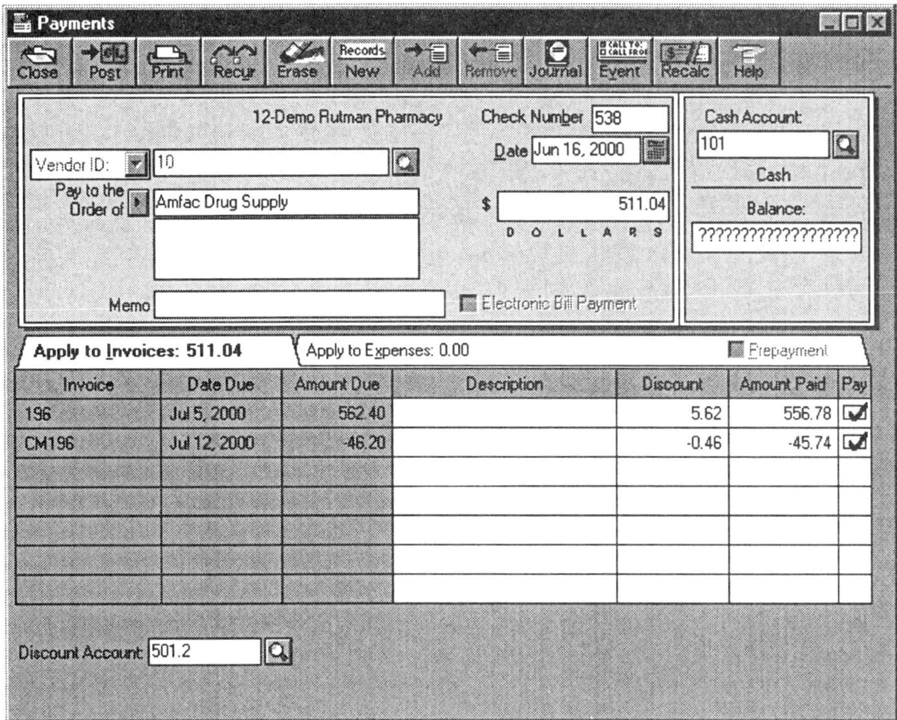

FIGURE 2.27 Payment Windows (Applying a Credit Memo to Payment)

Payment on Account (Apply to Invoices Tab):

- ▶ **Enter or select the Vendor ID number.**
- ▶ **Enter the Check Number.**
- ▶ **Enter the Date of the check.**
- ▶ **Under the Apply to Invoices tab, click on the Pay box for the invoice or invoices to be paid. Click on the Pay box for any credit memos that are to be applied to this payment.**
- ▶ **Click on Post to record the payment.**

  An example of a payment on account transaction is illustrated in Figure 2.28.

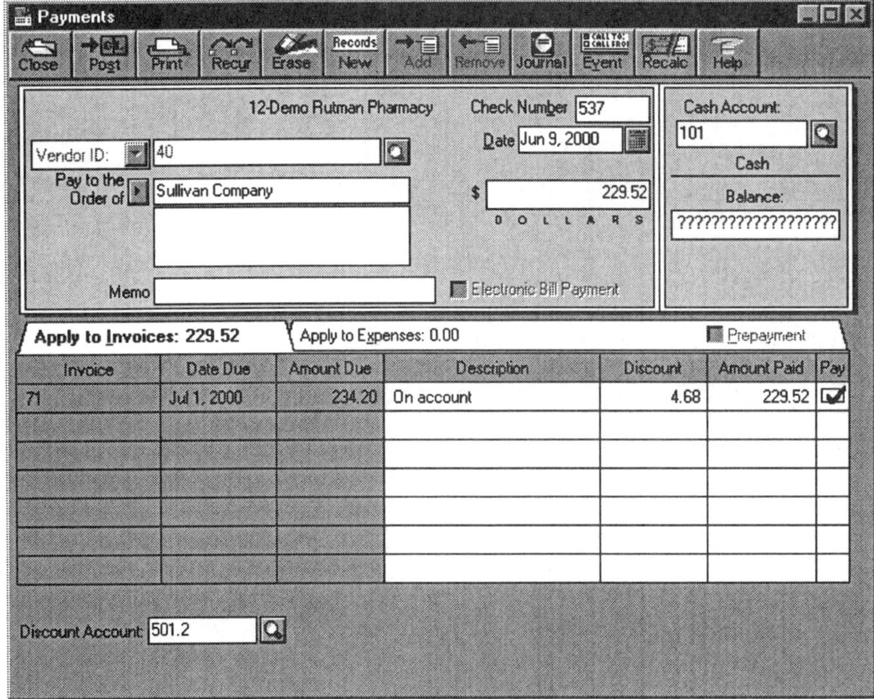

FIGURE 2.28 Payments Window (Payment on Account)

Direct Payment (Apply to Expenses Tab):

- **Enter the payee in the Pay to the Order of field. If none is available in the transaction statement, create one. For example, if the check is for rent, enter "Rent payment."**
- **Enter the Check Number.**
- **Enter the Date.**
- **Under the Apply to Expenses tab, enter a description of the transaction, the account number of the account to be debited, and the amount of the payment.**
- **Click Post to record the transaction.**

  A Payments window illustrating the recording of a direct payment for rent is illustrated in Figure 2.29.

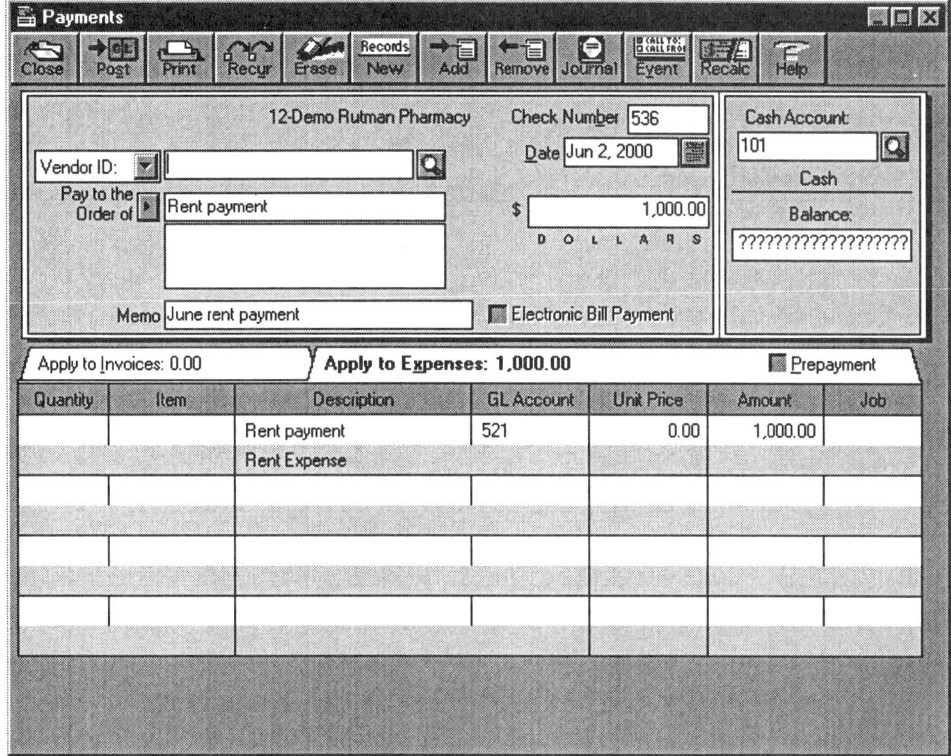

FIGURE 2.29 Payments Window (Direct Payment)

STEP 4: **Display a General Ledger Trial Balance Report.**

STEP 5: **From the Reports menu, select the Accounts Payable option and display a schedule of accounts payable, purchases journal, check register, and cash disbursements journal with titles reports.**

STEP 6: **If errors are detected on the reports, return to the appropriate data-entry window (Purchases/Receive Inventory or Payments) and use the Edit Icon Bar button to select the transaction in error and make corrections.**

See the solution section of this workbook for the solution to the demonstration problem.

PROBLEM 12A4

Freddy Flint owns a small retail business called Flint's Fantasy. The cash account has a balance of $20,000 on July 1. The following transactions occurred during July.

July 1 Issued check no. 414 in payment of July rent, $1,500.

1 Purchased merchandise on account from Tang's Toys, invoice no. 311, $2,700, terms 2/10, n/30.

3 Purchased merchandise on account from Sillas & Company, invoice no. 812, $3,100, terms 1/10, n/30.

5 Returned merchandise purchased from Tang's Toys, receiving a credit memo on the amount owed, $500.

8 Purchased merchandise on account from Daisy's Dolls, invoice no. 139, $1,900, terms 2/10, n/30.

11 Issued check no. 415 to Tang's Toys for merchandise purchased on account, less return of July 5 and less 2% discount.

13 Issued a check no. 416 to Sillas & Company for merchandise purchased on account, less 1% discount.

15 Returned merchandise purchased from Daisy's Dolls, receiving a credit memo on the amount owed, $400.

18 Issued check no. 417 to Daisy's Dolls for merchandise purchased on account, less return of July 15 and less 2% discount.

25 Purchased merchandise on account from Allied Business, invoice no. 489, $2,450, terms n/30.

26 Purchased merchandise on account from Tang's Toys, invoice no. 375, $1,980, terms 2/10, n/30.

29 Purchased merchandise on account from Sillas & Company, invoice no. 883, $3,460, terms 1/10, n/30.

31 Freddy Flint withdrew cash for personal use, $2,000. Issued check no. 418.

31 Issued check no. 419 to Glisan Distributors for a cash purchase of merchandise, $975.

REQUIRED

1. Enter the transactions in a purchases journal, a cash payments journal, and a general journal. Total and rule the purchases and cash payments journals. Prove the cash payments journal.
2. Post from the journals to the general ledger and accounts payable ledger accounts.

In the Problem 124A you will use the Peachtree Accounting software to process purchases and cash payments, and to display a trial balance, schedule of accounts payable, purchases journal, check register, and cash disbursements journal. Follow the steps listed to complete the problem.

STEP 1: Open the data file for Problem 12A4.

STEP 2: From the Tasks menu, select the Purchases/Receive Inventory option and enter the purchases on account and returns or allowance transactions.

STEP 3: From the Tasks menu, select the Payments option and enter the cash payment transactions.

Note: Vendor credits for returns and allowances must be applied to the appropriate payment. For example, on the 11th, the amount of the check is $2,154.00. The $2,154.00 is arrived at by applying invoice number 311 for $2,700.00 less the credit of $500.00 less the discount. The discount is $54.00 on the original invoice amount of $2,700.00 minus the discount credit of $10.00 yielding a net discount of $44.00. ($2,700.00 – 500.00 – 44.00 = $2,154,00).

STEP 4: From the Reports menu, select the General Ledger option and display a General Ledger Trial Balance Report.

STEP 5: From the Reports menu, select the Accounts Payable option and display a schedule of accounts payable, purchases journal, check register, cash disbursements journal with titles, reports, and vendor ledgers.

PROBLEM 12B4

Debbie Mueller owns a small retail business called Debbie's Doll House. The cash account has a balance of $20,000 on July 1. The following transactions occurred during July.

July	1	Issued check no. 314 for July rent, $1,400.
	1	Purchased merchandise on account from Topper's Toys, invoice no. 211, $2,500, terms 2/10, n/30.
	3	Purchased merchandise on account from Jones & Company, invoice no. 812, $2,800, terms 1/10, n/30.
	5	Returned merchandise purchased from Topper's Toys receiving a credit memo on the amount owed, $400.
	8	Purchased merchandise on account from Downtown Merchants, invoice no. 159, $1,600, terms 2/10, n/30.
	11	Issued check no. 315 to Topper's Toys for merchandise purchased on account, less return of July 5 and less 2% discount.
	13	Issued check no. 316 to Jones & Company for merchandise purchased on account, less 1% discount.
	15	Returned merchandise purchased from Downtown Merchants receiving a credit memo on the amount owed, $600.
	18	Issued check no. 317 to Downtown Merchants for merchandise purchased on account, less return of July 15 and less 2% discount.
	25	Purchased merchandise on account from Columbia Products, invoice no. 468, $3,200, terms n/30.
	26	Purchased merchandise on account from Topper's Toys, invoice no. 395, $1,430, terms 2/10, n/30.
	29	Purchased merchandise on account from Jones & Company, invoice no. 853, $2,970, terms 1/10, n/30.
	31	Mueller withdrew cash for personal use, $2,500. Issued check no. 318.
	31	Issued check no. 319 to Burnside Warehouse for a cash purchase of merchandise, $1,050.

REQUIRED

1. Enter the transactions in a purchases journal, a cash payments journal, and a general journal. Total and rule the purchases and cash payments journals. Prove the cash payments journal.
2. Post from the journals to the general ledger and accounts payable ledger accounts. Use general ledger account numbers as shown in the chapter.

In Problem 12B4, you will use the Peachtree Accounting software to process purchases and cash payments, and to display a trial balance, schedule of accounts payable, purchases journal, check register, and cash disbursements. Follow the steps listed to complete the problem.

STEP 1: **Open the data file for Problem 12B4.**

STEP 2: **From the Tasks menu, select the Purchases/Receive Inventory option and enter the purchases on account and returns or allowance transactions.**

STEP 3: **From the Tasks menu, select the Payments option and enter the cash payment transactions.**

STEP 4: **From the Reports menu, select the General Ledger option and display a General Ledger Trial Balance Report.**

STEP 5: **From the Reports menu, select the Accounts Payable option and display a schedule of accounts payable, purchases journal, check register, cash disbursements journal reports, and vendor ledgers.**

CHAPTER 12 MASTERY PROBLEM

Michelle French owns and operates Books and More, a retail book store. Selected account balances on June 1 are as follows:

General Ledger	
Cash	$32,200.00
Accounts Payable	2,000.00
Michelle French, Drawing	18,000.00
Purchases	67,021.66
Purchases Returns and Allowances	2,315.23
Purchases Discounts	905.00
Freight-In	522.60
Rent Expense	3,125.00
Utilities Expense	1,522.87

Accounts Payable Ledger	
North-Eastern Publishing Co.	$2,000.00

The following purchases and cash payment transactions took place during the month of June:

June 1 Purchased books on account from Irving Publishing Co., $2,100. Invoice no. 101, terms 2/10, n/30, FOB destination.

2 Issued check no. 300 to North-Eastern Publishing Co. for goods purchased on May 23, terms 2/10, n/30, $1,960 (the $2,000 invoice amount less the 2% discount).

3 Purchased books on account from Broadway Publishing, Inc., $2,880. Invoice no. 711, subject to 20% trade discount, and invoice terms of 3/10, n/30, FOB shipping point.

3 Issued check no. 301 to Mayday Shipping for delivery from Broadway Publishing, Inc., $250.

4 Issued check no. 302 for June rent, $625.

8 Purchased books on account from North-Eastern Publishing Co., $5,825. Invoice no. 268, terms 2/eom, n/60, FOB destination.

10 Received a credit memo from Irving Publishing Co., $550. Books had been returned because the covers were on upside down.

13 Issued check no. 304 to Broadway Publishing, Inc., for the purchase made on June 3. (Check no. 303 was voided because an error was made in preparing it.)

28 Made the following purchases:

Invoice No.	Company	Amount	Terms
579	Broadway Publishing, Inc.	$2,350	2/10, n/30 FOB destination
406	North-Eastern Publishing Co.	4,200	2/eom, n/60 FOB destination
964	Riley Publishing Co.	3,450	3/10, n/30 FOB destination

30 Issued check no. 305 to Taylor County Utility Co., for June utilities, $325.

30 French withdrew cash for personal use, $4,500. Issued check no. 306.

30 Issued check no. 307 to Irving Publishing Co. for purchase made on June 1 less returns made on June 10.

30 Issued check no. 308 to North-Eastern Publishing Co. for purchase made on June 8.

30 Issued check no. 309 for books purchased at an auction, $1,328.

REQUIRED

1. Enter the above transactions in the appropriate journals.
2. Total and rule the purchases journal and cash payments journal. Prove the cash payments journal.
3. Post from the journals to the general ledger accounts and the accounts payable ledger.
4. Prepare a schedule of accounts payable.
5. If merchandise inventory was $35,523 on January 1 and $42,100 as of June 30, prepare the cost of goods sold section of the income statement for the six months ended June 30, 20--.

In the Chapter 12 Mastery Problem, you will use the Peachtree Accounting software to process purchases and cash payments, and to display a trial balance, cost of goods sold statement, schedule of accounts payable, purchases journal, check register, and cash disbursements. Follow the steps listed to complete the problem.

STEP 1: Open the data file for the Chapter 12 Mastery Problem.

STEP 2 From the Tasks menu, select the Purchases/Receive Inventory option and enter the purchases on account and returns or allowance transactions.

STEP 3: From the Tasks menu, select the Payments option and enter the cash payment transactions.

Note: In the cash payment on the 2nd to North-Eastern Publishing Co., you must enter $40.00 discount manually. The computer will not automatically calculate it. For the cash payment on the 30th (check no. 309), make the check payable to Auction.

STEP 4: From the Reports menu, select the General Ledger option and display a Cost of Goods Sold Statement and a General Ledger Trial Balance Report.

STEP 5: From the Reports menu, select the Accounts Payable option and display a schedule of accounts payable, purchases journal, check register, and cash disbursements journal reports.

CHAPTER 13 DEMONSTRATION PROBLEM (13-DEMO)

Harpo, Inc., is a retail novelty store. The following transactions relate to operations for the month of March.

March 2 Issued voucher no. 313 to Tremont Rental for March rent, $500.

2 Issued check no. 450 to Tremont Rental, $500. Voucher no. 313.

3 Purchased merchandise from Gail's Gags, $550, terms 2/15, n/60. Voucher no. 314.

4 Purchased merchandise from Silly Sam's, $200, terms 2/10, n/60. Voucher no. 315.

10 Issued check no. 451 to Jerry's Jokes, $500 less $10 discount. Voucher no. 310.

12 Received a credit memo from Silly Sam's for returned merchandise that was purchased on March 4, $100.

14 Issued check no. 452 to Resource Supplies, $250. Voucher no. 311.

16 Purchased merchandise from Giggles, $700, terms 2/10, n/30. Voucher no. 316.

18 Issued check no. 453 to Gail's Gags for purchase made on March 3 less 2% discount. Voucher no. 314.

19 Issued check no. 454 to Donnelly's, $750. Voucher no. 312.

21 Purchased merchandise from Creations, $870, terms 3/15, n/50. Voucher no. 317.

25 Purchased supplies from Hal's Supply, $120, terms 3/10, n/30. Voucher no. 318.

31 Issued check no. 455 to Silly Sam's for purchase made on March 4 less returns made on March 12. Voucher no. 315.

31 Issued voucher no. 319 to Payroll in payment of March wages, $1,250.

31 Issued check no. 456 to Payroll, $1,250. Voucher no. 319.

REQUIRED Selected general ledger accounts and their opening balances as well as a portion of the voucher register for February are shown below.

1. Enter the transactions in the voucher register, check register, and general journal. Total, rule, and prove the voucher register and check register.
2. Post the transactions to the general ledger accounts.
3. Prepare a schedule of vouchers payable, and compare the March 31 balance to the balance of Vouchers Payable in the general ledger.

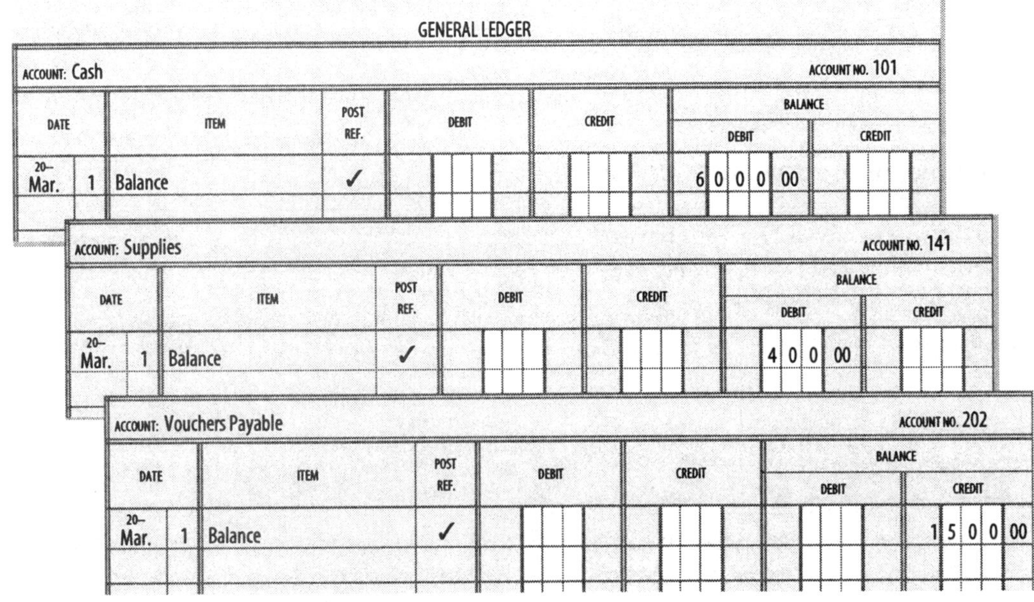

GENERAL LEDGER

ACCOUNT: Cash — ACCOUNT NO. 101

DATE		ITEM	POST REF.	DEBIT	CREDIT	BALANCE DEBIT	BALANCE CREDIT
20– Mar.	1	Balance	✓			6,000 00	

ACCOUNT: Supplies — ACCOUNT NO. 141

DATE		ITEM	POST REF.	DEBIT	CREDIT	BALANCE DEBIT	BALANCE CREDIT
20– Mar.	1	Balance	✓			400 00	

ACCOUNT: Vouchers Payable — ACCOUNT NO. 202

DATE		ITEM	POST REF.	DEBIT	CREDIT	BALANCE DEBIT	BALANCE CREDIT
20– Mar.	1	Balance	✓				1,500 00

ACCOUNT: Purchases						ACCOUNT NO. 501
DATE		ITEM	POST REF.	DEBIT	CREDIT	BALANCE	
						DEBIT	CREDIT
20-- Mar.	1	Balance	✓			4 2 5 0 00	

ACCOUNT: Purchases Returns and Allowances						ACCOUNT NO. 501.1
DATE		ITEM	POST REF.	DEBIT	CREDIT	BALANCE	
						DEBIT	CREDIT
20-- Mar.	1	Balance	✓				1 0 0 00

ACCOUNT: Purchases Discounts						ACCOUNT NO. 501.2
DATE		ITEM	POST REF.	DEBIT	CREDIT	BALANCE	
						DEBIT	CREDIT
20-- Mar.	1	Balance	✓				5 0 00

VOUCHER REGISTER

	DATE	VOUCHER NO.	ISSUED TO	PURCHASES DEBIT	
1	2/24/--	310	Jerry's Jokes	5 0 0 00	1
2	2/26/--	311	Resource Supplies		2
3	2/26/--	312	Donnelly's	7 5 0 00	3
4					4
5					5

The Chapter 13 Demonstration Problem involves processing accounts payable transactions using a voucher system. All vouchers as well as returns and allowances will be entered into the Purchases/Receive Inventory window. Payment of vouchers will be processed through the Payments window. Once all the transactions have been entered, the various accounts payable reports will be generated. Follow the step-by-step instructions provided to solve the problem.

STEP 1: Open the data file for the Chapter 13 Demonstration Problem.

STEP 2: From the Tasks menu, select the Purchases/Receive Inventory option and enter the vouchers and returns and allowance transactions.

Entering Voucher Transactions:

- **Enter or select the vendor number.**
- **Enter the Voucher Number in the Invoice Number field.**
- **Enter the Date of the transaction.**
- **Verify that the terms of the sale are correctly indicated. If not, click on the right arrow button at the end of the Terms field and a Term Information window will appear allowing you to enter the pertinent discount data.**

- **On the Apply to Purchases tab, enter a description of the transaction in the Description field. For example, enter "March rent" for the rent payment on March 2nd.**
- **Enter or select the account number of the account to be debited in the GL Account field.**
- **Enter the amount of the voucher in the Amount field.**
- **Click on Post to record the transaction.**

An example of the recording of a new voucher is illustrated in the Purchases/Receive Inventory window shown in Figure 2.30.

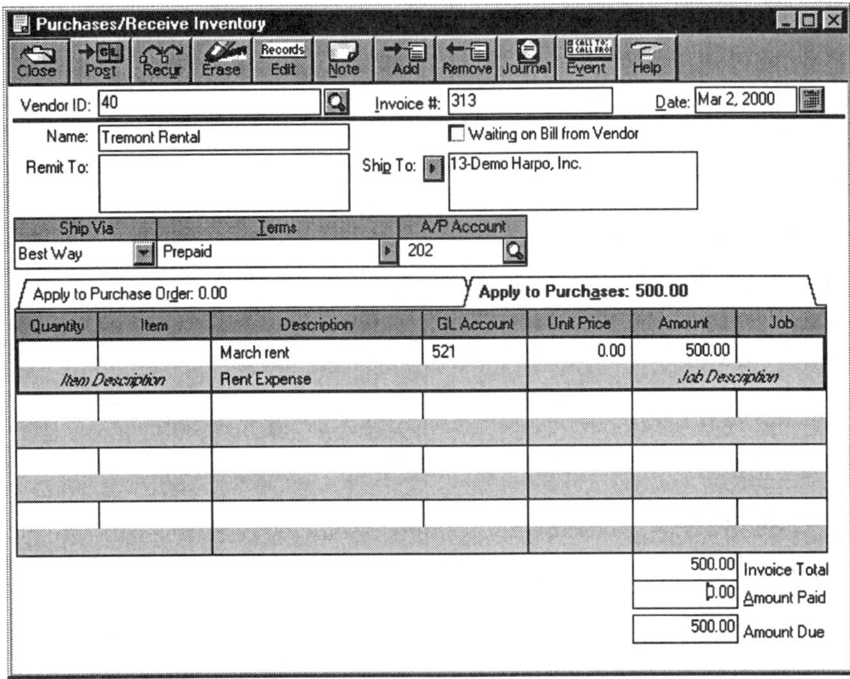

FIGURE 2.30 Purchases/Receive Inventory (New Voucher)

Entering Purchases Returns and Allowance Transactions:

- **Enter or select the Vendor ID number.**
- **Enter an Invoice Number consisting of CM plus the original voucher number.**
- **Verify that the terms of the sale are correct; if not, click on the right arrow button in the Terms field and enter correct terms.**
- **Enter "Credit memo" as the Description.**
- **Enter the Purchases Returns and Allowances Account Number in the GL Account field.**
- **Enter the amount of the credit memo received as a negative number.**
- **Click on Post to record the transaction.**

The recording of a Purchase Return transaction is illustrated in the Purchases/Receive Inventory window shown in Figure 2.31.

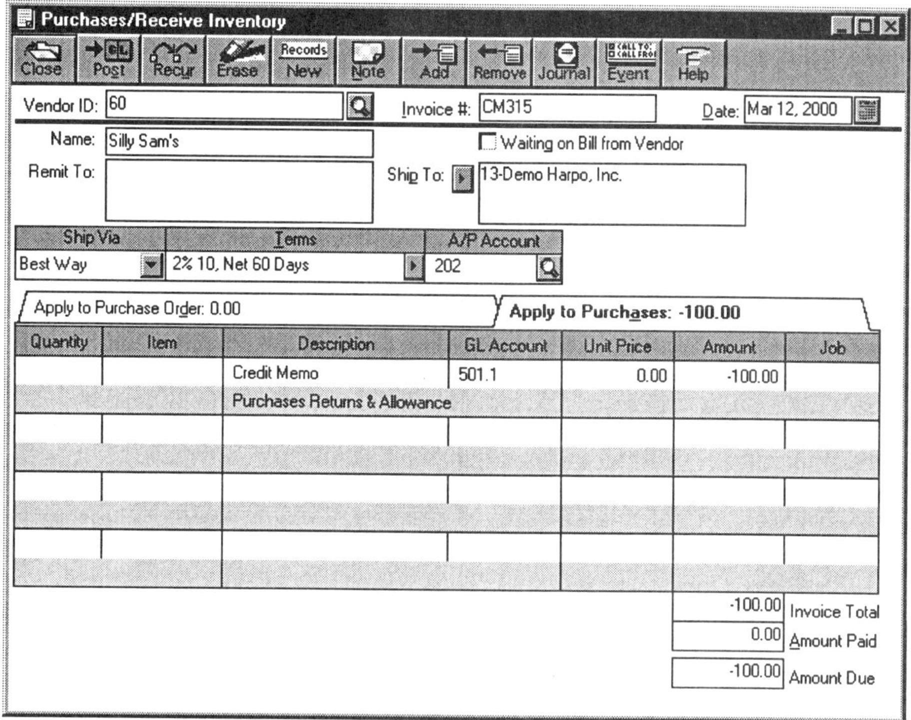

FIGURE 2.31 Purchases/Receive Inventory (Purchases Return)

STEP 3: From the Tasks menu, select the Payments option and enter the voucher payment transactions.

In the voucher system, all cash disbursements are vouchered and entered into the accounts payable system and later paid through the Payments window. There are no direct payments. Because all cash disbursements go through accounts payable, all voucher payments are, in effect, payments on account.

When entering voucher payments, you must select the vouchers you wish to pay and apply the appropriate credit memos to the voucher(s).

Voucher Payment (Apply to Invoices Tab):

- ▶ **Enter or select the Vendor ID number.**
- ▶ **Enter the Check Number.**
- ▶ **Enter the Date of the check.**
- ▶ **Under the Apply to Invoices tab, click on the Pay box for the voucher or vouchers to be paid. Click on the Pay box for any credit memos that are to be applied to this payment.**
- ▶ **Click on Post to record the payment.**

An example of a payment of a voucher transaction is illustrated in Figure 2.32.

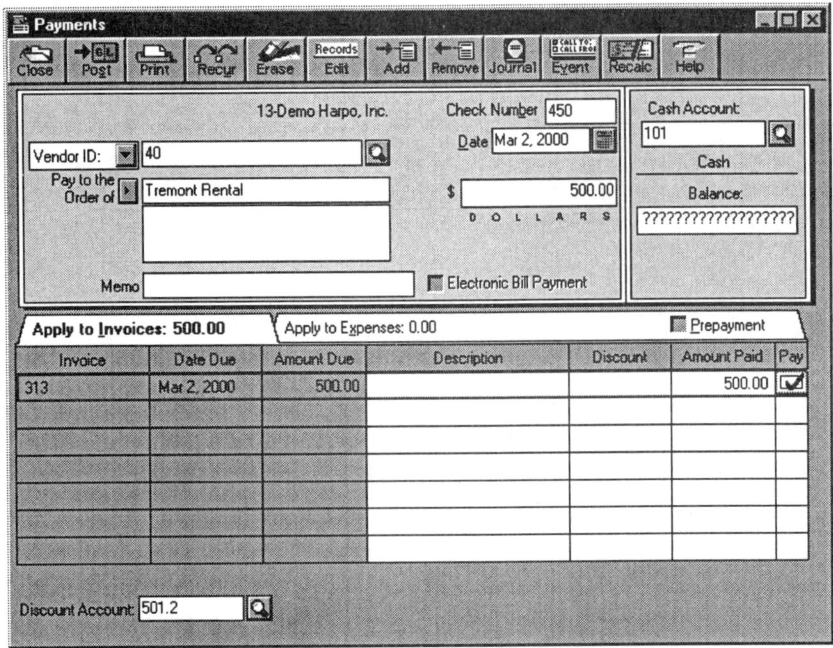

FIGURE 2.32 Payments Window (Payment of Voucher)

STEP 4: Display a General Ledger Trial Balance Report.

STEP 5: From the Reports menu, select the Accounts Payable option and display a schedule of vouchers payable, purchases journal, check register, and cash disbursements journal with titles reports.

STEP 6: If errors are detected on the reports, return to the appropriate data entry window (Purchases/Receive Inventory or Payments) and use the Edit Icon Bar button to select the transaction in error and make corrections.

See the solution section of this workbook for the solution to the demonstration problem.

PROBLEM 13A3

Betty Classic owns the Classic Candle Shop. The following transactions occurred during April 20--. The Classic Candle Shop uses a voucher register, a check register, and a general ledger. Unpaid vouchers are filed and listed at the end of the month. General ledger account balances on April 1 were: Cash, $5,189; and Supplies, $408.

Date	Voucher No.	Issued To	Amount	Purpose	Terms
4/1	1101	Landmark Realty	$ 500	April rent	
4/3	1102	Wax House	280	Merchandise	2/10, n/30
4/5	1103	Designs West	490	Merchandise	2/10, n/30
4/9	1104	Crane Stationers	180	Office supplies	
4/11	1105	Magic Solutions	600	Merchandise	2/10, n/30
4/15	1106	Payroll	1,500	Bimonthly payroll	
4/23	1107	Wax House	510	Merchandise	1/10, n/30
4/25	1108	Baskets & More	440	Merchandise	2/10, n/30
4/28	1109	Magic Solutions	450	Merchandise	2/10, n/30
4/30	1110	Payroll	1,500	Bimonthly payroll	

Checks issued:

Date	Check No.	Payee	Voucher No.	Amount
4/1	928	Landmark Realty	1101	$ 500
4/9	929	Crane Stationers	1104	180
4/11	930	Wax House	1102	280
4/15	931	Payroll	1106	1,500
4/19	932	Designs West	1103	490
4/30	933	Payroll	1110	1,500

REQUIRED

1. Enter the transactions for April in the voucher register. Total, rule, and prove the register. Update the Payment column when vouchers are paid.
2. Enter the transactions for April in the check register. Be sure to take discounts where appropriate. Total, rule, and prove the register.
3. Post the voucher register and the check register to the general ledger.
4. Prepare a schedule of vouchers payable.

In Problem 13A3, all vouchers as well as returns and allowances will be entered into the Purchases/Receive Inventory window. Payment of vouchers will be processed through the Payments window. Once all the transactions have been entered, the various accounts payable reports will be generated. Follow the step-by-step instructions provided to solve the problem.

STEP 1: **Open the data file for Problem 13A3.**

STEP 2: **From the Tasks menu, select the Purchases/Receive Inventory option and enter the vouchers and returns and allowance transactions. Verify that the default terms on the Purchases window are correct. If not, enter the correct terms for that transaction.**

STEP 3: **From the Tasks menu, select the Payments option and enter the voucher payment transactions.**

STEP 4: **Display a General Ledger Trial Balance Report.**

STEP 5: **From the Reports menu, select the Accounts Payable option and display a schedule of vouchers payable, purchases journal, check register, and cash disbursements journal with titles reports.**

STEP 6: **If errors are detected on the reports, return to the appropriate data entry window (Purchases/Receive Inventory or Payments) and use the Edit Icon Bar button to select the transaction in error and make corrections.**

PROBLEM 13B3

Jane Hledik is owner of Hledik Lawn Supply. The following transactions occurred during April 20--. Hledik Lawn Supply uses a voucher register, a check register, and a general ledger. Unpaid vouchers are filed and listed at the end of the month. General ledger account balances on April 1 were: Cash, $5,189; and Supplies, $408.

Vouchers issued:

Date	Voucher No.	Issued To	Amount	Purpose	Terms
4/2	662	Brenner's	$600	April rent	
4/4	663	Lawn Care Wholesale	300	Merchandise	2/10, n/30
4/7	664	Southern Supply	128	Office supplies	
4/10	665	Clay's Chemicals	420	Merchandise	1/20, n/30
4/13	666	Mendel & Son	530	Merchandise	2/10, n/30
4/15	667	Payroll	950	Bimonthly payroll	
4/19	668	Lawn Care Wholesale	570	Merchandise	1/10, n/30
4/27	669	Southern Supply	99	Office supplies	
4/29	670	Lakeside Fertilizer	280	Merchandise	2/10, n/30
4/30	671	Payroll	950	Bimonthly payroll	

Checks issued:

Date	Check No.	Payee	Voucher No.	Amount
4/2	748	Brenner's	662	$600
4/7	749	Southern Supply	664	128
4/11	750	Lawn Care Wholesale	663	300
4/15	751	Payroll	667	950
4/20	752	Mendel & Son	666	530
4/30	753	Payroll	671	950

REQUIRED

1. Enter the transactions for April in the voucher register. Total, rule, and prove the register. Update the Payment column when vouchers are paid.
2. Enter the transactions for April in the check register. Be sure to take discounts where appropriate. Total, rule, and prove the register.
3. Post the voucher register and the check register to the general ledger.
4. Prepare a schedule of vouchers payable.

In Problem 13B3, all vouchers as well as returns and allowances will be entered into the Purchases/Receive Inventory window. Payment of vouchers will be processed through the Payments window. Once all the transactions have been entered, the various accounts payable reports will be generated. Follow the step-by-step instructions provided to solve the problem.

STEP 1: **Open the data file for Problem 13B3.**

STEP 2: **From the Tasks menu, select the Purchases/Receive Inventory option and enter the vouchers and returns and allowance transactions. Verify that the default terms in the Purchases window are correct. If not, enter the correct terms for that transaction.**

STEP 3: **From the Tasks menu, select the Payments option and enter the voucher payment transactions.**

STEP 4: **Display a General Ledger Trial Balance Report.**

STEP 5: **From the Reports menu, select the Accounts Payable option and display a schedule of vouchers payable, purchases journal, check register, and cash disbursements journal with titles reports.**

STEP 6: **If errors are detected on the reports, return to the appropriate data entry window (Purchases/Receive Inventory or Payments) and use the Edit Icon Bar button to select the transaction in error and make corrections.**

CHAPTER 13 MASTERY PROBLEM

Sunshine Flower Shop began operations in the month of July. The following transactions occurred during the first month of the business.

July 1 Purchased merchandise from Thorny Wholesale, $600. Voucher no. 1.

2 Issued check no. 1 to Strongs Rental for July rent, $1,000. Voucher no. 2

3 Purchased merchandise from Flowerbed, Inc., $470, terms 2/15, n/60, FOB shipping point. Voucher no. 3.

7 Issued check no. 2 to Thorny Wholesale in partial payment for goods purchased on July 1, $300. Voucher no. 1. Issued new voucher nos. 4 and 5.

9 Issued check no. 3 to Charlie's Trucking for shipping charges, $20. Voucher no. 6.

15 Issued check no. 4 to Payroll for wages, $600. Voucher no. 7.

16 Purchased merchandise from Petals Co., $377, terms 2/15, n/30. Voucher no. 8.

17 Purchased merchandise from Weeds Plus, $436, terms 3/15, n/60. Voucher no. 9.

18 Issued check no. 5 to Flowerbed, Inc., for goods purchased on July 3 less discount. Voucher no. 3.

23 Purchased supplies from Staples Supply, $150. Voucher no. 10.

25 Received a credit memo from Weeds Plus for returned merchandise that was purchased on July 17, $80.

31 Issued check no. 6 to Petals Co. for goods purchased on July 16 less discount. Voucher no. 8.

31 Issued check no. 7 to Payroll for wages, $600. Voucher no. 11.

REQUIRED The general ledger accounts are listed below. The $6,000 with which the Flower Shop began business is entered in the cash account. Only this account has a beginning balance.

Cash	101
Supplies	141
Vouchers Payable	202
Purchases	501
Purchases Returns and Allowances	501.1
Purchases Discounts	501.2
Freight-In	502
Wages Expense	511
Rent Expense	521

1. Enter all transactions in the voucher register, check register, and general journal. Total, rule, and prove the voucher register and check register.
2. Post the transactions to the general ledger.
3. Prepare a schedule of vouchers payable and compare the July 31 total to the balance of Vouchers Payable in the general ledger.

In the Chapter 13 Mastery Problem, all vouchers as well as returns and allowances will be entered into the Purchases/Receive Inventory window. Payment of vouchers will be processed through the Payments window. Once all the transactions have been entered, the various accounts payable reports will be generated. Follow the step-by-step instructions provided to solve the problem.

STEP 1: **Open the data file for the Chapter 13 Mastery Problem.**

STEP 2: **From the Tasks menu, select the Purchases/Receive Inventory option and enter the vouchers and returns and allowance transactions.**

Note: Because a voucher system is being used, all cash disbursements must be first recorded in the Purchase/Receive Inventory window before payment is made.

STEP 3: **From the Tasks menu, select the Payments option and enter the voucher payment transactions.**

Note: The transaction on the 7th of July involves a partial payment to Thorny Wholesale. In the manual solution, the original voucher 1 is canceled and two new vouchers are issued to make the partial payments. With the Peachtree Accounting software, you simply specify the partial payment of $300.00. The software will handle the remaining payment. There is no need to issue the 2 additional vouchers.

STEP 4: **Display a General Ledger Trial Balance Report.**

STEP 5: **From the Reports menu, select the Accounts Payable option and display a schedule of vouchers payable, purchases journal, check register, and cash disbursements journal with titles reports.**

STEP 6: **If errors are detected on the reports, return to the appropriate data entry window (Purchases/Receive Inventory or Payments) and use the Edit Icon Bar button to select the transaction in error and make corrections.**

PROBLEM 14A1

The trial balance for the Seaside Kite Shop, a business owned by Joyce Kennington, is shown on the next page. Year-end adjustment information is as follows:

(a, b) Merchandise inventory costing $30,000 is on hand as of December 31, 20--.

(c) Supplies remaining at the end of the year, $2,700.

(d) Unexpired insurance on December 31, $2,900.

(e) Depreciation expense on the building for 20--, $5,000.

(f) Depreciation expense on the store equipment for 20--, $3,200.

(g) Unearned rent revenue as of December 31, $2,200.

(h) Wages earned but not paid as of December 31, $900.

REQUIRED

1. Complete the Adjustments columns, identifying each adjustment with its corresponding letter.
2. Complete the worksheet.
3. Enter the adjustments in a general journal.

Seaside Kite Shop
Trial Balance
December 31, 20 - -

ACCOUNT TITLE	DEBIT BALANCE	CREDIT BALANCE
Cash	20,000.00	
Accounts Receivable	14,000.00	
Merchandise Inventory	25,000.00	
Supplies	8,000.00	
Prepaid Insurance	5,400.00	
Land	30,000.00	
Building	50,000.00	
Accumulated Depreciation—Building		20,000.00
Store Equipment	35,000.00	
Accumulated Depreciation—Store Equipment		14,000.00
Accounts Payable		9,600.00
Wages Payable		
Sales Tax Payable		5,900.00
Unearned Rent Revenue		8,900.00
Mortgage Payable		45,000.00
Joyce Kennington, Capital		65,410.00
Joyce Kennington, Drawing	26,000.00	
Income Summary		
Sales		118,000.00
Sales Returns and Allowances	1,700.00	
Rent Revenue		
Purchases	27,000.00	
Purchases Returns and Allowances		1,400.00
Purchases Discounts		1,800.00
Freight-In	2,100.00	
Wages Expense	32,000.00	
Advertising Expense	3,600.00	
Supplies Expense		
Telephone Expense	1,350.00	
Utilities Expense	8,000.00	
Insurance Expense		
Depreciation Expense —Building		
Depreciation Expense —Store Equipment		
Miscellaneous Expense	860.00	
	290,010.00	290,010.00

In Problem 14A1, you will enter the adjusting entries and display the financial statements for a merchandising business. When the Peachtree Accounting software prepares the income statement, it assumes that you are using a perpetual inventory and a cost of goods sold account approach. The income statement in the problems utilize a physical inventory approach whereby the cost of goods sold is calculated based on beginning inventory, cost accounts, and ending inventory. This can easily be circumvented by simply adding a cost account titled "Inventory Adjustment" and adjusting the merchandise inventory account to this account rather than the income summary account. This will allow the computer to total up a cost of goods sold figure on the income statement as shown in Figure 2.33. The inventory adjustment account gets closed to equity at the end of the period in the same way that Income Summary would in a manual system.

Cost of Goods Sold

Purchases	27,000.00
Purchases Returns and Allowances	<1,400.00>
Purchases Discounts	<1,800.00>
Freight-In	2,100.00
Inventory Adjustment	<5,000.00>
Total Cost of Goods Sold	20,900.00

FIGURE 2.33 Cost of Goods Sold Section of Income Statement

STEP 1: **Open the data file for Problem 14A1.**

STEP 2: **Enter the adjusting entries for this problem. Use the worksheet letters (a), (b), etc., as the reference for the adjusting general journal entries.**

STEP 3: **Display the General Journal Entries with Titles Report.**

STEP 4: **Display a Trial Balance Report.**

STEP 5: **Display the financial statements: Basic Income Statement, Owner's Equity Statement, and Balance Sheet.**

PROBLEM 14A2

The trial balance for Cascade Bicycle Shop, a business owned by David Lamond, is shown on the next page. Year-end adjustment information is provided:

(a, b) Merchandise inventory costing $22,000 is on hand as of December 31, 20--.

(c) Supplies remaining at the end of the year, $2,400.

(d) Unexpired insurance on December 31, $1,750.

(e) Depreciation expense on the building for 20--, $4,000.

(f) Depreciation expense on the store equipment for 20--, $3,600.

(g) Unearned storage revenue as of December 31, $1,950.

(h) Wages earned but not paid as of December 31, $750.

REQUIRED

1. Complete the Adjustments columns, identifying each adjustment with its corresponding letter.
2. Complete the worksheet.
3. Enter the adjustments in the general journal.

Cascade Bicycle Shop
Trial Balance
December 31, 20 - -

ACCOUNT TITLE	DEBIT BALANCE	CREDIT BALANCE
Cash	23,000.00	
Accounts Receivable	15,000.00	
Merchandise Inventory	31,000.00	
Supplies	7,200.00	
Prepaid Insurance	4,600.00	
Land	28,000.00	
Building	53,000.00	
Accumulated Depreciation—Building		17,000.00
Store Equipment	27,000.00	
Accumulated Depreciation—Store Equipment		9,000.00
Accounts Payable		3,800.00
Wages Payable		
Sales Tax Payable		3,050.00
Unearned Storage Revenue		5,600.00
Mortgage Payable		42,000.00
David Lamond, Capital		165,760.00
David Lamond, Drawing	33,000.00	
Income Summary		
Sales		51,000.00
Sales Returns and Allowances	2,400.00	
Storage Revenue		
Purchases	21,000.00	
Purchases Returns and Allowances		1,300.00
Purchases Discounts		1,900.00
Freight-in	1,800.00	
Wages Expense	35,000.00	
Advertising Expense	5,700.00	
Supplies Expense		
Telephone Expense	2,200.00	
Utilities Expense	9,600.00	
Insurance Expense		
Depreciation Expense—Building		
Depreciation Expense—Store Equipment		
Miscellaneous Expense	910.00	
	300,410.00	300,410.00

In Problem 14A2, you will enter the adjusting entries and display the financial statements for a merchandising business. Follow the steps listed below to complete the problem.

STEP 1: Open the data file for Problem 14A2.

STEP 2: Enter the adjusting entries for this problem. Use the worksheet letter (a), (b), etc., as the general journal reference for the adjusting entries.

STEP 3: Display the General Journal Entries with Titles Report.

STEP 4: Display a Trial Balance Report.

STEP 5: Display the financial statements: Basic Income Statement, Owner's Equity Statement, and Balance Sheet.

PROBLEM 14B1

A trial balance for the Basket Corner, a business owned by Linda Palermo, is shown on the next page. Year-end adjustment information is provided:

(a, b) Merchandise inventory costing $24,000 is on hand as of December 31, 20--.

(c) Supplies remaining at the end of the year, $2,100.

(d) Unexpired insurance on December 31, $2,600.

(e) Depreciation expense on the building for 20--, $5,300.

(f) Depreciation expense on the store equipment for 20--, $3,800.

(g) Unearned decorating revenue as of December 31, $1,650.

(h) Wages earned but not paid as of December 31, $750.

REQUIRED

1. Complete the Adjustments columns, identifying each adjustment with its corresponding letter.
2. Complete the worksheet.
3. Enter the adjustments in a general journal.

Basket Corner
Trial Balance
December 31, 20 - -

ACCOUNT TITLE	DEBIT BALANCE	CREDIT BALANCE
Cash	25,000 00	
Accounts Receivable	8,100 00	
Merchandise Inventory	32,000 00	
Supplies	7,100 00	
Prepaid Insurance	3,600 00	
Land	40,000 00	
Building	45,000 00	
Accumulated Depreciation—Building		16,000 00
Store Equipment	27,000 00	
Accumulated Depreciation—Store Equipment		5,500 00
Accounts Payable		3,600 00
Wages Payable		
Sales Tax Payable		6,200 00
Unearned Decorating Revenue		6,300 00
Mortgage Payable		36,000 00
Linda Palermo, Capital		112,050 00
Linda Palermo, Drawing	31,000 00	
Income Summary		
Sales		125,000 00
Sales Returns and Allowances	2,600 00	
Decorating Revenue		
Purchases	38,000 00	
Purchases Returns and Allowances		2,200 00
Purchases Discounts		1,700 00
Freight-In	1,900 00	
Wages Expense	38,000 00	
Advertising Expense	4,200 00	
Supplies Expense		
Telephone Expense	1,870 00	
Utilities Expense	8,400 00	
Insurance Expense		
Depreciation Expense —Building		
Depreciation Expense —Store Equipment		
Miscellaneous Expense	780 00	
	314,550 00	314,550 00

In Problem 14B1, you will enter the adjusting entries and display the financial statements for a merchandising business. Follow the steps listed below to complete the problem.

STEP 1: Open the data file for Problem 14B1.

STEP 2: Enter the adjusting entries for this problem. Use the worksheet letters (a), (b), etc., as the general journal reference for the adjusting entries.

STEP 3: Display the General Journal Entries with Titles Report.

STEP 4: Display a Trial Balance Report.

STEP 5: Display the financial statements: Basic Income Statement, Owner's Equity Statement, and Balance Sheet.

PROBLEM 14B2

The trial balance for Oregon Bike Company, a business owned by Craig Moody, is shown on the next page. Year-end adjustment information is provided:

(a, b) Merchandise inventory costing $26,000 is on hand as of December 31, 20--.

(c) Supplies remaining at the end of the year, $2,500.

(d) Unexpired insurance on December 31, $1,820.

(e) Depreciation expense on the building for 20--, $6,400.

(f) Depreciation expense on the store equipment for 20--, $2,800.

(g) Unearned rent revenue as of December 31, $2,350.

(h) Wages earned but not paid as of December 31, $1,100.

REQUIRED

1. Complete the Adjustments columns, identifying each adjustment with its corresponding letter.
2. Complete the worksheet.
3. Enter the adjustments in a general journal.

Oregon Bike Company
Trial Balance
December 31, 20 - -

ACCOUNT TITLE	DEBIT BALANCE	CREDIT BALANCE
Cash	27,000.00	
Accounts Receivable	12,000.00	
Merchandise Inventory	39,000.00	
Supplies	6,200.00	
Prepaid Insurance	5,800.00	
Land	32,000.00	
Building	58,000.00	
Accumulated Depreciation—Building		27,000.00
Store Equipment	31,000.00	
Accumulated Depreciation—Store Equipment		14,000.00
Accounts Payable		4,900.00
Wages Payable		2,900.00
Sales Tax Payable		
Unearned Rent Revenue		6,100.00
Mortgage Payable		49,000.00
Craig Moody, Capital		169,500.00
Craig Moody, Drawing	36,000.00	
Income Summary		
Sales		58,000.00
Sales Returns and Allowances	3,300.00	
Rent Revenue		
Purchases	19,000.00	
Purchases Returns and Allowances		900.00
Purchases Discounts		1,450.00
Freight-In	800.00	
Wages Expense	47,000.00	
Advertising Expense	6,200.00	
Supplies Expense		
Telephone Expense	1,860.00	
Utilities Expense	8,100.00	
Insurance Expense		
Depreciation Expense —Building		
Depreciation Expense —Store Equipment		
Miscellaneous Expense	490.00	
	333,750.00	333,750.00

In Problem 14B2, you will enter the adjusting entries and display the financial statements for a merchandising business. Follow the steps listed below to complete the problem.

STEP 1: **Open the data file for Problem 14B2.**

STEP 2: **Enter the adjusting entries for this problem. Use the worksheet letters (a), (b), etc., as the general journal reference for the adjusting entries.**

STEP 3: **Display the General Journal Entries with Titles Report.**

STEP 4: **Display a Trial Balance Report.**

STEP 5: **Display the financial statements: Basic Income Statement, Owner's Equity Statement, and Balance Sheet.**

CHAPTER 14 MASTERY PROBLEM

John Neff owns and operates the Waikiki Surf Shop. A year-end trial balance is shown on the next page. Year-end adjustment data for the Waikiki Surf Shop is as follows:

(a, b) A physical count shows merchandise inventory costing $45,000 on hand as of December 31, 20--.

(c) Supplies remaining at the end of the year, $600.

(d) Unexpired insurance on December 31, $900.

(e) Depreciation expense on the building for 20--, $6,000.

(f) Depreciation expense on the store equipment for 20--, $4,500.

(g) Wages earned but not paid as of December 31, $675.

(h) Unearned boat rental revenue as of December 31, $3,000.

REQUIRED 1. Prepare a year-end worksheet.

2. Journalize the adjusting entries.

Waikiki Surf Shop
Trial Balance
December 31, 20--

ACCOUNT TITLE	DEBIT BALANCE	CREDIT BALANCE
Cash	30,000.00	
Accounts Receivable	22,500.00	
Merchandise Inventory	57,000.00	
Supplies	2,700.00	
Prepaid Insurance	3,600.00	
Land	15,000.00	
Building	135,000.00	
Accumulated Depreciation—Building		24,000.00
Store Equipment	75,000.00	
Accumulated Depreciation—Store Equipment		22,500.00
Notes Payable		7,500.00
Accounts Payable		15,000.00
Wages Payable		
Unearned Boat Rental Revenue		33,000.00
John Neff, Capital		233,700.00
John Neff, Drawing	30,000.00	
Income Summary		
Sales		300,750.00
Sales Returns and Allowances	1,800.00	
Boat Rental Revenue		
Purchases	157,500.00	
Purchases Returns and Allowances		1,200.00
Purchases Discounts		1,500.00
Freight-In	450.00	
Wages Expense	63,000.00	
Advertising Expense	11,250.00	
Supplies Expense		
Telephone Expense	5,250.00	
Utilities Expense	18,000.00	
Insurance Expense		
Depreciation Expense—Building		
Depreciation Expense—Store Equipment		
Miscellaneous Expense	10,875.00	
Interest Expense	225.00	
	639,150.00	639,150.00

In the Chapter 14 Mastery Problem, you will enter the adjusting entries and display the financial statements for a merchandising business. Follow the steps listed below to complete the problem.

STEP 1: **Open the data file for the Chaper 14 Mastery Problem.**

STEP 2: **Enter the adjusting entries. Use the letters (a), (b), etc., as the general journal reference for the adjusting entries.**

STEP 3: **Display the General Journal Entries with Titles Report.**

STEP 4: **Display a Trial Balance Report.**

STEP 5: **Display the financial statements: Basic Income Statement, Owner's Equity Statement, and Balance Sheet.**

CHAPTER 15 DEMONSTRATION PROBLEM (15-DEMO)

Tom McKinney owns and operates McK's Home Electronics. He has a store where he sells and repairs televisions and stereo equipment. A completed worksheet for 20-1 is provided on the next page. McKinney made a $20,000 additional investment during 20-1. The current portion of Mortgage Payable is $1,000. Credit sales for 20-1 were $200,000, and the balance of Accounts Receivable on January 1 was $26,000.

REQUIRED

1. Prepare a multiple-step income statement.
2. Prepare a statement of owner's equity.
3. Prepare a balance sheet.
4. Compute the following measures of performance and financial condition for 20-1:
   a. current ratio,
   b. quick ratio,
   c. working capital,
   d. return on owner's equity,
   e. accounts receivable turnover and the average number of days required to collect receivables, and
   f. inventory turnover and the average number of days required to sell inventory.
5. Prepare adjusting entries and indicate which should be reversed and why.
6. Prepare closing entries.
7. Prepare reversing entries for the adjustments where appropriate.

McK's Home Electronics
Work Sheet
For Year Ended December 31, 20-1

	ACCOUNT TITLE	TRIAL BALANCE DEBIT	TRIAL BALANCE CREDIT	ADJUSTMENTS DEBIT	ADJUSTMENTS CREDIT	ADJUSTED TRIAL BALANCE DEBIT	ADJUSTED TRIAL BALANCE CREDIT	INCOME STATEMENT DEBIT	INCOME STATEMENT CREDIT	BALANCE SHEET DEBIT	BALANCE SHEET CREDIT	
1	Cash	10 000 00				10 000 00				10 000 00		1
2	Accounts Receivable	22 500 00				22 500 00				22 500 00		2
3	Merchandise Inventory	39 000 00		(b) 45 000 00	(a) 39 000 00	45 000 00				45 000 00		3
4	Supplies	2 700 00			(c) 2 100 00	600 00				600 00		4
5	Prepaid Insurance	3 600 00			(d) 2 700 00	900 00				900 00		5
6	Land	15 000 00				15 000 00				15 000 00		6
7	Building	135 000 00				135 000 00				135 000 00		7
8	Accum. Depr.—Building		24 000 00		(e) 6 000 00		30 000 00				30 000 00	8
9	Store Equipment	75 000 00				75 000 00				75 000 00		9
10	Accum. Depr.—Store Equipment		22 500 00		(f) 4 500 00		27 000 00				27 000 00	10
11	Notes Payable		7 500 00				7 500 00				7 500 00	11
12	Accounts Payable		15 000 00				15 000 00				15 000 00	12
13	Wages Payable				(g) 675 00		675 00				675 00	13
14	Sales Tax Payable		2 250 00				2 250 00				2 250 00	14
15	Unearned Repair Fees		18 000 00	(h) 15 000 00			3 000 00				3 000 00	15
16	Mortgage Payable		45 000 00				45 000 00				45 000 00	16
17	Tom McKinney, Capital		151 600 00				151 600 00				151 600 00	17
18	Tom McKinney, Drawing	30 000 00				30 000 00				30 000 00		18
19	Income Summary			(a) 39 000 00	(b) 45 000 00	39 000 00	45 000 00	39 000 00	45 000 00			19
20	Sales		300 750 00				300 750 00		300 750 00			20
21	Sales Returns and Allowances	1 800 00				1 800 00		1 800 00				21
22	Repair Fees				(h) 15 000 00		15 000 00		15 000 00			22
23	Interest Revenue		1 350 00				1 350 00		1 350 00			23
24	Purchases	157 500 00				157 500 00		157 500 00				24
25	Purchases Returns and Allowances		1 200 00				1 200 00		1 200 00			25
26	Purchases Discounts		1 500 00				1 500 00		1 500 00			26
27	Freight-In	450 00				450 00		450 00				27
28	Wages Expense	63 000 00		(g) 675 00		63 675 00		63 675 00				28
29	Advertising Expense	3 750 00				3 750 00		3 750 00				29
30	Supplies Expense			(c) 2 100 00		2 100 00		2 100 00				30
31	Telephone Expense	5 250 00				5 250 00		5 250 00				31
32	Utilities Expense	18 000 00				18 000 00		18 000 00				32
33	Insurance Expense			(d) 2 700 00		2 700 00		2 700 00				33
34	Depr. Expense—Building			(e) 6 000 00		6 000 00		6 000 00				34
35	Depr. Expense—Store Equipment			(f) 4 500 00		4 500 00		4 500 00				35
36	Miscellaneous Expense	3 375 00				3 375 00		3 375 00				36
37	Interest Expense	4 725 00				4 725 00		4 725 00				37
38		590 650 00	590 650 00	114 975 00	114 975 00	646 825 00	646 825 00	312 825 00	364 800 00	334 000 00	282 025 00	38
39	Net Income							51 975 00			51 975 00	39
40								364 800 00	364 800 00	334 000 00	334 000 00	40

In the Chapter 15 Demonstration Problem, you will enter the adjusting entries and display the financial statements for a merchandising business. After the financial statements have been prepared, you will close out the accounting period, and enter the reversing entries.

STEP 1: **Open the data file for the Chapter 15 Demonstration Problem.**

STEP 2: **Enter the adjusting entries from the worksheet illustrated in the problem. Use the worksheet letters (a), (b), etc., as the reference for the adjusting general journal entries.**

STEP 3: **Display the General Journal Entries with Titles Report.**

STEP 4: **Display a Trial Balance Report.**

STEP 5: **Display the financial statements: Basic Income Statement, Owner's Equity Statement, and Balance Sheet.**

STEP 6: **Close out the accounting period by changing the accounting period to be "January 1, 2001, to January 31, 2001." To change the accounting period, select the System option from the Tasks menu and then choose the Change Accounting Period submenu option.**

STEP 7: **Display a Post-Closing Trial Balance Report.**

STEP 8: **Enter the reversing entries.**

STEP 9: **Display the General Journal Entries with Titles Report to display the reversing entries.**

See the solution section of this workbook for the solution to the demonstration problem.

PROBLEM 15A1

Ellis Fabric Store shows the following trial balance as of December 31, 20--.

At the end of the year, the following adjustments need to be made:

(a, b) Merchandise Inventory as of December 31, $28,900.

(c) Unused supplies on hand, $1,350.

(d) Insurance expired, $300.

(e) Depreciation expense for the year, $500.

(f) Wages earned but not paid (Wages Payable), $480.

REQUIRED
1. Prepare a worksheet.
2. Prepare adjusting entries.
3. Prepare closing entries.
4. Prepare a post-closing trial balance.
5. Prepare reversing entries.

Ellis Fabric Store
Trial Balance
For Year Ended December 31, 20 - -

ACCOUNT TITLE	ACCOUNT NO.	DEBIT BALANCE	CREDIT BALANCE
Cash		28,000.00	
Accounts Receivable		14,200.00	
Merchandise Inventory		33,000.00	
Supplies		1,600.00	
Prepaid Insurance		900.00	
Equipment		6,600.00	
Accumulated Depreciation—Equipment			1,000.00
Accounts Payable			16,620.00
Wages Payable			
Sales Tax Payable			850.00
W. P. Ellis, Capital			71,200.00
W. P. Ellis, Drawing		21,610.00	
Income Summary			
Sales			78,500.00
Sales Returns and Allowances		1,850.00	
Interest Revenue			1,200.00
Purchases		41,500.00	
Purchases Returns and Allowances			1,800.00
Purchases Discounts			830.00
Freight-In		660.00	
Wages Expense		14,880.00	
Advertising Expense		810.00	
Supplies Expense			
Telephone Expense		1,210.00	
Utilities Expense		3,240.00	
Insurance Expense			
Depreciation Expense—Equipment			
Miscellaneous Expense		920.00	
Interest Expense		1,020.00	
		172,000.00	172,000.00

In Problem 15A1, you will enter the adjusting entries and display the financial statements for a merchandising business. After the financial statements have been prepared, you will close out the accounting period and enter the reversing entries.

STEP 1: **Open the data file for Problem 15A1.**

STEP 2: **Enter the adjusting entries for this problem. Use the worksheet letters (a), (b), etc., as the reference for the adjusting general journal entries.**

STEP 3: **Display the General Journal Entries with Titles Report.**

STEP 4: **Display a Trial Balance Report.**

STEP 5: **Display the financial statements: Basic Income Statement, Owner's Equity Statement, and Balance Sheet.**

STEP 6: **Close out the accounting period by changing the accounting period to be "January 1, 2001, to January 31, 2001."**

STEP 7: **Display a Post-Closing Trial Balance Report.**

STEP 8: **Enter the reversing entries.**

STEP 9: **Display the General Journal Entries with Titles Report to display the reversing entries.**

PROBLEM 15B1

The trial balance for Darby Kite Store as of December 31, 20-- is shown on the next page.

At the end of the year, the following adjustments need to be made:

(a, b) Merchandise inventory as of December 31, $23,600.

(c) Unused supplies on hand, $1,050.

(d) Insurance expired, $250.

(e) Depreciation expense for the year, $400.

(f) Wages earned but not paid (Wages Payable), $360.

REQUIRED

1. Prepare a worksheet.
2. Prepare adjusting entries.
3. Prepare closing entries.
4. Prepare a post-closing trial balance.
5. Prepare reversing entries.

Darby Kite Store
Trial Balance
For Year Ended December 31, 20 - -

ACCOUNT TITLE	ACCOUNT NO.	DEBIT BALANCE		CREDIT BALANCE	
Cash		11,700	00		
Accounts Receivable		11,200	00		
Merchandise Inventory		25,000	00		
Supplies		1,200	00		
Prepaid Insurance		800	00		
Equipment		5,400	00		
Accumulated Depreciation—Equipment				800	00
Accounts Payable				7,600	00
Wages Payable					
Sales Tax Payable				250	00
M. D. Akins, Capital				50,000	00
M. D. Akins, Drawing		10,500	00		
Income Summary					
Sales				57,990	00
Sales Returns and Allowances		1,450	00		
Purchases		34,500	00		
Purchases Returns and Allowances				1,100	00
Purchases Discounts				630	00
Freight-In		360	00		
Wages Expense		10,880	00		
Advertising Expense		740	00		
Supplies Expense					
Telephone Expense		1,100	00		
Utilities Expense		2,300	00		
Insurance Expense					
Depreciation Expense—Equipment					
Miscellaneous Expense		320	00		
Interest Expense		920	00		
		118,370	00	118,370	00

In Problem 15B1, you will enter the adjusting entries and display the financial statements for a merchandising business. After the financial statements have been prepared, you will close out the accounting period, and enter the reversing entries.

STEP 1: **Open the data file for the Problem 15B1.**

STEP 2: **Enter the adjusting entries for this problem. Use the worksheet letters (a), (b), etc., as the reference for the adjusting general journal entries.**

STEP 3: **Display the General Journal Entries with Titles Report.**

STEP 4: **Display a Trial Balance Report.**

STEP 5: **Display the financial statements: Basic Income Statement, Owner's Equity Statement, and Balance Sheet.**

STEP 6: **Close out the accounting period by changing the accounting period to be "January 1, 2001, to January 31, 2001."**

STEP 7: **Display a Post-Closing Trial Balance Report.**

STEP 8: **Enter the reversing entries.**

STEP 9: **Display the General Journal Entries with Titles Report to display the reversing entries.**

CHAPTER 15 MASTERY PROBLEM

Dominique Fouque owns and operates Dominique's Doll House. She has a small shop in which she sells new and antique dolls. She is particularly well known for her collection of antique Ken and Barbie dolls. A completed worksheet for 20-3 is shown on the next page. Fouque made no additional investments during the year, and the long-term note payable is due in 20-9. No portion of the long-term note is due within the next year. Net credit sales for 20-3 were $35,300 and receivables on January 1 were $2,500.

REQUIRED

1. Prepare a multiple-step income statement.
2. Prepare a statement of owner's equity.
3. Prepare a balance sheet.
4. Compute the following measures of performance and financial condition for 20-3:
    a. current ratio,
    b. quick ratio,
    c. working capital,
    d. return on owner's equity,
    e. accounts receivable turnover and average number of days required to collect receivables, and
    f. inventory turnover and the average number of days required to sell inventory.
5. Prepare adjusting entries, and indicate which should be reversed and why.
6. Prepare closing entries.
7. Prepare reversing entries for the adjustments where appropriate.

Dominique's Doll House
Work Sheet
For Year Ended December 31, 20 -3

	ACCOUNT TITLE	TRIAL BALANCE		ADJUSTMENTS		ADJUSTED TRIAL BALANCE		INCOME STATEMENT		BALANCE SHEET		
		DEBIT	CREDIT	DEBIT	CREDIT	DEBIT	CREDIT	DEBIT	CREDIT	DEBIT	CREDIT	
1	Cash	5,200.00				5,200.00				5,200.00		1
2	Accounts Receivable	3,200.00				3,200.00				3,200.00		2
3	Merchandise Inventory	22,300.00		(b) 24,600.00	(a) 22,300.00	24,600.00				24,600.00		3
4	Office Supplies	800.00			(c) 600.00	200.00				200.00		4
5	Prepaid Insurance	1,200.00			(d) 400.00	800.00				800.00		5
6	Store Equipment	85,000.00				85,000.00				85,000.00		6
7	Accum. Depr.—Store Equipment		15,000.00		(e) 5,000.00		20,000.00				20,000.00	7
8	Notes Payable		6,000.00				6,000.00				6,000.00	8
9	Accounts Payable		5,500.00				5,500.00				5,500.00	9
10	Wages Payable				(g) 200.00		200.00				200.00	10
11	Sales Tax Payable		850.00				850.00				850.00	11
12	Unearned Rent Revenue		1,000.00	(f) 700.00			300.00				300.00	12
13	Long-Term Note Payable		10,000.00				10,000.00				10,000.00	13
14	Dominique Fouque, Capital		75,800.00				75,800.00				75,800.00	14
15	Dominique Fouque, Drawing	21,000.00				21,000.00				21,000.00		15
16	Income Summary			(a) 22,300.00	(b) 24,600.00	22,300.00	24,600.00	22,300.00	24,600.00			16
17	Sales		130,500.00				130,500.00		130,500.00			17
18	Sales Returns and Allowances	900.00				900.00		900.00				18
19	Rent Revenue		25,000.00		(f) 700.00		25,700.00		25,700.00			19
20	Purchases	72,000.00				72,000.00		72,000.00				20
21	Purchases Discounts		750.00				750.00		750.00			21
22	Freight-In	1,200.00				1,200.00		1,200.00				22
23	Wages Expense	42,000.00		(g) 200.00		42,200.00		42,200.00				23
24	Rent Expense	6,000.00				6,000.00		6,000.00				24
25	Office Supplies Expense			(c) 600.00		600.00		600.00				25
26	Telephone Expense	1,500.00				1,500.00		1,500.00				26
27	Utilities Expense	7,600.00				7,600.00		7,600.00				27
28	Insurance Expense			(d) 400.00		400.00		400.00				28
29	Depr. Expense—Store Equipment			(e) 5,000.00		5,000.00		5,000.00				29
30	Interest Expense	500.00				500.00		500.00				30
31		270,400.00	270,400.00	53,800.00	53,800.00	300,200.00	300,200.00	160,200.00	181,550.00	140,000.00	118,650.00	31
32	Net Income							21,350.00			21,350.00	32
33								181,550.00	181,550.00	140,000.00	140,000.00	33

In the Chapter 15 Mastery Problem, you will enter the adjusting entries and display the financial statements for a merchandising business. After the financial statements have been prepared, you will close out the accounting period and enter the reversing entries.

STEP 1: **Open the data file for the Chapter 15 Mastery Problem.**

STEP 2: **Enter the adjusting entries from the worksheet illustrated in the problem. Use the worksheet letters (a), (b), etc., as the reference for the adjusting general journal entries.**

STEP 3: **Display the General Journal Entries with Titles Report.**

STEP 4: **Display a Trial Balance Report.**

STEP 5: **Display the financial statements: Basic Income Statement, Owner's Equity Statement, and Balance Sheet.**

STEP 6: **Close out the accounting period by changing the accounting period to be "January 1, 2001, to January 31, 2001."**

STEP 7: **Display a Post-Closing Trial Balance Report.**

STEP 8: **Enter the reversing entries.**

STEP 9: **Display the General Journal Entries with Titles Report to display the reversing entries.**

SECTION 3

Setting Up a New Company

This section describes the process of setting up a new company. The process is very different depending on whether or not you have access to a CD-ROM drive.

COMPLETING NEW COMPANY SETUP WITH A CD-ROM

If you have a CD-ROM drive, you can run New Company Setup using the Peachtree Accounting CD-ROM, which provides a guided tour of the setup process and explains how your selections will affect the company you set up. Follow the steps below to complete the setup process:

- ▶ **Insert the Peachtree Accounting CD-ROM disk into the CD-ROM drive.**
- ▶ **From the File menu, choose the New Company option (or choose the Set up button from the Startup screen).**
- ▶ **An animated character will appear providing detailed step-by-step instructions for completing the setup.**
- ▶ **At various points in the presentation, you will be directed to enter specific company information.**
- ▶ **Click on the Help button or press the F1 key if you need additional help with a particular topic at any point within the setup.**
- ▶ **Once the company files are created, follow the instructions in the Setup Checklist section under Completing New Company Setup without a CD-ROM.**

COMPLETING NEW COMPANY SETUP WITHOUT A CD-ROM

If you do not have a CD-ROM drive or you do not wish to use the CD-ROM method, follow the step-by-step instructions below to complete a company setup.

- ▶ **From the File menu, choose the New Company option (or choose the Set up button from the Startup Screen).**
- ▶ **If you have a CD-ROM drive but aren't using the Peachtree CD to complete setup, you will get the message telling you to insert the Peachtree Accounting CD. Click Ok to continue.**
- ▶ **When the message asking if you would like to run the text only version of Setup appears, click on the Text Setup button.**
- ▶ **A welcome screen will appear, providing additional instructions. Click on the Next button in the upper right corner to proceed.**
- ▶ **As each data entry window appears, it will be accompanied by a full explanation of the data to be keyed. Follow these on-screen instructions and key the required setup data. Click Next to proceed to each new screen.**

  When the process is completed, a dialog will appear asking if you wish to create the files or go back and make changes to setup data. Click on the Create button to create the files and return to Peachtree Accounting. Click on Go Back to make corrections.

SETUP CHECKLIST

- **The Setup Checklist window will appear. To complete setup, click on each applicable option in the Setup Checklist and enter the appropriate data. Each of the Setup Checklist options is described in the following sections. As each data entry window appears, click on the Help button (or press F1) for a complete description of how to enter the data for that particular window. You do not have to complete the entire setup process in one session. You can return to the setup checklist at any time by choosing the Setup Checklist option from the Maintain menu.**

GENERAL LEDGER CHECKLIST

- **Enter general ledger default settings.** This option lets you set up an account to be used by customized financials that use rounding. In most cases, you will leave it blank.
- **Enter general ledger chart of accounts.** This window is used to set up an Account ID, Description and Account Type (Cash, Accounts Payable, Retained Earnings, etc.). You can also enter budget amounts for each accounting period, and copy the budget amounts into the next year. Click on the Help button for a detailed explanation of the various data fields.
- **Enter general ledger account beginning balances.** This screen allows you to select an account and enter the starting balance for that account.

ACCOUNTS PAYABLE CHECKLIST

- **Enter vendor default settings.** In this window, you set up default information for payment terms, account aging, and custom field labels. In most cases, the account aging and custom fields may be omitted. Again, remember to click on the Help button for detailed information about entering the data.
- **Enter vendor records.** In this window, enter the basic information about vendors, including address, the contact person, the terms of sale, and the tax authority for sales tax.
- **Enter vendor beginning balances.** In this window, enter the beginning balances for the vendors.

ACCOUNTS RECEIVABLE CHECKLIST

- **Enter customer default settings.** This data entry window allows you to set up default settings for terms of sale by customer, finance charges, account aging, custom fields, and payment types.
- **Enter statement/invoice default settings.** Enter the statement and invoice print options and dunning messages.

- **Enter customer records.** In this data entry window, you enter customer name and address information, including ship-to address (if different from regular address) and a Type code to use in categorizing customers. You can specify a general ledger account to use for sales to the customer, and a sales tax code, as well as terms of sale for each customer.
- **Enter customer beginning balances.** In this window, enter open invoices by customer. Optionally, you can simply enter the current balance with an invoice number of "Balance."
- **Enter employee default settings.** This window allows you to establish the unemployment percentage for your company, the state and locality you are in, and whether you deduct for 401K, Meals, or Tips. You can also set up default information for general employee information, pay levels, employee fields, employer fields, and custom field types. You can also enter the default cash account for payroll, define additional payroll fields, and assign fields for the W-2 forms.
- **Enter employee records.** In this screen, enter basic employee information including address, phone number, social security number, filing statuses, and pay information. Remember that you can press F1 or click on the Help button at any time to receive detailed information about a particular data entry window.
- **Enter employee year-to-date earnings and withholdings.** Enter year-to-date earnings and withholding amounts for up to 52 payroll periods.

INVENTORY CHECKLIST

- **Enter inventory default settings.** Enter the defaults for custom field types, item tax type, and ship methods.
- **Enter inventory items and assemblies.** In this window, enter your inventory account numbers—sales, merchandise inventory, and purchases. You may also enter the preferred vendor for each item and create a bill of materials for inventory items tracked as assembled items.
- **Enter the inventory.**
- **Enter inventory beginning quantities.** Enter the beginning quantities, unit costs, and total cost for each of the inventory items.

JOBS CHECKLIST

- **Enter jobs default settings.** This window allows you to set up labels for the customer fields to be used when entering jobs for the job costing system.
- **Enter jobs.** In this window, you can set up jobs and enter the customer, start date, and ending date.
- **Enter job beginning balances.** Enter the beginning balances for jobs. Enter the amount as a negative if it represents revenue.

SECTION 4

Demonstration Problem Solutions

Chapter 2 Demonstration Problem Solution

02-Demo Home and Away Inspections
Chart of Accounts
As of Dec 31, 2000
Filter Criteria includes: Report order is by ID. Report is printed with Accounts having Zero Amounts and in Detail Format.

Account ID	Account Description	Activ	Account Type
101	Cash	Yes	Cash
102	Accounts Receivable	Yes	Accounts Receivable
103	Supplies	Yes	Other Current Assets
104	Prepaid Insurance	Yes	Other Current Assets
105	Tools	Yes	Fixed Assets
106	Truck	Yes	Fixed Assets
201	Accounts Payable	Yes	Accounts Payable
300	Beginning Balance Equity	Yes	Equity-doesn't close
301	Damon Young, Capital	Yes	Equity-Retained Earnings
303	Damon Young, Drawing	Yes	Equity-gets closed
401	Inspection Fees	Yes	Income
501	Wages Expense	Yes	Expenses
503	Rent Expense	Yes	Expenses
505	Telephone Expense	Yes	Expenses
507	Utilities Expense	Yes	Expenses

02-Demo Home and Away Inspections
Balance Sheet
December 31, 2000

ASSETS

Assets				
Cash	$	7,665.00		
Accounts Receivable		1,300.00		
Supplies		300.00		
Prepaid Insurance		600.00		
Tools		3,000.00		
Truck		8,000.00		
Total Assets			$	20,865.00

LIABILITIES AND CAPITAL

Liabilities				
Accounts Payable	$	2,200.00		
Total Liabilities				2,200.00
Capital				
Damon Young, Capital		15,000.00		
Damon Young, Drawing		<500.00>		
Net Income		4,165.00		
Total Capital				18,665.00
Total Liabilities & Capital			$	20,865.00

02-Demo Home and Away Inspections
Income Statement
For the Month Ending December 31, 2000

		Year to Date
Revenues		
Inspection Fees	$	5,000.00
Total Revenues		5,000.00
Expenses		
Wages Expense		450.00
Rent Expense		300.00
Telephone Expense		35.00
Utilities Expense		50.00
Total Expenses		835.00
Net Income	$	4,165.00

02-Demo Home and Away Inspections
Statement of Owner's Equity
December 31, 2000

Capital, Beginning of Period			15,000.00
Net Income for the Period	4,165.00		
Less Withdrawals for Period	500.00		
Increase in Capital			3,665.00
Capital, End of Period		$	18,665.00

Chapter 3 Demonstration Problem Solution

03-Demo We-Buy, You-Pay Shopping Serv.
Balance Sheet
December 31, 2000

ASSETS

Assets		
Cash	$ 20,010.00	
Accounts Receivable	8,400.00	
Office Equipment	10,000.00	
Computer Equipment	4,800.00	
Total Assets		$ 43,210.00

LIABILITIES AND CAPITAL

Liabilities		
Accounts Payable	$ 6,000.00	
Notes Payable	4,000.00	
Total Liabilities		10,000.00
Capital		
Celia Pints, Capital	33,210.00	
Net Income	0.00	
Total Capital		33,210.00
Total Liabilities & Capital		$ 43,210.00

03-Demo We-Buy, You-Pay Shopping Serv.
Income Statement
For the Month Ending December 31, 2000

		Year to Date
Revenues		
Shopping Fees	$	18,400.00
Total Revenues		18,400.00
Expenses		
Rent Expense		500.00
Telephone Expense		90.00
Commissions Expense		10,500.00
Utilities Expense		600.00
Travel Expense		1,500.00
Total Expenses		13,190.00
Net Income	$	5,210.00

03-Demo We-Buy, You-Pay Shopping Serv.
Statement of Owner's Equity
December 31, 2000

Capital, Beginning of Period			30,000.00
Net Income for the Period	5,210.00		
Less Withdrawals for Period	2,000.00		
Increase in Capital			3,210.00
Capital, End of Period		$	33,210.00

Chapter 4 Demonstration Problem Solution

Page: 1

04-Demo George Fielding Fin. Conslt.

General Journal

For the Period From Dec 1, 2000 to Dec 31, 2000

Date	Account ID	Reference	Trans Description	Account Description	Debit Amt	Credit Amt
12/1/00	101		Owner's original investment	Cash	20,000.00	
	311		Owner's original investment	George Fielding, Capital		20,000.00
12/3/00	521		Paid rent for December	Rent Expense	1,000.00	
	101		Paid rent for December	Cash		1,000.00
12/4/00	101		Received cash for services	Cash	2,500.00	
	401		Received cash for services	Professional Fees		2,500.00
12/6/00	533		Paid utilities	Utilities Expense	75.00	
	101		Paid utilities	Cash		75.00
12/7/00	101		Received cash for services	Cash	2,000.00	
	401		Received cash for services	Professional Fees		2,000.00
12/12/00	538		Paid for gas and oil	Automobile Expense	60.00	
	101		Paid for gas and oil	Cash		60.00
12/14/00	511		Paid temporary secretaries	Wages Expense	600.00	
	101		Paid temporary secretaries	Cash		600.00
12/17/00	142		Purchases office supplies on accou	Office Supplies	280.00	
	202		Purchases office supplies on accou	Accounts Payable		280.00
12/20/00	525		Paid telephone bill	Telephone Expense	100.00	
	101		Paid telephone bill	Cash		100.00
12/21/00	312		Owner's withdrawal	George Fielding, Drawing	1,100.00	
	101		Owner's withdrawal	Cash		1,100.00
12/24/00	534		Contribution to National Multiple	Charitable Contribution Exp.	100.00	
	101		Contribution to National Multiple	Cash		100.00
12/27/00	101		Received cash for services rendere	Cash	2,000.00	
	401		Received cash for services rendere	Professional Fees		2,000.00
12/28/00	511		Paid temporary secretaries	Wages Expense	600.00	
	101		Paid temporary secretaries	Cash		600.00
12/29/00	202		Payment on account to Bowers Off	Accounts Payable	100.00	
	101		Payment on account to Bowers Off	Cash		100.00
		Total			**30,515.00**	**30,515.00**

04-Demo George Fielding Fin. Conslt.

General Ledger Trial Balance

As of Dec 31, 2000

Filter Criteria includes: Report order is by ID. Report is printed in Detail Format.

Account ID	Account Description	Debit Amt	Credit Amt
101	Cash	22,765.00	
142	Office Supplies	280.00	
202	Accounts Payable		180.00
311	George Fielding, Capital		20,000.00
312	George Fielding, Drawing	1,100.00	
401	Professional Fees		6,500.00
511	Wages Expense	1,200.00	
521	Rent Expense	1,000.00	
525	Telephone Expense	100.00	
533	Utilities Expense	75.00	
534	Charitable Contribution Exp	100.00	
538	Automobile Expense	60.00	
	Total:	**26,680.00**	**26,680.00**

04-Demo George Fielding Fin. Conslt.

General Ledger

For the Period From Dec 1, 2000 to Dec 31, 2000

Filter Criteria includes: Report order is by ID. Report is printed in Detail Format.

Account ID Account Description	Date Reference	Jrnl	Trans Description	Debit Amt	Credit Amt	Balance
101 Cash	12/1/00		Beginning Balance			
	12/1/00	GENJ	Owner's original investment	20,000.00		
	12/3/00	GENJ	Paid rent for December		1,000.00	
	12/4/00	GENJ	Received cash for services	2,500.00		
	12/6/00	GENJ	Paid utilities		75.00	
	12/7/00	GENJ	Received cash for services	2,000.00		
	12/12/00	GENJ	Paid for gas and oil		60.00	
	12/14/00	GENJ	Paid temporary secretaries		600.00	
	12/20/00	GENJ	Paid telephone bill		100.00	
	12/21/00	GENJ	Owner's withdrawal		1,100.00	
	12/24/00	GENJ	Contribution to National Multiple Sclerosis Society		100.00	
	12/27/00	GENJ	Received cash for services rendered	2,000.00		
	12/28/00	GENJ	Paid temporary secretaries		600.00	
	12/29/00	GENJ	Payment on account to Bowers Office Supply		100.00	
			Current Period Change	26,500.00	3,735.00	22,765.00
	12/31/00		**Ending Balance**			**22,765.00**
142 Office Supplies	12/1/00		Beginning Balance			
	12/17/00	GENJ	Purchases office supplies on account from Bowers Office Supply	280.00		
			Current Period Change	280.00		280.00
	12/31/00		**Ending Balance**			**280.00**
202 Accounts Payable	12/1/00		Beginning Balance			
	12/17/00	GENJ	Purchases office supplies on account from Bowers Office Supply		280.00	
	12/29/00	GENJ	Payment on account to Bowers Office Supply	100.00		
			Current Period Change	100.00	280.00	-180.00
	12/31/00		**Ending Balance**			**-180.00**
311 George Fielding, Capital	12/1/00		Beginning Balance			
	12/1/00	GENJ	Owner's original investment		20,000.00	

04-Demo George Fielding Fin. Conslt.

General Ledger

For the Period From Dec 1, 2000 to Dec 31, 2000

Filter Criteria includes: Report order is by ID. Report is printed in Detail Format.

Account ID Account Description	Date Reference	Jrnl	Trans Description	Debit Amt	Credit Amt	Balance
			Current Period Change		20,000.00	-20,000.00
	12/31/00		**Ending Balance**			**-20,000.00**
312 George Fielding, Drawing	12/1/00		Beginning Balance			
	12/21/00	GENJ	Owner's withdrawal	1,100.00		
			Current Period Change	1,100.00		1,100.00
	12/31/00		**Ending Balance**			**1,100.00**
401 Professional Fees	12/1/00		Beginning Balance			
	12/4/00	GENJ	Received cash for services		2,500.00	
	12/7/00	GENJ	Received cash for services		2,000.00	
	12/27/00	GENJ	Received cash for services rendered		2,000.00	
			Current Period Change		6,500.00	-6,500.00
	12/31/00		**Ending Balance**			**-6,500.00**
511 Wages Expense	12/1/00		Beginning Balance			
	12/14/00	GENJ	Paid temporary secretaries	600.00		
	12/28/00	GENJ	Paid temporary secretaries	600.00		
			Current Period Change	1,200.00		1,200.00
	12/31/00		**Ending Balance**			**1,200.00**
521 Rent Expense	12/1/00		Beginning Balance			
	12/3/00	GENJ	Paid rent for December	1,000.00		
			Current Period Change	1,000.00		1,000.00
	12/31/00		**Ending Balance**			**1,000.00**
525 Telephone Expense	12/1/00		Beginning Balance			
	12/20/00	GENJ	Paid telephone bill	100.00		
			Current Period Change	100.00		100.00
	12/31/00		**Ending Balance**			**100.00**

04-Demo George Fielding Fin. Conslt.

General Ledger

For the Period From Dec 1, 2000 to Dec 31, 2000

Filter Criteria includes: Report order is by ID. Report is printed in Detail Format.

Account ID Account Description	Date Reference	Jrnl	Trans Description	Debit Amt	Credit Amt	Balance
533 Utilities Expense	12/1/00		Beginning Balance			
	12/6/00	GENJ	Paid utilities	75.00		
			Current Period Change	75.00		75.00
	12/31/00		**Ending Balance**			**75.00**
534 Charitable Contribution Ex	12/1/00		Beginning Balance			
	12/24/00	GENJ	Contribution to National Multiple Sclerosis Society	100.00		
			Current Period Change	100.00		100.00
	12/31/00		**Ending Balance**			**100.00**
538 Automobile Expense	12/1/00		Beginning Balance			
	12/12/00	GENJ	Paid for gas and oil	60.00		
			Current Period Change	60.00		60.00
	12/31/00		**Ending Balance**			**60.00**

Chapter 5 Demonstration Problem Solution

Page: 1

05-Demo Justin Park Legal Services

General Journal

For the Period From Dec 1, 2000 to Dec 31, 2000

Date	Account ID	Reference	Trans Description	Account Description	Debit Amt	Credit Amt
12/31/00	523		Adjusting Entry	Office Supplies Expense	500.00	
	142		Adjusting Entry	Office Supplies		500.00
	541		Adjusting Entry	Depr. Expense--Office Equip.	3,000.00	
	181.1		Adjusting Entry	Accum. Depr.--Office Equipment		3,000.00
	542		Adjusting Entry	Depr. Expense--Computer Equip.	1,000.00	
	187.1		Adjusting Entry	Accum. Depr.--Computer Equip.		1,000.00
	535		Adjusting Entry	Insurance Expense	100.00	
	145		Adjusting Entry	Prepaid Insurance		100.00
	511		Adjusting Entry	Wages Expense	300.00	
	219		Adjusting Entry	Wages Payable		300.00
		Total			**4,900.00**	**4,900.00**

Page: 1

05-Demo Justin Park Legal Services

Income Statement

For the Twelve Months Ending December 31, 2000

	Year to Date
Revenues	
Client Fees	$ 40,000.00
Total Revenues	40,000.00
Expenses	
Wages Expense	12,300.00
Rent Expense	5,000.00
Office Supplies Expense	500.00
Telephone Expense	1,000.00
Utilities Expense	3,900.00
Insurance Expense	100.00
Depr. Expense--Office Equip.	3,000.00
Depr. Expense--Computer Equip.	1,000.00
Total Expenses	26,800.00
Net Income	$ 13,200.00

05-Demo Justin Park Legal Services
Statement of Owner's Equity
December 31, 2000

Capital, Beginning of Period		11,400.00
Net Income for the Period	13,200.00	
Less Withdrawals for Period	5,000.00	
Increase in Capital		8,200.00
Capital, End of Period		$ 19,600.00

05-Demo Justin Park Legal Services
Balance Sheet
December 31, 2000

ASSETS

Assets		
Cash	$ 7,000.00	
Office Supplies	300.00	
Prepaid Insurance	1,100.00	
Office Equipment	15,000.00	
Accum. Depr.--Office Equipment	<3,000.00>	
Computer Equipment	6,000.00	
Accum. Depr.--Computer Equip.	<1,000.00>	
Total Assets		$ 25,400.00

LIABILITIES AND CAPITAL

Liabilities		
Notes Payable	$ 5,000.00	
Accounts Payable	500.00	
Wages Payable	300.00	
Total Liabilities		5,800.00
Capital		
Justin Park, Capital	11,400.00	
Justin Park, Drawing	<5,000.00>	
Net Income	13,200.00	
Total Capital		19,600.00
Total Liabilities & Capital		$ 25,400.00

Chapter 6 Demonstration Problem Solution

Page: 1

06-Demo Hard Copy Printers

General Journal

For the Period From Dec 1, 2000 to Dec 31, 2000

Date	Account ID	Reference	Trans Description	Account Description	Debit Amt	Credit Amt
12/31/00	543		Adjusting Entry	Paper Supplies Expense	3,550.00	
	151		Adjusting Entry	Paper Supplies		3,550.00
	547		Adjusting Entry	Insurance Expense	505.00	
	155		Adjusting Entry	Prepaid Insurance		505.00
	541		Adjusting Entry	Wages Expense	30.00	
	219		Adjusting Entry	Wages Payable		30.00
	546		Adjusting Entry	Depr. Exp.--Printing Equipment	1,200.00	
	185.1		Adjusting Entry	Accum. Depr.--Printing Equip.		1,200.00
		Total			5,285.00	5,285.00

Page: 1

06-Demo Hard Copy Printers

General Ledger Trial Balance

As of Dec 31, 2000

Filter Criteria includes: Report order is by ID. Report is printed in Detail Format.

Account ID	Account Description	Debit Amt	Credit Amt
111	Cash	1,180.00	
151	Paper Supplies	50.00	
155	Prepaid Insurance	495.00	
185	Printing Equipment	5,800.00	
185.1	Accum. Depr.--Printing Equ		1,200.00
211	Accounts Payable		500.00
219	Wages Payable		30.00
311	Timothy Chang, Capital		10,000.00
312	Timothy Chang, Drawing	13,000.00	
411	Printing Fees		35,100.00
541	Wages Expense	12,000.00	
542	Rent Expense	7,500.00	
543	Paper Supplies Expense	3,550.00	
544	Telephone Expense	550.00	
545	Utilities Expense	1,000.00	
546	Depr. Exp.--Printing Equip	1,200.00	
547	Insurance Expense	505.00	
	Total:	46,830.00	46,830.00

06-Demo Hard Copy Printers
Statement of Owner's Equity
December 31, 2000

Capital, Beginning of Period			10,000.00
Net Income for the Period	8,795.00		
Less Withdrawals for Period	13,000.00		
Increase in Capital			<4,205.00>
Capital, End of Period		$	5,795.00

06-Demo Hard Copy Printers
Balance Sheet
December 31, 2000

ASSETS

Assets				
Cash	$	1,180.00		
Paper Supplies		50.00		
Prepaid Insurance		495.00		
Printing Equipment		5,800.00		
Accum. Depr.--Printing Equip.		<1,200.00>		
Total Assets			$	6,325.00

LIABILITIES AND CAPITAL

Liabilities				
Accounts Payable	$	500.00		
Wages Payable		30.00		
Total Liabilities				530.00
Capital				
Timothy Chang, Capital		10,000.00		
Timothy Chang, Drawing		<13,000.00>		
Net Income		8,795.00		
Total Capital				5,795.00
Total Liabilities & Capital			$	6,325.00

06-Demo Hard Copy Printers
Income Statement
For the Month Ended December 31, 2000

Revenues		
Printing Fees	$	35,100.00
Total Revenues		35,100.00
Expenses		
Wages Expense		12,000.00
Rent Expense		7,500.00
Paper Supplies Expense		3,550.00
Telephone Expense		550.00
Utilities Expense		1,000.00
Depr. Exp.--Printing Equipment		1,200.00
Insurance Expense		505.00
Total Expenses		26,305.00
Net Income	$	8,795.00

06-Demo Hard Copy Printers
General Ledger Trial Balance
As of Jan 31, 2001

Filter Criteria includes: Report order is by ID. Report is printed in Detail Format.

Account ID	Account Description	Debit Amt	Credit Amt
111	Cash	1,180.00	
151	Paper Supplies	50.00	
155	Prepaid Insurance	495.00	
185	Printing Equipment	5,800.00	
185.1	Accum. Depr.--Printing Equ		1,200.00
211	Accounts Payable		500.00
219	Wages Payable		30.00
311	Timothy Chang, Capital		5,795.00
	Total:	**7,525.00**	**7,525.00**

Chapter 7 Demonstration Problem Solution

07-Demo Vietor Financial Planning

General Journal

For the Period From Dec 1, 2000 to Dec 31, 2000

Filter Criteria includes: Report order is by Date. Report is printed with Accounts having Zero Amounts and with Truncated Transaction Description Detail Format.

Date	Account ID	Reference	Trans Description	Account Description	Debit Amt	Credit Amt
12/1/00	101		Original investment by	Cash	20,000.00	
	311		Original investment by	Maria Vietor, Capital		20,000.00
12/3/00	521		Paid rent	Rent Expense	1,000.00	
	101		Paid rent	Cash		1,000.00
12/4/00	101		Fee for services	Cash	2,500.00	
	401		Fee for services	Professional Fees		2,500.00
12/6/00	533		Paid utilities	Utilities Expense	75.00	
	101		Paid utilities	Cash		75.00
12/7/00	101		Fee for services	Cash	2,000.00	
	401		Fee for services	Professional Fees		2,000.00
12/12/00	526		Gas & oil	Automobile Expense	60.00	
	101		Gas & oil	Cash		60.00
12/14/00	511		Secretarial services	Wages Expense	600.00	
	101		Secretarial services	Cash		600.00
12/17/00	142		Cleat Office Supply	Office Supplies	280.00	
	202		Cleat Office Supply	Accounts Payable		280.00
12/20/00	525		Long distance service	Telephone Expense	100.00	
	101		Long distance service	Cash		100.00
12/21/00	312		Owner withdrawal	Maria Vietor, Drawing	1,100.00	
	101		Owner withdrawal	Cash		1,100.00
12/24/00	534		National Multiple Scler	Charitable Contributions Exp.	100.00	
	101		National Multiple Scler	Cash		100.00
12/27/00	101		Fee for services	Cash	2,000.00	
	401		Fee for services	Professional Fees		2,000.00
12/28/00	511		Secretarial services	Wages Expense	600.00	
	101		Secretarial services	Cash		600.00
12/29/00	202		Cleat Office Supply	Accounts Payable	100.00	
	101		Cleat Office Supply	Cash		100.00
		Total			**30,515.00**	**30,515.00**

07-Demo Vietor Financial Planning

General Ledger Trial Balance

As of Dec 31, 2000

Filter Criteria includes: Report order is by ID. Report is printed in Detail Format.

Account ID	Account Description	Debit Amt	Credit Amt
101	Cash	22,765.00	
142	Office Supplies	280.00	
202	Accounts Payable		180.00
311	Maria Vietor, Capital		20,000.00
312	Maria Vietor, Drawing	1,100.00	
401	Professional Fees		6,500.00
511	Wages Expense	1,200.00	
521	Rent Expense	1,000.00	
525	Telephone Expense	100.00	
526	Automobile Expense	60.00	
533	Utilities Expense	75.00	
534	Charitable Contributions Ex	100.00	
	Total:	**26,680.00**	**26,680.00**

Chapter 8 Demonstration Problem Solution

Page: 1

08-Demo Kuhn's Wilderness Outfitters
Account Register
For the Period From Mar 1, 2000 to Mar 31, 2000
101 - Cash

Filter Criteria includes: Report order is by Date.

Date	Trans No	Type	Trans Desc	Deposit Amt	Withdrawal Amt	Balance
			Beginning Balance			4,870.57
3/31/00		Other	Bank service charge		4.10	4,866.47
3/31/00		Other	Error on check no. 456		54.00	4,812.47
3/31/00		Other	ATM withdrawal		100.00	4,712.47
3/31/00	477	Withdrawal	Petty Cash		197.45	4,515.02
			Total		**355.55**	

Page: 1

08-Demo Kuhn's Wilderness Outfitters
Account Reconciliation
As of Mar 31, 2000
101 - Cash
Bank Statement Date: March 31, 2000

Filter Criteria includes: Report is printed in Detail Format.

Beginning GL Balance				4,870.57
Add: Cash Receipts				
Less: Cash Disbursements				<197.45>
Add <Less> Other				<158.10>
Ending GL Balance				4,515.02
Ending Bank Balance				5,419.00
Add back deposits in transit				
	Feb 12, 2000	3/12/00	926.10	
Total deposits in transit				926.10
<Less> outstanding checks				
	Feb 1, 2000	462	<524.26>	
	Feb 5, 2000	465	<213.41>	
	Feb 22, 2000	473	<543.58>	
	Feb 22, 2000	476	<351.38>	
	Mar 31, 2000	477	<197.45>	
Total outstanding checks				<1,830.08>
Add <Less> Other				
Total other				
Unreconciled difference				0.00
Ending GL Balance				4,515.02

Chapter 9 Demonstration Problem Solution

Page: 1

09-Demo Canine Coiffures

Check Register

For the Period From Jan 15, 1998 to Jan 21, 1998

Filter Criteria includes: Report order is by Check Date. Report is printed in Detail Format.

Reference	Date	Employee	Amount
811	1/21/98	Katie DeNourie	408.11
812	1/21/98	Pete Garriott	360.12
813	1/21/98	Sheila Martinez	395.17
814	1/21/98	Nancy Parker	396.89
815	1/21/98	John Shapiro	340.68
		1/15/98 thru 1/21/98	1,900.97
		1/15/98 thru 1/21/98	1,900.97

09-Demo Canine Coiffures

Payroll Journal

For the Period From Jan 15, 1998 to Jan 31, 1998

Filter Criteria includes: Report order is by Check Date. Report is printed in Detail Format.

Date Employee	GL Acct ID	Reference	Debit Amt	Credit Amt
1/21/98	511	811	460.00	
Katie DeNourie	511		69.00	
	211			56.13
	212			32.80
	213			7.67
	215			5.29
	216			4.00
	217			15.00
	212			32.80
	213			7.67
	219			4.23
	219			21.69
	513		32.80	
	513		7.67	
	513		4.23	
	513		21.69	
	101			408.11
1/21/98	511	812	480.00	
Pete Garriott	211			45.61
	212			29.76
	213			6.96
	215			4.80
	216			14.00
	218			18.75
	212			29.76
	213			6.96
	219			3.84
	219			19.68
	513		29.76	
	513		6.96	
	513		3.84	
	513		19.68	
	101			360.12
1/21/98	511	813	487.50	
Sheila Martinez	211			31.15
	212			30.23
	213			7.07
	215			4.88
	216			4.00
	217			15.00
	212			30.23
	213			7.07
	219			3.90
	219			19.99
	513		30.23	
	513		7.07	
	513		3.90	
	513		19.99	
	101			395.17
1/21/98	511	814	440.00	
Nancy Parker	511		33.00	

09-Demo Canine Coiffures

Payroll Journal

For the Period From Jan 15, 1998 to Jan 31, 1998

Filter Criteria includes: Report order is by Check Date. Report is printed in Detail Format.

Date Employee	GL Acct ID	Reference	Debit Amt	Credit Amt
	211			21.19
	212			29.33
	213			6.86
	215			4.73
	216			14.00
	212			29.33
	213			6.86
	219			3.78
	219			19.39
	513		29.33	
	513		6.86	
	513		3.78	
	513		19.39	
	101			396.89
1/21/98	511	815	460.00	
John Shapiro	211			45.78
	212			28.52
	213			6.67
	215			4.60
	217			15.00
	218			18.75
	212			28.52
	213			6.67
	219			3.68
	219			18.86
	513		28.52	
	513		6.67	
	513		3.68	
	513		18.86	
	101			340.68
			2,734.41	**2,734.41**

09-Demo Canine Coiffures

Payroll Register

For the Period From Jan 15, 1998 to Jan 21, 1998

Filter Criteria includes: Report order is by Check Date. Report is printed in Detail Format.

Employee ID Employee SS No Reference Date	Pay Type	Pay Hrs	Pay Amt	Amount	Gross Local Soc_Sec_ER	Fed_Income Health Ins. Medicare_E	Soc_Sec Cred. Union FUTA_ER	Medicare Saving Bo SUI_ER
1	Regular	40.00	460.00	408.11	529.00	-56.13	-32.80	-7.67
Katie DeNourie	Overtime	4.00	69.00		-5.29	-4.00	-15.00	
436-44-2712					-32.80	-7.67	-4.23	-21.69
811								
1/21/98								
2	Regular	40.00	480.00	360.12	480.00	-45.61	-29.76	-6.96
Pete Garriott					-4.80	-14.00		-18.75
568-88-8722					-29.76	-6.96	-3.84	-19.68
812								
1/21/98								
3	Regular	39.00	487.50	395.17	487.50	-31.15	-30.23	-7.07
Sheila Martinez					-4.88	-4.00	-15.00	
455-73-3478					-30.23	-7.07	-3.90	-19.99
813								
1/21/98								
4	Regular	40.00	440.00	396.89	473.00	-21.19	-29.33	-6.86
Nancy Parker	Overtime	2.00	33.00		-4.73	-14.00		
423-28-2769					-29.33	-6.86	-3.78	-19.39
814								
1/21/98								
5	Regular	40.00	460.00	340.68	460.00	-45.78	-28.52	-6.67
John Shapiro					-4.60		-15.00	-18.75
877-228214					-28.52	-6.67	-3.68	-18.86
815								
1/21/98								
Summary Total	Regular	199.00	2,327.50	1,900.97	2,429.50	-199.86	-150.64	-35.23
1/15/98 thru 1/21/98	Overtime	6.00	102.00		-24.30	-36.00	-45.00	-37.50
					-150.64	-35.23	-19.43	-99.61
Report Date Final Total	Regular	199.00	2,327.50	1,900.97	2,429.50	-199.86	-150.64	-35.23
1/15/98 thru 1/21/98	Overtime	6.00	102.00		-24.30	-36.00	-45.00	-37.50
					-150.64	-35.23	-19.43	-99.61

Chapter 10 Demonstration Problem Solution

Page: 1

10-Demo Hart Company

General Journal

For the Period From Dec 1, 2000 to Dec 31, 2000

Filter Criteria includes: Report order is by Date. Report is printed with Accounts having Zero Amounts and with Truncated Transaction Descriptions and in Detail Format.

Date	Account ID	Reference	Trans Description	Account Description	Debit Amt	Credit Amt
12/31/00	511	1 (a)	Record Dec. 31 payroll	Wages and Salaries Expense	3,800.00	
	211		Record Dec. 31 payroll	Employee Income Tax Payable		380.00
	212		Record Dec. 31 payroll	Social Security Tax Payable		235.60
	213		Record Dec. 31 payroll	Medicare Tax Payable		55.10
	216		Record Dec. 31 payroll	Health Insurance Premium Pay.		50.00
	217		Record Dec. 31 payroll	United Way Contribution Pay.		100.00
	101		Record Dec. 31 payroll	Cash		2,979.30
12/31/00	513	1 (b)	Employer payroll taxes	Payroll Taxes Expense	315.50	
	212		Employer payroll taxes	Social Security Tax Payable		235.60
	213		Employer payroll taxes	Medicare Tax Payable		55.10
	219		Employer payroll taxes	FUTA Tax Payable		3.20
	220		Employer payroll taxes	SUTA Tax Payable		21.60
12/31/00	510	3	Adjustment fo insurance prem	Workers' Comp. Ins. Expense	18.00	
	221		Adjustment fo insurance prem	Workers' Comp. Ins. Payable		18.00
		Total			**4,133.50**	**4,133.50**

Page: 1

10-Demo Hart Company

General Journal

For the Period From Jan 1, 2001 to Jan 31, 2001

Filter Criteria includes: Report order is by Date. Report is printed with Accounts having Zero Amounts and with Truncated Transaction Descriptions and in Detail Format.

Date	Account ID	Reference	Trans Description	Account Description	Debit Amt	Credit Amt
1/31/01	211	2 (a)	Deposit employee taxes	Employee Income Tax Payable	1,520.00	
	212		Deposit employee taxes	Social Security Tax Payable	1,847.00	
	213		Deposit employee taxes	Medicare Tax Payable	433.00	
	101		Deposit employee taxes	Cash		3,800.00
1/31/01	219	2 (b)	Paid FUTA tax	FUTA Tax Payable	27.20	
	101		Paid FUTA tax	Cash		27.20
1/31/01	220	2 (c)	Paid SUTA tax	SUTA Tax Payable	183.60	
	101		Paid SUTA tax	Cash		183.60
		Total			**4,010.80**	**4,010.80**

10-Demo Hart Company

General Ledger Trial Balance

As of Jan 31, 2001

Filter Criteria includes: Report order is by ID. Report is printed in Detail Format.

Account ID	Account Description	Debit Amt	Credit Amt
101	Cash	64,156.52	
103	Accounts Receivable	21,250.00	
142	Office Supplies	1,200.00	
143	Prepaid Insurance	560.00	
180	Equipment	178,575.00	
180.1	Accum. Depr.--Equipment		40,286.00
201	Accounts Payable		8,165.00
216	Health Insurance Premium		50.00
217	United Way Contribution Pa		100.00
221	Workers' Comp. Ins. Payabl		18.00
311	Beatrice Hart, Capital		217,122.52
	Total:	265,741.52	265,741.52

Chapter 11 Demonstration Problem Solution

Page: 1

11-Demo Hunt's Audio-Video Store

Sales Journal

For the Period From Apr 1, 2000 to Apr 30, 2000

Filter Criteria includes: Report order is by Invoice Date. Report is printed in Detail Format.

Date	Account ID	Invoice No	Line Description	Account Description	Debit Amnt	Credit Amnt
4/3/00	231	41	MO: Missouri 7% sales tax	Sales Tax Payable		11.17
	401		Merchandise	Sales		159.50
	122		Susan Haberman	Accounts Receivable	170.67	
4/4/00	231	42	MO: Missouri 7% sales tax	Sales Tax Payable		21.00
	401		Merchandise	Sales		299.95
	122		Goro Kimura	Accounts Receivable	320.95	
4/7/00	231	CM1	MO: Missouri 7% sales tax	Sales Tax Payable	2.80	
	401.1		Credit Memo	Sales Returns & Allowance	39.95	
	122		Kenneth Watt	Accounts Receivable		42.75
4/11/00	231	43	MO: Missouri 7% sales tax	Sales Tax Payable		35.00
	401		Merchandise	Sales		499.95
	122		Victor Cardona	Accounts Receivable	534.95	
4/17/00	231	44	MO: Missouri 7% sales tax	Sales Tax Payable		26.60
	401		Merchandise	Sales		379.95
	122		Susan Haberman	Accounts Receivable	406.55	
4/19/00	231	45	MO: Missouri 7% sales tax	Sales Tax Payable		4.20
	401		Merchandise	Sales		59.95
	122		Tera Scherrer	Accounts Receivable	64.15	
4/21/00	231	CM2	MO: Missouri 7% sales tax	Sales Tax Payable	3.50	
	401.1		Credit Memo	Sales Returns & Allowance	49.95	
	122		Goro Kimura	Accounts Receivable		53.45
4/25/00	231	46	MO: Missouri 7% sales tax	Sales Tax Payable		12.57
	401		Merchandise	Sales		179.50
	122		Kellie Cokley	Accounts Receivable	192.07	
4/28/00	231	47	MO: Missouri 7% sales tax	Sales Tax Payable		3.50
	401		Merchandise	Sales		49.95
	122		Kenneth Watt	Accounts Receivable	53.45	
		Total			**1,838.99**	**1,838.99**

11-Demo Hunt's Audio-Video Store

Cash Receipts Journal

For the Period From Apr 1, 2000 to Apr 30, 2000

Date	Account ID	Transaction Ref	Line Description	Account Description	Debit Amnt	Credit Amnt
4/6/00	122	1	Invoice: Balance	Accounts Receivable		69.50
	101		Tera Scherrer	Cash	69.50	
4/10/00	122	2	Invoice: Balance	Accounts Receivable		99.95
	101		Kellie Cokley	Cash	99.95	
4/14/00	122	3	Invoice: Balance	Accounts Receivable		199.75
	122		Invoice: CM1	Accounts Receivable	42.75	
	101		Kenneth Watt	Cash	157.00	
4/24/00	122	4	Invoice: Balance	Accounts Receivable		299.95
	101		Victor Cardona	Cash	299.95	
4/26/00	122	5	Invoice: Balance	Accounts Receivable		79.98
	122		Invoice: 41	Accounts Receivable		170.67
	101		Susan Haberman	Cash	250.65	
4/30/00	231	6	MO: Missouri 7% sales tax	Sales Tax Payable		85.40
	401		Credit card receipts	Sales		1,220.00
	231		Credit card expense	Sales Tax Payable	65.27	
	101		Credit card receipts	Cash	1,240.13	
4/30/00	231	7	MO: Missouri 7% sales tax	Sales Tax Payable		140.00
	401		Cash sales	Sales		2,000.00
	101		Cash sales	Cash	2,140.00	
					4,365.20	**4,365.20**

11-Demo Hunt's Audio-Video Store

Invoice Register

For the Period From Apr 1, 2000 to Apr 30, 2000

Filter Criteria includes: Report order is by Invoice Number.

Invoice No	Date	Quote No	Name	Amount
41	4/3/00		Susan Haberman	170.67
42	4/4/00		Goro Kimura	320.95
43	4/11/00		Victor Cardona	534.95
44	4/17/00		Susan Haberman	406.55
45	4/19/00		Tera Scherrer	64.15
46	4/25/00		Kellie Cokley	192.07
47	4/28/00		Kenneth Watt	53.45
CM Kimura	4/21/00		Goro Kimura	-53.45
CM Watt	4/7/00		Kenneth Watt	-42.75
Total				**1,646.59**

11-Demo Hunt's Audio-Video Store

Customer Ledgers

For the Period From Apr 1, 2000 to Apr 30, 2000

Filter Criteria includes: Report order is by ID. Report is printed in Detail Format.

Customer ID Customer	Date	Trans No	Typ	Debit Amt	Credit Amt	Balance
10	4/1/00	Balance Fwd				299.95
Victor Cardona	4/11/00	43	SJ	534.95		834.90
	4/24/00	4	CRJ		299.95	534.95
20	4/1/00	Balance Fwd				99.95
Kellie Cokley	4/1/00	46	SJ	192.07		292.02
	4/10/00	2	CRJ		99.95	192.07
30	4/1/00	Balance Fwd				79.98
Susan Haberman	4/3/00	41	SJ	170.67		250.65
	4/17/00	44	SJ	406.55		657.20
	4/26/00	5	CRJ		250.65	406.55
40	4/1/00	Balance Fwd				379.50
Goro Kimura	4/4/00	42	SJ	320.95		700.45
	4/21/00	CM2	SJ		53.45	647.00
50	4/1/00	Balance Fwd				149.50
Tera Scherrer	4/6/00	1	CRJ		69.50	80.00
	4/19/00	45	SJ	64.15		144.15
60	4/1/00	Balance Fwd				199.75
Kenneth Watt	4/7/00	CM1	SJ		42.75	157.00
	4/14/00	3	CRJ		157.00	0.00
	4/28/00	47	SJ	53.45		53.45

Chapter 12 Demonstration Problem Solution

Page: 1

12-Demo Rutman Pharmacy
General Ledger Trial Balance
As of Jun 30, 2000

Filter Criteria includes: Report order is by ID. Report is printed in Detail Format.

Account ID	Account Description	Debit Amt	Credit Amt
101	Cash	5,481.74	
202	Accounts Payable		952.12
311	Jodi Rutman, Capital		26,264.48
501	Purchases	16,378.27	
501.1	Purchases Returns & Allow		412.53
501.2	Purchases Discounts		230.88
521	Rent Expense	6,000.00	
	Total:	**27,860.01**	**27,860.01**

Page: 1

12-Demo Rutman Pharmacy
Schedule of Accounts Payable
As of Jun 30, 2000

Vendor	Invoice No	Amount Due
Flites Pharmaceuticals	675	638.47
Flites Pharmaceuticals		**638.47**
University Drug Co.	914A	367.35
	CM914A	-53.70
University Drug Co.		**313.65**
		952.12

12-Demo Rutman Pharmacy

Purchase Journal

For the Period From Jun 1, 2000 to Jun 30, 2000

Filter Criteria includes: Report order is by Date. Report is printed in Detail Format.

Date	Account ID Account Description	Invoice #	Line Description	Debit Amount	Credit Amount
6/1/00	501 Purchases	71	Merchandise	234.20	
	202 Accounts Payable		Sullivan Company		234.20
6/5/00	501 Purchases	196	Merchandise	562.40	
	202 Accounts Payable		Amfac Drug Supply		562.40
6/7/00	501 Purchases	914A	Merchandise	367.35	
	202 Accounts Payable		University Drug Co.		367.35
6/12/00	501.1 Purchases Returns & Allowanc	CM106	Credit Memo		46.20
	202 Accounts Payable		Amfac Drug Supply	46.20	
6/14/00	501 Purchases	745	Merchandise	479.40	
	202 Accounts Payable		Mutual Drug Company		479.40
6/15/00	501.1 Purchases Returns & Allowanc	CM914A	Credit Memo		53.70
	202 Accounts Payable		University Drug Co.	53.70	
6/27/00	501 Purchases	675	Merchandise	638.47	
	202 Accounts Payable		Flites Pharmaceuticals		638.47
				2,381.72	**2,381.72**

12-Demo Rutman Pharmacy
Check Register
For the Period From Jun 1, 2000 to Jun 30, 2000

Filter Criteria includes: Report order is by Date.

Check #	Date	Payee	Cash Account	Amount
536	6/2/00	Rent Payment	101	1,000.00
537	6/9/00	Sullivan Company	101	229.52
538	6/16/00	Amfac Drug Supply	101	511.04
539	6/23/00	Mutual Drug Company	101	469.81
540	6/29/00	Merchandise	101	270.20
541	6/30/00	Vashon Medical Supply	101	1,217.69
Total				**3,698.26**

12-Demo Rutman Pharmacy
Cash Disbursements Journal
For the Period From Jun 1, 2000 to Jun 30, 2000

Filter Criteria includes: Report order is by Date. Report is printed in Detail Format.

Date	Check #	Account ID	Line Description	Account Description	Debit Amount	Credit Amount
6/2/00	536	521	Rent payment	Rent Expense	1,000.00	
		101	Rent Payment	Cash		1,000.00
6/9/00	537	501.2	Discounts Taken	Purchases Discounts		4.68
		202	Invoice: 71	Accounts Payable	234.20	
		101	Sullivan Company	Cash		229.52
6/16/00	538	501.2	Discounts Taken	Purchases Discounts		5.16
		202	Invoice: 196	Accounts Payable	562.40	
		202	Invoice: CM106	Accounts Payable		46.20
		101	Amfac Drug Supply	Cash		511.04
6/23/00	539	501.2	Discounts Taken	Purchases Discounts		9.59
		202	Invoice: 745	Accounts Payable	479.40	
		101	Mutual Drug Company	Cash		469.81
6/29/00	540	501	Cash Purchase Merchandise	Purchases	270.20	
		101	Merchandise	Cash		270.20
6/30/00	541	202	Invoice: Balance	Accounts Payable	1,217.69	
		101	Vashon Medical Supply	Cash		1,217.69
	Total				**3,763.89**	**3,763.89**

Chapter 13 Demonstration Problem Solution

Page: 1

13-Demo Harpo, Inc.
General Ledger Trial Balance
As of Mar 31, 2000

Filter Criteria includes: Report order is by ID. Report is printed in Detail Format.

Account ID	Account Description	Debit Amt	Credit Amt
101	Cash	2,121.00	
141	Supplies	520.00	
202	Vouchers Payable		1,690.00
301	Capital Stock		12,500.00
501	Purchases	6,570.00	
501.1	Purchases Returns & Allow		200.00
501.2	Purchases Discounts		71.00
511	Wages Expense	3,750.00	
521	Rent Expense	1,500.00	
	Total:	**14,461.00**	**14,461.00**

Page: 1

13-Demo Harpo, Inc.
Schedule of Vouchers Payable
As of Mar 31, 2000

Vendor ID Vendor	Invoice No	Amount Due
70 Giggles	316	700.00
70 Giggles		**700.00**
80 Creations	317	870.00
80 Creations		**870.00**
90 Hal's Supply	318	120.00
90 Hal's Supply		**120.00**
Report Total		**1,690.00**

13-Demo Harpo, Inc.
Purchase Journal
For the Period From Mar 1, 2000 to Mar 31, 2000

Filter Criteria includes: Report order is by Date. Report is printed in Detail Format.

Date	Account ID Account Description	Invoice #	Line Description	Debit Amount	Credit Amount
3/2/00	521 Rent Expense	313	March rent	500.00	
	202 Vouchers Payable		Tremont Rental		500.00
3/3/00	501 Purchases	314	Merchandise	550.00	
	202 Vouchers Payable		Gail's Gags		550.00
3/4/00	501 Purchases	315	Merchandise	200.00	
	202 Vouchers Payable		Silly Sam's		200.00
3/12/00	501.1 Purchases Returns & Allowanc	CM315	Credit memo		100.00
	202 Vouchers Payable		Silly Sam's	100.00	
3/16/00	501 Purchases	316	Merchandise	700.00	
	202 Vouchers Payable		Giggles		700.00
3/21/00	501 Purchases	317	Merchandise	870.00	
	202 Vouchers Payable		Creations		870.00
3/25/00	141 Supplies	318	Merchandise	120.00	
	202 Vouchers Payable		Hal's Supply		120.00
3/31/00	511 Wages Expense	319	Payroll	1,250.00	
	202 Vouchers Payable		Payroll		1,250.00
				4,290.00	**4,290.00**

13-Demo Harpo, Inc.
Check Register
For the Period From Mar 1, 2000 to Mar 31, 2000

Filter Criteria includes: Report order is by Date.

Check #	Date	Payee	Cash Account	Amount
450	3/2/00	Tremont Rental	101	500.00
451	3/10/00	Jerry's Jokes	101	490.00
452	3/14/00	Resource Supplies	101	250.00
453	3/18/00	Gail's Gags	101	539.00
454	3/19/00	Donnelly's	101	750.00
455	3/31/00	Silly Sam's	101	100.00
456	3/31/00	Payroll	101	1,250.00
Total				**3,879.00**

Chapter 15 Demonstration Problem Solution

Page: 1

15-Demo McK's Home Electronics

General Journal

For the Period From Dec 1, 2000 to Dec 31, 2000

Date	Account ID	Reference	Trans Description	Account Description	Debit Amt	Credit Amt
12/31/00	503	(a)	Adjusting Entry	Inventory Adjustment	39,000.00	
	131		Adjusting Entry	Merchandise Inventory		39,000.00
12/31/00	131	(b)	Adjusting Entry	Merchandise Inventory	45,000.00	
	503		Adjusting Entry	Inventory Adjustment		45,000.00
12/31/00	521	(c)	Adjusting Entry	Supplies Expense	2,100.00	
	141		Adjusting Entry	Supplies		2,100.00
12/31/00	527	(d)	Adjusting Entry	Insurance Expense	2,700.00	
	145		Adjusting Entry	Prepaid Insurance		2,700.00
12/31/00	529	(e)	Adjusting Entry	Depr. Expense--Building	6,000.00	
	190.1		Adjusting Entry	Accum. Depr.--Building		6,000.00
12/31/00	531	(f)	Adjusting Entry	Depr. Expense--Store Equipment	4,500.00	
	195.1		Adjusting Entry	Accum. Depr.--Store Equipment		4,500.00
12/31/00	511	(g)	Adjusting Entry	Wages Expense	675.00	
	214		Adjusting Entry	Wages Payable		675.00
12/31/00	221	(h)	Adjusting Entry	Unearned Repair Fees	15,000.00	
	601		Adjusting Entry	Repair Fees		15,000.00
		Total			114,975.00	114,975.00

15-Demo McK's Home Electronics

General Ledger Trial Balance

As of Dec 31, 2000

Filter Criteria includes: Report order is by ID. Report is printed in Detail Format.

Account ID	Account Description	Debit Amt	Credit Amt
101	Cash	10,000.00	
102	Accounts Receivable	22,500.00	
131	Merchandise Inventory	45,000.00	
141	Supplies	600.00	
145	Prepaid Insurance	900.00	
185	Land	15,000.00	
190	Building	135,000.00	
190.1	Accum. Depr.--Building		30,000.00
195	Store Equipment	75,000.00	
195.1	Accum. Depr.--Store Equip		27,000.00
201	Notes Payable		7,500.00
202	Accounts Payable		15,000.00
214	Wages Payable		675.00
219	Sales Tax Payable		2,250.00
221	Unearned Repair Fees		3,000.00
285	Mortgage Payable		45,000.00
311	Tom McKinney, Capital		151,600.00
312	Tom McKinney, Drawing	30,000.00	
401	Sales		300,750.00
401.1	Sales Returns & Allowance	1,800.00	
501	Purchases	157,500.00	
501.1	Purchases Returns & Allow		1,200.00
501.2	Purchases Discounts		1,500.00
502	Freight-In	450.00	
503	Inventory Adjustment		6,000.00
511	Wages Expense	63,675.00	
518	Advertising Expense	3,750.00	
521	Supplies Expense	2,100.00	
523	Telephone Expense	5,250.00	
524	Utilities Expense	18,000.00	
527	Insurance Expense	2,700.00	
529	Depr. Expense--Building	6,000.00	
531	Depr. Expense--Store Equip	4,500.00	
534	Miscellaneous Expense	3,375.00	
601	Repair Fees		15,000.00
602	Interest Revenue		1,350.00
701	Interest Expense	4,725.00	
	Total:	**607,825.00**	**607,825.00**

15-Demo McK's Home Electronics
Income Statement
For the Period Ending December 31, 2000

Revenues		
Sales	$	300,750.00
Sales Returns & Allowance		<1,800.00>
Total Revenues		298,950.00
Cost of Goods Sold		
Purchases		157,500.00
Purchases Returns & Allowance		<1,200.00>
Purchases Discounts		<1,500.00>
Freight-In		450.00
Inventory Adjustment		<6,000.00>
Total Cost of Goods Sold		149,250.00
Gross Profit		149,700.00
Expenses		
Wages Expense		63,675.00
Advertising Expense		3,750.00
Supplies Expense		2,100.00
Telephone Expense		5,250.00
Utilities Expense		18,000.00
Insurance Expense		2,700.00
Depr. Expense--Building		6,000.00
Depr. Expense--Store Equipment		4,500.00
Miscellaneous Expense		3,375.00
Total Expenses		109,350.00
Income from Operations		40,350.00
Other Revenue		
Repair Fees		15,000.00
Interest Revenue		1,350.00
Other Expenses		
Interest Expense		4,725.00
Net Income	$	51,975.00

15-Demo McK's Home Electronics
Statement of Owner's Equity
December 31, 2000

Capital, Beginning of Period			151,600.00
Net Income for the Period	54,975.00		
Less Withdrawals for Period	30,000.00		
Increase/Decrease in Capital			24,975.00
Capital, End of Period		$	176,575.00

15-Demo McK's Home Electronics
Balance Sheet
December 31, 2000

ASSETS

Current Assets		
Cash	$ 10,000.00	
Accounts Receivable	22,500.00	
Merchandise Inventory	45,000.00	
Supplies	600.00	
Prepaid Insurance	900.00	
Total Current Assets		79,000.00
Property and Equipment		
Building	135,000.00	
Accum. Depr.--Building	<30,000.00>	
Store Equipment	75,000.00	
Accum. Depr.--Store Equipment	<27,000.00>	
Total Property and Equipment		153,000.00
Other Assets		
Land	15,000.00	
Total Other Assets		15,000.00
Total Assets		$ 247,000.00

LIABILITIES AND CAPITAL

Current Liabilities		
Notes Payable	$ 7,500.00	
Accounts Payable	15,000.00	
Wages Payable	675.00	
Sales Tax Payabe	2,250.00	
Total Current Liabilities		25,425.00
Long-Term Liabilities		
Mortgage Payable	45,000.00	
Total Long-Term Liabilities		45,000.00
Total Liabilities		70,425.00
Capital		
Tom McKinney, Capital	151,600.00	
Tom McKinney, Drawing	<30,000.00>	
Net Income	54,975.00	
Total Capital		176,575.00
Total Liabilities & Capital		$ 247,000.00

15-Demo McK's Home Electronics

General Ledger Trial Balance

As of Jan 31, 2001

Filter Criteria includes: Report order is by ID. Report is printed in Detail Format.

Account ID	Account Description	Debit Amt	Credit Amt
101	Cash	10,000.00	
102	Accounts Receivable	22,500.00	
131	Merchandise Inventory	45,000.00	
141	Supplies	600.00	
145	Prepaid Insurance	900.00	
185	Land	15,000.00	
190	Building	135,000.00	
190.1	Accum. Depr.--Building		30,000.00
195	Store Equipment	75,000.00	
195.1	Accum. Depr.--Store Equip		27,000.00
201	Notes Payable		7,500.00
202	Accounts Payable		15,000.00
214	Wages Payable		675.00
219	Sales Tax Payabe		2,250.00
285	Mortgage Payable		45,000.00
311	Tom McKinney, Capital		176,575.00
	Total:	**304,000.00**	**304,000.00**

15-Demo McK's Home Electronics

General Journal

For the Period From Jan 1, 2001 to Jan 31, 2001

Date	Account ID	Reference	Trans Description	Account Description	Debit Amt	Credit Amt
1/1/01	214		Reversing Entry	Wages Payable	675.00	
	511		Reversing Entry	Wages Expense		675.00
		Total			**675.00**	**675.00**